From Taverns to Gastropubs

From Taverns to Gastropubs

Food, Drink, and Sociality in England

Christel Lane

OXFORD
UNIVERSITY PRESS

OXFORD
UNIVERSITY PRESS

Great Clarendon Street, Oxford, OX2 6DP,
United Kingdom

Oxford University Press is a department of the University of Oxford.
It furthers the University's objective of excellence in research, scholarship,
and education by publishing worldwide. Oxford is a registered trade mark of
Oxford University Press in the UK and in certain other countries

© Christel Lane 2018

The moral rights of the author have been asserted

First Edition published in 2018

Impression: 1

All rights reserved. No part of this publication may be reproduced, stored in
a retrieval system, or transmitted, in any form or by any means, without the
prior permission in writing of Oxford University Press, or as expressly permitted
by law, by licence or under terms agreed with the appropriate reprographics
rights organization. Enquiries concerning reproduction outside the scope of the
above should be sent to the Rights Department, Oxford University Press, at the
address above

You must not circulate this work in any other form
and you must impose this same condition on any acquirer

Published in the United States of America by Oxford University Press
198 Madison Avenue, New York, NY 10016, United States of America

British Library Cataloguing in Publication Data

Data available

Library of Congress Control Number: 2017963136

ISBN 978–0–19–882618–7

Printed and bound by
CPI Group (UK) Ltd, Croydon, CR0 4YY

Links to third party websites are provided by Oxford in good faith and
for information only. Oxford disclaims any responsibility for the materials
contained in any third party website referenced in this work.

Acknowledgements

In doing the field work for this book and in writing it, I incurred many debts of gratitude.

My first and largest debt is to the forty publicans interviewed who ran the gastropubs and often were their head chefs as well. They were generous with their time, making room in their extremely busy lives, and they responded frankly to my many questions. As a result, these visits entailed not merely work but were a real pleasure, further enhanced by the pubs' individual and welcoming environment and their good food. I am also grateful to the group of men who led their village communities in order to rescue their village pub, and talked to me about these efforts as well as revealing the reasons for their deep attachment to their pubs.

I owe thanks also to some of my friends who read and helpfully commented on some of the chapters, causing me to make some revisions. Among them are Peter Burke and Maria Lucia Pallares Burke, Jocelyn Probert, and Kate Wright. Mike Lane has been a stalwart friend, reading and commenting on the whole manuscript and giving me the impetus to make some much-needed cuts. I additionally owe a deep gratitude to the four anonymous readers appointed by Oxford University Press who were exceptionally helpful in spotting weaknesses and making suggestions for improvement. Any remaining weaknesses are my own responsibility. Another very positive experience during the writing process has been the interaction with my editor at Oxford University Press, Adam Swallow, who, from my first approach to him, has been consistently constructive and extremely supportive.

Last, but not least, I would like to thank my husband, David Lane, who accompanied me on many of the trips all over Britain and who gave me support throughout the long gestation period for the book.

Contents

List of Tables   ix

Introduction   1

Part I. A Historical Perspective

1. The Historical Development of Taverns, Inns, and Public Houses   19
2. The Social Identity of Hosts and Patrons   37
3. Eating Out in the Seventeenth and Eighteenth Centuries: The Contest between English and French Food   71
4. Eating Out in the Nineteenth and Twentieth Centuries: Changes in Food and in Social Identities   98

Part II. The Rise of the Gastropub

5. Publicans Between the State and the Brewers: A Subordinate Relationship   125
6. The Gastropub and its Divided Identity: Drink, Food, and Sociality   142
7. Social and National Identity: A Focus on Class, Gender, and Nation   169
8. The Future of the Pub: Are Gastropubs the Saviour or the Nemesis of the Traditional Pub?   195

Appendix I. The Concept of Class in Historical Analysis   211
Appendix II. Class Classification Schemes   215
Appendix III. Pubs Interviewed   216
Appendix IV. Dual or Divided Organizational Identity   217

Index   219

List of Tables

5.1.	Pub ownership in 2014	134
6.1.	Period when licensees started their current business	144
6.2.	Proportion of pub classics/bar snacks of all food offered (in %)	150
6.3.	Number of covers pubs can cater for	153
6.4.	Weekly number of covers actually served	153
6.5.	Chefs' culinary style	154
6.6.	Labels adopted by publicans	164
7.1.	Types of ownership	170

Introduction

Pubs have been an integral part of English history and a prominent social institution. They form as much part of English identity as roast beef, cricket, and the village green. Sociologists Alan Warde and Lydia Martens[1] agree, as they describe the pub 'as a principal symbolic site of English recreation'. Anthropologist Kate Fox[2] goes as far as claiming that 'it would be impossible even to attempt to understand Englishness without spending a lot of time in pubs'. The *Sunday Mirror*, a long-time campaigner on behalf of the British pub, enjoined the then Prime Minister David Cameron to honour his promise to be pub-friendly and to take urgent action 'to protect a treasured national institution'.[3] The pub—its architecture, décor, and particularly the nature of its sociality (the state or quality of being social)—is also internationally recognized as something peculiarly English or (now more often) British, and many tourist visits to Britain include at least one pub visit to experience its peculiar ambience. Under a variety of names, such as alehouse and tavern, as well as public house and pub, it can boast a very long history, going back, according to some authors, to the twelfth century.[4]

Moulded by the changing economy and society (nature of production, class system, consumption patterns, gender relations, and national identification), as well as by government regulation and relations with breweries, the institution of the pub has both maintained a remarkable continuity and adapted constantly to its changing social and economic environment. The public house has not merely been a place for drinking and informal sociality. At different points in history, it has additionally assumed a multitude of community functions: affording a place for popular games or music, offering a facility for both working class and bourgeois clubs and associations, as well as serving as labour exchange, law court, theatre, and dance hall—to mention only some of its uses. More episodically, pubs have offered shelter from floods, accommodated religious services, and served as morale-boosting gathering places during World War II. All this has given pubs a seemingly cross-class appeal and the character of a generally well-loved community institution. Pubs have long been tightly woven into the fabric of British social life.

However, this long-lived capacity for adaptation and persistence of pubs through many social and economic upheavals can no longer be taken for granted. Most recently, pubs have been seen to enter a period of crisis and have become, in some eyes, 'an endangered species'.[5] Being a well-loved institution is no longer enough. The escalating dying of pubs (through demolition and change of purpose)—they have closed at the rate of thirty a week in recent years, according to CAMRA (Campaign for Real Ale)[6]—has caused great alarm in many quarters. This alarm is often motivated by a generalized fear of the substitution of a community-oriented society with a more individualistic and atomized society. Usually, the concern is prompted by the actual disappearance of a pub from a locality where it has been the only place for informal sociality and a focus of neighbourhood life.

This accelerating decline has alerted many individuals and organizations to defend the institution of the pub. By various means, they have attempted to stem the decline and even to revitalize the pub. Among the most notable is CAMRA, which, among several strategies, has tried to upgrade the pub's quintessential drink: beer. Even more remarkable has been the intervention by the state, which has been concerned with the loss of community focus, particularly in rural areas. Historically, the state has been an enemy that has viewed pubs as sources of political subversion and social disorder and, accordingly, has imposed on them heavy regulation, as well as punitive taxation (see Chapter 5). However, most recently the state has presented itself as the pub's protector, and the historically much maligned institution has now become a valued part of British 'cultural patrimony'. The pub has become politically justified as a traditional and authentic cultural institution worthy of (albeit limited) state protection.

What is being overlooked in this lament about the threatened extinction of the pub is that it is once again engaged in a process of adaptation, rather than disappearance. The number of pubs has certainly been decreasing significantly, and backstreet boozers, particularly, have declined at great speed. However, their more refined brethren, at the upper end of the scale, are being transformed into upmarket food-led pubs, also referred to as gastropubs. Such pubs serve meals to a high standard of quality, to match top restaurant standards, and food, usually locally sourced, has become as, or even more, important than drink in generating turnover. However, beer and other beverages are still served at the bar for those in search of only liquid refreshment.

The term 'gastropub' is a portmanteau term joining gastronomy and public house that indicates the style of a pub. The term appeared first in 1991, when David Eyre and Mike Belben, two workers in the West End restaurant industry, took over the Eagle pub in Clerkenwell and transformed it into a pub selling robust, locally sourced food, inspired by currently fashionable chefs such as Alistair Little, Rowley Leigh, and the River Café. They had insufficient capital to acquire a conventional restaurant but also felt well able to dispense with some of the trappings of an upmarket restaurant. Belben calls it 'casual and deliberately scruffy, but high standard'.[7] The actual coining of the term gastropub, according to Mike Belben, is attributable to Charles Campion, the then food writer for the *Evening Standard*.

Gastropubs have been variously defined, ranging from fairly neutral definitions that merely link the terms 'pub' and 'restaurant' to ones expressing considerable disdain for this new institution. Elizabeth Carter, then editor of the British *Good Food Guide*, in the 2011 edition of the *Guide* rejected the term as confused and confusing. She vowed that the term would no longer be used by the *Good Food Guide*. Others, who share her view, poke fun with phrases such as, 'It's really an expensive restaurant hiding behind half-timbered charm',[8] or liken it to a hermit crab in that it is 'a restaurant occupying the dead shell of a pub'.[9]

Controversy around the term relates to what kind of food such pubs specialize in, what clientele they attract, and whether they will destroy or revitalize the traditional pub. Gastropubs provide high-quality food that is freshly made on the premises from mostly locally sourced produce. Such pubs are not merely food-led, but aspire to serving gastronomically ambitious food. Hence, food may be inventive, as the term 'gastro' indicates, but it is not necessarily so. Some pub chefs aim to provide more simple food from a British tradition, albeit at a high level of quality in terms of sourcing, preparation, and presentation. Yet, because of the suggestion of something 'gastronomic'—whatever this may be—there is a suspicion that the gastropub will not revitalize, but replace the traditional pub. The question is essentially whether gastropubs will remain pubs or become restaurants. By turning simply into a restaurant under another name, it is claimed, the gastropub is likely to deprive drinkers of their traditional refuge.

However, many industry insiders see the trend towards gastropubs highly positively. They emphasize not only a positive transformation of food, but also of the beer served. Thus, chef and gastropub owner Tom Kerridge, host to the 2015 Top50 Pubs Awards, claimed: 'We are the future of dining. The pub sector in many circles is talked about in a negative fashion, with many pubs closing, but in terms of craft ale, small distilleries and fantastic food-led businesses, the pub industry goes from strength to strength... As a collective force, we are building a world-wide reputation and becoming a world-wide movement.'[10] An article on gastropubs in the 'food and drink' industry magazine, *Restaurant*, also embraces the term, but, at the same time, wants to clarify its meaning and rescue it from becoming a catch-all term.[11] A Guardian journalist, too, is enthusiastic about gastropubs: 'If you want pure progress, from a bad place to a better place, consider the gastropub.'[12]

Today's gastropub has several historical forebears. At certain points in history alehouses/public houses, inns, and taverns were clearly distinguished from each other. All three types of establishment date back to the late medieval period, but had their distinctiveness confirmed only in the late sixteenth century, when the government of the day officially designated them by their names. The three-fold categorization of alehouse, tavern, and inn became recognized in statute and common law in the way that premises were licenced and the legal obligations of their landlords defined.[13] As Burke notes: 'each place had its social and professional "tone" and gathered about it men of like tastes and sympathies'.[14]

During periods of transition, however, the distinctions between the various types of hostelries became blurred. In many cases, one institution gave way to another, while names lingered or became even resurrected at a later time. Thus, for example, in the early eighteenth century the new descriptor of 'public house' was applied not only to former alehouses, but also to taverns and smaller inns.[15]

The blurring of traditional distinctions became particularly pronounced during the early nineteenth century when the three establishments also had to compete with new institutions providing food and drink, such as 'eating houses' and 'dining rooms' and, later in the century, restaurants.[16] Rylance, writing in 1815, mentions several establishments that had two designations, such as Tavern and Public House or Tavern and Eating House, or Inn and Tavern. (The word 'restaurant' only entered the English language in the last quarter of the nineteenth century.) A confusing multiplicity of labels is again encountered today, particularly in relation to high-end, food-led pubs—the main focus of this study.

In this historical context, the tavern is an institution of particular interest because, similar to the gastropub, it is also a hostelry balancing the provision of food and drink, even though the type of sociality it afforded was very much sui generis, and the main drink sold was wine rather than beer. The inn originally differed in that its primary objective was the provision of accommodation, although food and drink were always available and the former grew in importance over time. However, as travel by horse and carriage gave way to the railways, and inns largely lost their original function, many of the survivors changed to become either pubs or taverns. But even after the inn had disappeared as a major institution, a developing coaching inn mythology has kept its image alive. Much copying of its architectural features by pubs has been notable through subsequent centuries. As Haydon suggests,[17] this mythology perhaps has provided a link for Britain's mainly urban dwellers to a mythical rural past that we have lost.

Many of today's pubs have their historical origin in either a tavern or an inn, particularly in rural areas, and several retain the label 'inn'.[18] In some cases, this indicates that they have added the 'small hotel' function to that of providing good food in a pub environment. In many cases, however, the terms 'tavern' and 'inn' have been adopted to benefit from the symbolic value of the terms. Take, for example, the Merchant's Tavern in Shoreditch, Jason Atherton's Berner's Tavern, or the pub companies calling themselves Punch Taverns, Cirrus Inns, and Enterprise Inns. Thus, public houses, inns, and taverns have had overlapping identities and functions, making the tracing of differences and continuity from tavern (and often inn) to gastropub a meaningful exercise. I shall take all three types of hostelry, though particularly the tavern, as forerunners of the gastropub, while taking care not to obliterate the historical distinctiveness of each.

This is a sociological study of the pub that will place it in its social, economic, and, to a lesser degree, political-regulatory context. My examination of its historical evolution and character, spanning the period from the second half of the seventeenth century to the beginning of the twenty-first century, tries to capture the impact of its constantly changing environment and how it moulds both the pub and its relationship with the other hospitality venues. My focus is the change in the identity of the various hostelries over time, culminating in the most recent transformation: the change towards food-led gastropubs—the most fully elaborated identity in the book. This identity is not exhausted by the move to high-quality food alone, but has ramifications for sociality, elaborated both in the historical section and in chapters on the gastropub.

Hence, the contemporary gastropub/pub restaurant will be my prime topic. My study of the gastropub compares its food and drink offerings, as well as its ambience and the type of sociality it fosters, to those of other hostelries serving food. Examining the constantly changing constellation of drink, food, and sociality that motivates pub visits, I shall concentrate predominantly on its food offering, but the other two aspects will not be neglected. Among the questions addressed are: What social and economic developments have contributed to its rise at the turn from the twentieth to the twenty-first century? What characterizes its organizational identity, viewed though the lenses of class, gender, and nation? The concern with social identity focuses both on the level of individual patrons and publicans and on the level of organization, i.e. that of the pub and, historically, of the tavern/inn. It is assumed that individual social identity shapes organizational identity. Food, drink, and sociality are considered the mediums through which individual social and organizational identity are expressed.

Food, in particular, is one aspect that lends gastropubs their distinctiveness, lifting them above the many pub chains that provide food. My interest is in both the material and the symbolic aspect of food. Has the pub's famously informal sociality been successfully combined with both a distinctive and high-quality food offering, rivalling that of upmarket restaurants? Have gastropubs managed to preserve a more English/British cuisine than other types of eateries? Have they contributed to the reinvigoration of what is identified as a style of cuisine called 'Modern British'? How do publicans juggle the difficult balance between drinking at the bar and dining in a style more akin to an upmarket restaurant? How do chefs manage to combine the offer of traditional bar food with the more refined and imaginative food served in pubs' dining rooms? In other words, how much pub and how much gastronomic indulgence do we find in today's gastropubs? Or, how do the different types of food contribute to pubs' organizational identity?

My study is mindful of the fact that food represents a powerful symbolic resource for the expression of patterns of differentiation. In this context, the following questions are addressed: Has the rise of the gastropub provided fuel for the rise of a British gastro-nationalism?[19] Has food consumption in pubs become connected, as it was in earlier centuries, with the demarcation and sustenance of the emotive power of national tradition and attachment? Another set of issues to be explored is whether gastropubs have maintained the alleged cross-class appeal and social mixing that pubs are often associated with by historians, and whether and how the gastropub reflects social relations between the sexes and, to a lesser extent, between age cohorts. The book thus examines the pub's role in establishing or breaching social distinctions, connected with class, gender, and nationality.

A set of wider issues always in the background of posing the above questions are the following: Has the gastropub become just another type of restaurant? Or does it preserve some of the pub's historical distinctiveness and even invigorated British pub culture? Cause and effect are difficult to disentangle empirically, and hence these questions about the pub's resilience receive only tentative answers.

To understand the historical resilience and, more lately, the economic fragility of the pub, its study has to go beyond a consideration of only its social functions. This book therefore analyses also some business aspects of running a pub. It views the pub as a small and entrepreneurial business, variously buffeted by big business in the form of powerful breweries and, more lately, pub companies operating a chain model. Pub-keeping has been a heavily regulated business, and, historically, the position of publicans vis-à-vis the state, compared with that of brewers, has been extremely weak. However, despite the importance of these economic issues, the gastropub, in common with all pubs, is very much a cultural institution that provides social experiences and facilitates social mixing. In the process, it both transcends and erects social barriers.

Methodological Approach

The public house has been a very popular subject of study for historians, and there is little need for yet another historical study. This work differs in that a historical analysis provides only the background that puts current developments into perspective. A historical focus not only underlines stark differences between historical periods. It additionally highlights continuity and even the current reappearance of trends deeply embedded in English history and society. To trace these continuities and divergences, historical development—the focus on inns, taverns, and alehouses/public houses—is studied through the same sociological lenses as the contemporary gastropub.

However, this is primarily a sociological work and, as such, has few competitors. In its analysis of food-led pubs, and particularly of gastropubs or pub restaurants, it breaks fresh ground. It adopts a new perspective not only in the study of pubs, but also in that of food and eating out and their intimate relation with different types of sociality and, indeed, with class, gender, and nation. The close link between food and nationalism, in particular, according to Rogers,[20] has not been much studied by sociologists.

The book focuses predominantly on England. During Victorian times and subsequent centuries, however, it is more appropriate to focus on 'England and Britain'.[21] When dealing with current-day developments, the descriptor 'British' is, most of the time, appropriate.

The historical analysis will be based mainly on secondary sources. This includes use also of little known, centuries' old diary accounts of visits to taverns, inns, and public houses, as well as opinions on food. It starts in the middle of the seventeenth century (after the Restoration in 1660), when the beginnings of capitalism and the rise of new cultural pursuits and consumption patterns led, among other trends, to the expansion of inns and taverns and the gradual improvement of public houses. The historical analysis concludes with the end of the twentieth century, when the decline of drinking and the large-scale closure of pubs created the conditions for the emergence of gastropubs.

I will explore the contemporary gastropub, or pub restaurant, by means of forty semi-structured interviews in different types of food-led pubs, both independent and owned by breweries or, more recently, by pub companies. The geographical focus of my study is on England only, and the pubs visited are located in London and in fifteen counties. Gastropubs are more often in rural than in urban areas, excepting London, and they are more often located in villages characterized by a population with an above average level of income and education. However, in both rural and urban areas, the population is not homogenous but contains members from various social classes. Interviews lasted at least one hour and often went well beyond this time. (For a list of pubs in which interviews were conducted in 2015 and 2016, please see Appendix III.)

My selection of pubs for interview of their licensee and/or head chef was guided by their high rating by contemporary pub guides. The great majority of pubs are taken from the Michelin guide, *Eating Out in Pubs*, that considers both their food and beer as well as their ambience. It includes only pubs offering high-quality food. The Michelin guide is sufficiently professional to convince users about the level of food quality[22] and thereby obviates reliance on my own, necessarily subjective evaluation. Personal observation, by eating in these pubs as well as analysing their menus, form two further strands of my methodological approach. Both helped me to check and complement the information gained from interviewees. The careful analysis of all the pubs' menus, in particular, allows me to make some judgments about the nature of the food served, beyond issues of its quality. Last, a few interviews with pub regulars, selected from among those who have stepped in to save their local pub by turning it into a Community Asset, will complement the other interviews, particularly on the issue of sociality.

However, most of the information about customers' class and gender comes from licensees, and national identification is judged by customers' choices of food, as conveyed by interviewees. Publicans' social categorization of customers serves to simplify an abundance of information, but constitutes only a lay conception of social structural issues. Furthermore, as such categorizations define their establishment to a significant degree, they may not always be objective. However, there is sufficient agreement among informants, as well as with corroborating information, to engender some confidence in the results. In most historical accounts, excepting the diary recordings, social identities are assigned by authors, and care is taken to rely always on several sources.

Theoretical Perspectives

The theoretical lenses for studying the gastropub, as well as its historical forebears, are the concepts of *social* and *organizational identity*. *Social identity* answers the question of 'Who am I?', and people tend to classify themselves into various social categories or assign others to such categories.[23] Categories are defined by prototypical characteristics abstracted from members, and construction of categories occurs during repeated social interaction. Such categories serve to distinguish members from other social groups and are helpful in ordering the social environment. They are therefore relational and comparative.[24] Individuals' identity is 'an amalgam of loosely coupled identities',[25] and in this work the concern is with distinctions between people, based on class, gender, and nation. Identification with such categories, in turn, is a vague perception of oneness with or belonging to a social group.

It has both antecedents and consequences,[26] in that classifications have a significant effect on social interactions.[27]

It is assumed that, in small organizations such as taverns, inns, and public houses, the social identity of the landlord/lady largely defines the organizational identity of their establishment. Patrons attracted to a given establishment then further reinforce this identity. In addition to patrons' assigned social identity, I therefore consider also the self-identity revealed by the owner/manager of the hostelry.

Organizational identity, according to Albert and Whetten,[28] is about an organization's goals and values and answers questions such as 'Who are we?' and 'What do we want to be?'. It consists of those attributes that members feel are fundamental to and uniquely descriptive of the organization and that persist in the organization over time.[29] Adoption of an identity, at the same time, involves developing a distinction from other organizations in the same broad market,[30] as well as striving to attain a positive image or gain legitimacy.[31] (See Appendix IV for an elaboration of the notion of dual or divided organizational identity.)

I will use the above concepts to examine how class, gender, and nation are expressed by seeking sustenance and sociality in the different types of hostelry and thereby shape the organizational identity of the pub. The emphasis on social identity draws attention to the fact that the pub is primarily a place where social bonds are forged, maintained, and reinforced, as is vividly expressed in today's designation of the pub as the centre of a local community. I am therefore not viewing 'identity' in individual terms, but in collective terms, focusing on class, gender, and nation. It has long been held that those who eat and drink together are by this very act tied to another by a bond of friendship or, more loosely, companionship. The buying of drinks and food and sociality support each other. Hence, I will consider the sociality fostered by the pub and the types of social linkages it affords, paying attention to variation both between the three types of hostelry and between periods. Social bonds have been created both between patrons and between patrons and landlords/ladies or tavern- and inn-keepers. Paradoxically, pubs are viewed in the literature as both blurring or glossing over social distinctions and as expressing them. The former belief is more widely held than the latter and undergirds the notion of the pub as a centre of a local community. My focus on divisions of class, gender, and, to a lesser extent, age will query the adequacy of this one-sided and somewhat romantic notion of pub sociality.

Class

The way the pub has both shaped and reflected class identity and class relations is of particular interest. The issue of whether the pub has had and still enjoys cross-class appeal and facilitates easy social mixing is examined. I agree with Warde[32] that class has remained a good explanation of habit and practice in the field of food. Like Warde, I am assuming that class differentiation in relation to eating out remains pronounced in British society, even if such differentiation is no longer asserting superiority and inferiority. The class categories applied to make sense of the social categorizations employed by publicans are based on the class schema of National Statistics on Socio-Economic Categories (NS-SEC),[33] originating in sociology and taken up by government in the census of 2011. They are based mainly on occupational status and the disposable income this yields. However, my interviewees additionally refer to the possession of property in land, businesses, houses, and cars. Class is thus perceived as a social category 'which refers to lived relations, surrounding social relations of production, exchange and consumption'.[34] Although class is reproduced every day largely by unreflected-upon cultural practices, including consumption practices, class shaped by the possession of cultural capital is only rarely considered by interviewees.

Historical analysis of class, particularly in the seventeenth and eighteenth centuries, raises many complexities and calls for a different approach. In historical analysis, classes in the seventeenth and eighteenth centuries, are largely seen as absent and/or as lowly articulated, and alternative terms like 'ranks', 'sorts', and 'orders' are used. This approach to social categorization is further explicated and critically examined in Appendix I. Here, it suffices to say that an incipient crystallization of what can only be called class identity—albeit mainly in cultural and more rarely in political terms—became often expressed in culinary identity. Furthermore, it frequently became linked to gender and national identity. Despite historians' valid claim that a consciousness of class identity and class opposition was rarely articulated in the seventeenth and eighteenth centuries, I shall argue that, for the middling classes, however vaguely delineated, class identity was expressed and acted out in the cultural field. This was particularly evident around sociality and drink and food taken in the various types of hostelries. Nevertheless, the terms 'middling sorts' or 'ranks' are sometimes useful to indicate the lack of clear definition when referring to this social category in the earlier centuries.

Gender

By examining the presence/absence of women in taverns and pubs and their relationships to male drinkers, I will add to the sociology of gender relations. Gender is a social category to do with lived relationships between men and women. They are the means by which sexual divisions are constructed, organized, and maintained, based on definitions of femininity and masculinity.[35]

I explore the shaping and expression of masculinity and femininity and the extent of women's exclusion from pubs and other eating-out venues at different points in history. I study how and to what extent women's changed position in the labour market and in the wider society, together with a changed gender ideology that emphasizes inclusion rather than exclusion, manifests itself in patterns of sociality around drinking and dining in the contemporary gastropub.

Food and National Identification

As Beardsworth and Keil point out, 'the absorption of a given food, particularly when occurring repeatedly, can have the effect of transferring certain symbolic properties of that food into the very being of the eater'.[36]

Symbolic threats against British food and food practices, in some quarters, are still regarded as assaults on heritage and culture that demand the assertion of British foodways, even though most people happily embrace globally inspired meals. I will examine whether the claim by Rogers, with reference to the seventeenth and eighteenth centuries, that food may both express and deny national identity, among the middling classes and the aristocracy respectively, is also applicable to later centuries.

In addition to pursuing this topic historically, I shall explore whether the rise of the gastropub has any significance for forging a connection between food and national identity.

National identity, because often dormant for long stretches of time and only re-energized at certain historical moments, is often overlooked in societal analysis. In the context of modern Britain, moreover, it is often claimed that the English have never expressed any national identity.[37] I agree instead with McCrone and Bechhofer, who hold that national identity in England is being expressed, but that it has always held a stronger cultural than political dimension.[38] While McCrone and Bechhofer focus mainly on contemporary nationalist sentiment, Newman offers a detailed theoretical and empirical analysis of cultural nationalism,[39] directed against the French during the period of 1740–1830, and distinguishes it from mere patriotism.

While most analysts of national identity envisage and explore a variety of markers of identity, and of behaviours motivated by them, Fischler focuses solely on culinary identity. He studies the way incorporation of food may become an important marker of both inclusion in a nation and opposition to another nation, whose cuisine is viewed as a threat to national culinary identity. Rogers suggests: 'If food helps to mark out all social distinctions, it is particularly important to national ones ... Food, after language, is the most important bearer of national identity.'[40]

National cuisines may be viewed as a set of classifications and rules, such as what ingredients are cooked together, what mode of preparation is matched with a particular food stuff, and what flavour principles are embraced, and these rules have both practical material and symbolic value. Meals are mostly consumed in the company of others. Culinary identity thus is closely linked to the type of sociality sought and, as will be shown later, therefore often overlaps with class identity.

Fischler[41] is well aware that both industrialization of food production and globalization have rendered the above classifications and rules less clear and compelling. They have induced uncertainty and insecurity around food consumption and its facility to connect the eater with a defined social community. In many cases, they have led to a search for reinsertion into a comprehensive system of classification, and for a recovery of meaning and identity. A close link between food and national identity is also encapsulated in the term of 'gastronationalism', coined by DeSoucey, who demonstrates how certain foodstuffs 'become valorized as a symbol...of national identity, history, and culinary culture'.[42] 'Food not only nourishes but also signifies.'[43]

Using the lens of national identity, it will be interesting to investigate whether a *Modern British* style of cooking, long aspired to but proving illusive to attain in high-end restaurants,[44] may be more readily achieved in the setting of the gastropub. The question thus becomes whether the strong association between the institution of the pub and Englishness will be able to spill over into food and affirmation of national identity.

It is often suggested that national identity has low salience for societal elites and that, instead, they express a cosmopolitanism in both their cultural and political preferences. A cleavage between cosmopolitanism by the social elite, on the one side, and an aggressive localism by sections of the middling classes, on the other, has been demonstrated for the later eighteenth century already by Newman.[45] Its expression in the choice of food and style of eating out is studied in chapters 3 and 4.

More recently, this cosmopolitan attitude was notoriously noted by George Orwell, who suggested in 1941 that 'England is perhaps the only country whose intellectuals are ashamed of their own nationality...and who snigger at every English institution, from horseracing to suet pudding'.[46] Contemporary social scientists, such as Hannerz and Urry,[47] have drawn renewed attention to such a cultural cosmopolitanism. This perspective entails relationships to a plurality of cultures understood as distinctive entities. My analysis of the various cuisines offered by contemporary gastropubs will focus on the constant tension regarding culinary style between globally oriented cosmopolitanism and localism. Such a tension is faced by both chefs of gastropubs and by gastropubs' patrons and often has a 'class' dimension.

Introduction

Structure of the Book

The book is divided into a historical part (chapters 1–4) and a contemporary part (chapters 5–8). Chapter 1 offers a descriptive account to acquaint the reader with the historical specificity and change over time of the three types of hostelries that form the focus of the book—the alehouse/public house, the tavern, and the inn. It draws attention to their divergent organizational identities, but also to the blurring of boundaries between them over the centuries and to the survival, in the twentieth century, of only the pub in a variety of forms. Chapter 2 adopts a sociological perspective and examines how class, gender, and national identity become expressed in the sociality distinguishing the three types of venues and how this has shaped organizational identity. In chapters 3 and 4, the focus moves to the food, and, to a lesser degree, the drink consumed in the pub, tavern, and inn and how it has become connected with class, gender, and national identity. Chapter 3 analyses the importance of national identification with food, as well as its connection with class and gender, during the seventeenth and eighteenth centuries. Chapter 4, on the nineteenth and twentieth centuries, continues this same focus on food, but is additionally concerned with the development of a striking diversity in eating-out venues, together with a growing homogenization of food. In both chapters, food is viewed in the context of the social, economic, and, to a lesser degree, political transformations of the wider society.

Chapter 5 links the historical and contemporary period, but mainly focuses on the pub's dependent relationships and ensuing economic fragility during the twenty-first century. The chapter takes a political economy approach and investigates the relationship of the pub with breweries, on the one side, and, on the other, with the state and its regulatory and taxing activity. Chapter 6 deals exclusively with the gastropub. An exploration of the gastropub's food, drink, and sociality during the twenty-first century develops the notion that it experiences a divided organizational identity. Chapter 7 is devoted to an analysis of how the gastropub's identity is shaped by and reflects patrons' class and gender identity, as well as the class origin of the publican. Chapter 8 has three sections. The first enquires about the contribution the gastropub has made to the pub landscape as a whole, as well as to community and food and dining out more generally in current-day Britain. The second section tries to answer the question, posed at the beginning of the book, about the historical continuities and divergences between the tavern and the gastropub. In the third section I provide a short conclusion to the book that summarizes its main findings in the light of the theoretical framework developed in the Introduction. Chapter 8 is followed by appendixes featuring a more extended discussion of some methodological and conceptual issues, as well as a table listing all the pubs visited.

Endnotes

1. Warde, A. and Martens, L. 2000, *Eating Out. Social differentiation, consumption and pleasure*. Cambridge: Cambridge University Press.
2. Fox, K. 2004, *Watching the English*, 88. London: Hodder & Stoughton.
3. *Sunday Mirror*, 12.09.2016.
4. Batchelor, D. 1996, *The English Inn*, 3. London: B.T. Batsford Ltd; Coysh, A.W. 1972, *Historic English Inns*. Newton Abbott: David and Charles.
5. *International New York Times*, 18.02.2014: 1, 16.
6. *The Daily Telegraph*, 31.03.2016.
7. Interview with Belben in 2015.
8. *The Guardian*, 29.08.2013: 32.
9. *Financial Times Magazine*, 2.11.2013: 93.
10. *Restaurant*, February 2015: 6.
11. *Restaurant*, July 2011: 46.
12. Williams, Z. 2016, 'Raising the bar', *The Guardian* 2, 28.01.2016: 12.
13. Clark, P. 1983, *The English Alehouse. A social history 1200–1830*, 3–5. London and New York: Longman.
14. Burke, T. 1947, *The English Inn*, 139. London: Herbert Jenkins Ltd. First published in 1930.
15. Clark, 1983.
16. Ing Freeman, J. ed. 2012, 'Introduction', *The Epicure's Almanack. Eating and drinking in Regency London*, xxxviii. London: The British Library. First published by Ralph Rylance under the title *Places of Alimentary Resort* in 1815.
17. Haydon, P. 2001[1995], *Beer and Britannia*, 128. Stroud: Sutton Publishing.
18. Interview Notes 2015–16.
19. DeSoucey, M. 2010, 'Gastronationalism: food traditions and authenticity politics in the European Union', *American Journal of Sociology*, 75, 3: 432–55.
20. Rogers, B. 2003, *Beef and Liberty*, 5. London: Chatto and Windus.
21. Tombs, R. 2015, *The English and their History*, 418. London: Penguin Books.
22. Lane, C. 2014, The *Cultivation of Taste. Chefs and the organization of fine dining*, chapter 10. Oxford: Oxford University Press.
23. Nkomo, S.M. and Cox, T. 1996, 'Diverse identities in organizations', S.R. Clegg, C. Hardy and W.R. Nord eds, *Handbook of Organization Studies*, 339. London: Sage Publications.
24. Ashforth, B.E. and Mael, F. 1989, 'Social identity theory and the organization', *Academy of Management Review*, 14: 20–2.
25. Ashforth and Mael, 1989, 30.
26. Ashforth and Mael, 1989, 35.
27. Nkomo and Cox, 1996, 339.
28. Albert, S. and Whetten D. 1985, 'Organizational identity', *Research in Organizational Behavior*, 7: 263–95, 264.
29. Albert and Whetten, 1985, 264.
30. Albert, S. and Whetten, D. 2004, 'Organizational identity', M.J. Hatch and M. Schultz eds, *Organizational Identity. A Reader*, 90. Oxford: Oxford University Press.

31. Whetten, D., Foreman, P. and Dyer, W.G. 2009, 'Organizational identity and family business', L. Melin, M. Nordqvist and P. Sham eds, *The Sage Handbook of Family Business*, 480. London: Sage Publications.
32. Warde, A. 1997, *Consumption, Food and Taste*, 39f., 109, 115, 170. London: Sage Publications.
33. See Appendix II.
34. Bradley, H. 2014, 'Class descriptors or class relations? Thoughts towards a critique of Savage et al.', *Sociology*, 48, 3: 3.
35. Bradley, H. 1996, *Fractured Identities. Changing patterns of inequality*, 19. Cambridge: Polity Press.
36. Beardsworth, A. and Keil, T. 1997, *Sociology on the Menu. An invitation to the study of food and society*, 54. London: Routledge.
37. Kumar, K. 2003, *The Making of English National Identity*. Cambridge: Cambridge University Press.
38. McCrone, D. and Bechhofer, F. 2015, *Understanding National Identity*, 20. Cambridge: Cambridge University Press.
39. Newman, G. 1987, *The Rise of English Nationalism. A cultural history 1740–1830*. London: Weidenfeld and Nicholson.
40. Rogers, 2003, 3.
41. Fischler, C. 1988, 'Food, self and identity', *Social Science Information*, 27: 290.
42. DeSoucey, 2010, 433.
43. Fischler, 1988, 276.
44. Lane, 2014, chapter 6.
45. Newman, 1987.
46. Orwell, G. 1941, 'England, your England', *The Lion and the Unicorn. Socialism and the English genius*. London: Secker and Warburg.
47. Hannerz, U. 1990, 'Cosmopolitans and locals in world culture', M. Featherstone ed., *Global Culture*. London: Sage Publications; Urry, J. 1994, *Consuming Places*. London: Routledge.

Part I
A Historical Perspective

1
The Historical Development of Taverns, Inns, and Public Houses

Each of the three types of hostelry, in different historical periods, has been of enormous economic, social, and political importance, and the functions each has fulfilled have both overlapped with and shaped those of the others. This chapter provides a broad-brush picture of their historical development and of their specific features and functions, charting both their separate and overlapping spheres of activity. Chapters 2–4 will then cover specific social and political themes.

All three hostelries facilitated a sociality which entailed much more than mere entertainment. Politically, they enabled citizens to develop a public sphere,[1] as well as being an important source of revenue for the state. Economically, all three facilitated and furthered business, by enabling meetings with like-minded people and with clients, as well as storage for goods. These hostelries have also accounted for a large part of out-of-home consumption. They 'emerged as barometers of shifting consumer preferences in the areas of drink and food'.[2]

The Inn

Burke views the inn as one symbol of Englishness 'similar to the oak, the ash and the village green, woven into its history and known to everyone'.[3] Batchelor endorses this when he says that the English inn 'is as much part of our national heritage as Newmarket, or the Boat Race, or All Fools' Day'.[4] The inn goes back to the Middle Ages when, initially, monasteries and, later, local lords or churches[5] provided beds for travellers. With the increase of economic activity, travel on horseback, and the development of roads, free private hospitality ceased. Both the Saxon ale-house and the Plantagenet church-house became the English inn,[6] constituting a commercial provider of sustenance and lodgings.[7] Early inns had no bars, no set dinner, and no dining room.[8] Guests of social pretension would order food to their room and had choices of meat, or they were invited to the innkeeper's table, providing the origin for the term *'table d'hote'*. More ordinary travellers, in contrast, were shown to the common table in the kitchen.[9] A sixteenth century law forbade locals to drink in an inn.[10]

By the beginning of the seventeenth century, the English inn was well established.[11] A further impetus towards inn building came between 1663 and 1710, when road building followed the first Turnpike Act.[12] Many of the inns built in the seventeenth and eighteenth centuries stood out by their architectural splendour and were described as the English equivalent of the Italian palazzo, as stately homes and even play houses.[13] The golden age of the inn came during the middle of the eighteenth century when travel by stage coach and post-chaise greatly increased long-distance travel.[14] At the beginning of the eighteenth century, London had around 200 major inns,[15] but they expanded also in provincial urban centres and resorts, catering both for the landed gentry and the rising bourgeoisie.[16] Inns were to be found all over England, at regular intervals along the main roads leading out from London. In large towns at that time 'inns were...as common a landmark as churches',[17] but they could also be found in small towns and villages, where they were often of high standard. Thus, the French traveller Rochefoucauld remarks: 'It is extraordinary what inns there are even in the smallest English village...they are incomparably better than the French.'[18]

During the sixteenth to eighteenth centuries, inns were considered important nodes of the road transport system, as well as significant centres of economic life where trade and commerce flourished.[19] Chartres[20] sees inns as catering for the needs of the emerging 'protoindustrial' economy. Inns not only provided lodgings for travellers, but also attracted merchants of all kinds who stored and/or sold their goods in these new 'market places'. Inns additionally were used for the meetings of petty courts, of local administrative bodies, and associations of various kinds. In smaller provincial towns, where dedicated administrative buildings were in very short supply, an inn would serve as a post office, excise office, lock-up, and court house as well as give room to petty and licensing sessions.

Inns additionally hosted political gatherings. In both Northampton and Norwich, for example, the meetings of each political party centred on a particular inn,[21] and inns were often party headquarters during elections.[22] During the eighteenth century, party candidates often held sumptuous dinners at well-known inns and ran up big bills for food and drink to gain supporters.

From the late seventeenth century, inns also became important social centres. With a rapidly urbanizing population and the growth of the urban leisured and professional classes, they came to cater for large-scale social occasions in a grand way, serving both drink and food.[23] Some urban inns had a considerable capacity and size, and London inns were particularly capacious.

In larger provincial towns, the social season attracted not only the country gentry who now took up residence there during the winter, but also the so-called town gentry, comprising the new professional occupations of various kinds.[24] Inns, says Chartres,[25] became 'social stages' for events ranging from public dining to club and race meetings. Inns were closely associated with the development of commercialized leisure, hosting concerts, theatre, recitals, and exhibitions.[26] Their yards presented the first music-halls and, later, the first play houses.[27]

In providing splendid meals for large parties of upper and upper-middle class guests, inns thus overlapped with and were competitors to taverns, particularly in London. Inns were, however, distinct from taverns in that they catered only for corporate bodies and not for individual diners. However, the cuisine they developed, as I will show in Chapters 3 and 4, nevertheless became an important part of the English culinary heritage.

Yet, not all social activities carried out in inns were genteel, and many provincial inns hosted such contests as cock-fighting, rat-catching, or prize-fighting with bare knuckles.[28] In several places, inns also hosted freak shows and exhibitions of various wild beasts that were immensely popular among all social groups.[29]

Inns improved greatly over the centuries as travel of all kinds grew and the public sphere expanded. Everitt, in his detailed study of Northampton, points to a distinct hierarchy among its inns. The largest had room for up to 400 horses and also accommodated up to 200 people for a special feast, and large scale was usually accompanied by high social status.[30] The three County Inns were at the top in the eighteenth century, patronized by the shire gentry, by titled magnates travelling through, and by the corporation and other public bodies on festive occasions.[31]

Inns receive a variety of evaluations by both English and foreign travellers. John Byng—a minor aristocrat who later became Lord Torrington—travelled regularly in different parts of England between 1781 and 1794. He, too, underlines the variability in quality between inns. In some inns, a traveller might be asked to share a room with a stranger or even sleep in a servant's bedroom, whereas in others it was possible to have supper served in one's own parlour.[32] The following only slightly exaggerates his most frequent impressions:

> The imposition in travelling is abominable; the innkeepers are insolent, the hostlers are sulky, the chambermaids are pert, and the waiters are impertinent; the meat is tough, the wine is foul, the bed is hard, the sheets are wet, the linen is dirty, and the knives are never clean'd![33]

Dickens, in *Pickwick Papers*, usually waxes lyrically about English inns. But as a paying customer, he was aware that there were some very poor and even unsavoury specimens. He refers disparagingly to an Ipswich inn as having 'such clusters of mouldy, ill-lighted rooms... a dying fire in a dirty grate, an hour's wait for dinner, and a waiter with a fortnight-old napkin'. He complains that, in an inn at Charing Cross, London, his bedroom 'smelt like a hackney coach and was shut up like a family vault'.[34]

Inns were not only loved by Englishmen but were also admired by foreign visitors. Thus, the Frenchman, Grosley, who did a tour of England in 1765, expressed great admiration for them:

> The towns and villages have excellent inns... at these an English lord is as well served as at his own house... Few inns in France can stand up to competition with the English.[35]

Another French upper-class traveller, Gustave d'Eichthal, staying in Britain for the year of 1828, in contrast, found some of the inns wanting, in both cleanliness and service. He complained that 'bedrooms are usually poorly furnished, the rooms are dirty and the staff... are dirtier still',[36] and 'guests are treated with indifference' and are received 'in a surly manner' by innkeepers.[37]

From the 1830s, the railway became a competitor to the coaching trade and its inns. By 1845, most long-distance travel was by railway. Some inns became public houses, others private residences. The disappearance of inns was particularly marked in London, whereas many more survived in the provinces.[38] Between the last quarter of the eighteenth century and the early years of the nineteenth century, dedicated buildings were to replace inns in carrying out the economic, administrative, and social functions that had centred on them.[39] By the middle of the nineteenth century, the inn had given way to the hotel.[40]

After World War I, the appearance of the motor car led to some revival of inns. Some old coaching inns were restored, and new ones were built. After World War II, brewing companies and hotel chains came to own most inns.[41] A description of Midland inns in the early 1950s[42] makes clear that a lot of inn buildings had not been destroyed, but were thriving as pubs, hotels, or pubs with rooms.

Even after the institution of the inn had become a historic relic, the label was still appropriated by some owners of other types of hostelries to indicate a socially superior status for what were essentially restaurants or pubs with rooms. Examples before World War II are John Fothergill's Spread Eagle at Thame, Barry Neames's Golden Hind at Hythe, Hampshire, and Gordon Russell's Lygon Arms at Broadway, Cotswolds. These self-styled innkeepers adopted a high degree of social selectivity in the class of guests they accommodated. John Fothergill, in particular, believed that it was as necessary to select the customers as to select the furniture or the wine. He declared: 'I have determined not only to have proper and properly cooked food but to have only either intelligent, beautiful or well-bred people to eat it.'[43]

In conclusion, inns had not only preserved centuries-old architecture and décor lending distinction to a village or part of town, but often constituted a valuable community asset. Some of these surviving inns, as I shall show in Chapter 6, have received a new incarnation as gastropubs.

The Tavern

The first legislation on taverns was introduced in 1553 when a strict division of functions was established between the tavernkeeper or vintner whose business was victualling, and the innkeeper whose business was to shelter travellers. Taverns had to become licensed and could not have amusements and gaming. They sold wine, rather than beer to the prosperous urban dwellers. In London, taverns were more numerous than inns but were outnumbered by far by alehouses. Outside London, taverns could be found in some large towns but, overall, were small in number. The reasons why taverns thrived in the seventeenth and eighteenth centuries were partly the early development of capitalism in England and the wealth this created. A second reason, given by Mennell et al.,[44] is that the meeting of Parliament in the spring and autumn of each year brought many of the landed elites into London. They sought a social as well as a political life and found taverns congenial places for this.

From the early seventeenth century onwards, taverns also came to provide increasingly elaborate hot meals to both individuals and parties.[45] In London, taverns became the main dining-out places to go to. Indeed, the seventeenth century is judged to have been the 'golden age of the tavern'.[46] Taverns, like inns, for much of the time became social centres. They catered both for individuals/smaller parties, and, in the larger taverns, particularly in London, also hosted many large-scale dinners and cultural events. Like inns, they served as meeting places for people with shared business, political, or cultural interests who mainly belonged to the middling and upper classes. Taverns were considered the most upmarket hostelries, where Londoners went for good food and drink and lively company.[47]

Most taverns had a big ground-floor called the bar room, buttery, or simply tavern. Here was the place for general eating and drinking. Then there were a striking number of private drinking/dining rooms, which might be used for business meetings, gambling, or amorous assignations.[48] Judging from pictures, tables usually had white table cloths and the rooms had some booths.[49]

The larger London taverns boasted grand assembly rooms suitable for large and small dinners. The Crown and Anchor, for example, could accommodate as many as 700 diners.[50]

Regarded as meeting places for polite conversation, taverns constituted an alternative to ale houses that were much more associated with uncouth drunkenness.[51] Although some taverns also came to be associated with less than polite behaviour. (For more details on the social background of both tavernkeepers and their guests, see Chapter 2.) However, the purpose of taverns was not exhausted by mere drinking and dining. They brought together (mainly) men for literary and political discussion, as well as for transacting business. Taverns became places for investments to be arranged and lawyers and physicians to be consulted,[52] and in smaller towns they even hosted book clubs.[53] The often lively literary and intellectual tenor of London tavern life is well captured in the following summary: 'Taverns were the centres of the arts, journalism, political debate, gossip, and of arguments on philosophy and religion.'[54]

During the seventeenth and, particularly, the eighteenth centuries, taverns attracted a host of literary, philosophical, and political luminaries, such as Ben Jonson, Jonathan Swift, Daniel Defoe, Dryden, Samuel Johnson, Oliver Goldsmith, David Garrick, Edmund Burke, Joseph Addison and Richard Steele. 'Each place had its social and professional "tone", and gathered about it men of like tastes and sympathies.'[55] That such men could also be boxers, an outlawed sport, was learnt by the French visitor to England, Gustave d'Eichthal, when he was shown a tavern 'which was the haunt of all the boxers and where you can learn the place of the next fight'.[56]

Taverns were thus meeting places used by men as they would later use private members' clubs. In 1764, Samuel Johnson formed what was later called the Literary Club that attracted many luminaries of the day.[57] Tombs[58] even calls the tavern 'an unofficial British academy' and, indeed, early meetings of what eventually became the Royal Society, occurred in London taverns. Taverns additionally hosted cultural events such as public meetings, special lectures, balls, and concerts, and rooms that could be hired for performances by both amateurs and professionals.[59] In London, taverns and inns thus were direct competitors, both as caterers and as forums for cultural events.

A few of the London taverns were singled out for the lavish banquets they provided. The London Tavern was even referred to as 'a temple of gastronomy'. Built on a space cleared by the fire of London of 1665, just within the City, it was once renowned both for its architectural splendour and for its food, particularly under its chef John Farley. (For more detail on the meals served, see the section on 'Food served' in Chapter 3.) 'From the beginning to its end, the London Tavern was what its name clearly intended to imply, the reflection of the City of London, and, although in many contrasting ways, of the interests of the city.'[60]

Several of the London taverns acquired considerable fame, either for their architectural splendour or for the famous men attending them and, much more rarely, for the quality of the meals they served. The London Tavern's architectural magnificence sometimes led to visitors mistaking it for the Bank of England.[61] The tavern was surprisingly large and could serve up to 2,500 people for a banquet and was known to have huge wine cellars. Other taverns famous for their banqueting were the White Hart Tavern, Holborn, and the Globe Tavern, Fleet Street, where Richard Briggs, author of the renowned cookery book, *The English Art of Cookery*, was *chef de cuisine* for a long time, together with the Crown and Anchor Tavern in the Strand, where Francis Collingwood and John Woollams, also connected with a best-selling cookery book, *The Universal Cook*, were the chefs.[62]

Until the second half of 1880s, taverns were quite traditional and unchanged, although at a point of transition. George Sims observes that even in the 1880s, people sat mainly at collective tables—separate tables were still unusual.[63] This arrangement made taverns very sociable places where good conversation was as important as good food and drink. Privacy was not yet high on the list of priorities.

Because of the high social or artistic reputation of some of their patrons, we mainly know about the more elegant taverns, but the appearance and social reputation of taverns was quite diverse. Some taverns attracted shady characters, such as highway men, footpads, and pickpockets.[64] Quite a few London taverns offered a retreat 'to receive prostitutes and their gallants'. Rooms were specifically set aside for this.[65]

The most famous ode to the tavern is that by Samuel Johnson, addressed to his friend Boswell in 1776, during a visit to a tavern in Blenheim:

> [T]here is no private house (said he) in which people can enjoy themselves so well, as at a capital tavern... at a tavern there is a general freedom from anxiety. You are sure you are welcome... no servants will attend to you with the alacrity the waiters do who are incited by the prospect of an immediate reward in proportion as they please. No sir; there is nothing which has yet been contrived by man, by which so much happiness is produced as by a good tavern or inn.[66]

Another bon mot attributed to Johnson is that 'a tavern chair was the throne of human felicity'.

The English have prided themselves on their taverns and extolled them in invidious comparisons with the French, who, until the end of the eighteenth century, had nothing comparable; and the French, for once, accepted that the English had a lead in this field. When one of the first restaurants was eventually opened in Paris, in 1782 by Antoine de Beauvilliers, it was named *La Grande Taverne de Londres*.

Taverns began to lose their reputation when, at the end of the eighteenth century, they became associated with vice. Coffee houses came to rival taverns as meeting places.[67] The prominent place occupied by London taverns as centres of intellectual activity lasted until the beginning of the nineteenth century. After that 'they were no longer the rendezvous for the principal men of the day'.[68] By the 1870s, taverns had passed into the hands of the brewer, and inn and tavern had merged.[69] By then, many taverns appear similar to pubs, with boisterous customers staying until late at night, and brawling not unknown.[70] The tavern had become deserted by its higher-class customers, who had created 'their own places'—the clubs—and wanted to exclude the general public.[71] This exodus caused the tavern to fall further in general esteem. Left to the working classes, it is said to have become gradually 'a social outcast' and, particularly in London, became referred to as 'pub'.

From the 1860s onwards, the appearance of the first London restaurants (outside hotels) further undermined taverns' substance by offering fine dining and a smart and exclusive new venue for the upper middle classes.[72] By the beginning of the twentieth century, those on comfortable incomes finally changed from eating in taverns to eating in 'dining rooms' or restaurants.[73] This was not universally viewed as progress. George Sims laments: 'With the passing of the old tavern life a great change has come over Fleet Street. The comradeship of the teacup and cigarette is not as the comradeship of the tankard and the pipe.'[74]

However, in a few places the tavern hung on tenaciously. Even in 1901, the year Newnham-Davies[75] published a kind of 'Good Food' guide to London, a few taverns are still mentioned. When Newnham-Davies wanted a more casual meal at the end of a working day, he went alone to the Cheddar Cheese. A detailed description of it makes clear that, in physical appearance, social arrangements, and food served, it still preserved many features of the tavern of old.

Taverns, it has become clear, had a very distinctive character and in their heyday differed in nearly all their features from pubs. The reason why I view them nevertheless as forerunners of gastropubs is that they combined the sale of drink with that of food and prided themselves on the special character of their buildings. A similar evaluation can be made of inns, which, moreover, were distinguished by providing accommodation. The kind of sociability both were able to foster, and the political importance they attained, was uniquely their own. Yet, the glamour and high social status attached to many of the taverns and inns is often aspired to by contemporary pubs and pub companies when they appropriate their titles.

The Alehouse/Public House

The alehouse is the oldest, as well as the most numerous of the three main establishments, with early mentions already in the twelfth century. As it turned eventually into the public house, it is also the most long-lived. Clark and Jennings both date the change in nomenclature from alehouse to public house in the late seventeenth century.[76] The public house, in turn, came to be referred to as simply the pub from around the 1850s onwards.

Only from the sixteenth century did the alehouse become a ubiquitous, central feature of the social world of ordinary folk.[77] Alehouses started as very modest places in private houses, and alehouse keepers brewed the ale they sold on the premises without requiring a licence. In early alehouses, a green bush—a clump of ivy and wine leaves to signify Bacchus—over the door or on a pole signified that ale was available for sale.

Ale was made solely from fermented malt. Beer with hops added first appeared in the late fifteenth century, particularly in London and somewhat later in the provinces.[78] Alehouses also provided rather basic food, such as bread and cheese, and they additionally provided very basic accommodation for the lower orders.[79] They were considered much less respectable than inns and taverns,[80] and Wrightson describes numerous campaigns to get them repressed.[81]

From the late seventeenth century onwards, alehouse premises became less rudimentary than they had been in the past. By the mid-eighteenth century, larger alehouses or, more often now, public houses had come to predominate.[82]

In the eighteenth century, gin shops gained ground and became regarded as a severe social menace. They were becoming competitors to public houses and constituted a threat to breweries. Brewers countered the competition by increasing the number of alehouses. As beer was thought to be far less harmful than gin, the Beer Act of 1830 introduced a new lower-tier establishment, the beer house. This, too, was generally located in private homes, and own brewing was permitted. As it was easier to gain a licence for a beer house than for a pub, they expanded rapidly. This led to greatly increased drunkenness and public disorder.[83] Most beer houses eventually became pubs, and the name virtually disappeared towards the end of the nineteenth century. The coffee house, first introduced around 1809, also became a competitor to the pub, but its influence was temporary, and the pub outlived it.

By 1830, the public house was slowly becoming recognizable as a modern institution. Builders, brewers, and publicans began to construct purpose-built pubs with special facades, and the old adapted dwelling houses began to disappear. Landlords came to copy taverns and inns, with some even adopting their names. Such confusion reflected both the growing size of pubs and the decline of taverns and inns by the end of the eighteenth century.[84] Such levelling up in scale and value of public houses occurred across the whole country, even in villages.[85]

The golden age of public drinking in England and Wales was between 1831 and 1881, when the number of public houses rose by nearly half.[86] This rise is attributed to the effects of industrialization and urbanization, the rising wages the new industrial working class could command, and the increased spending power they now possessed. Public houses were considered to play a huge part in public life, greater than friendly societies or churches.

The physical layout of public houses also changed significantly over time. Whereas in the seventeenth and eighteenth centuries, drinkers mainly took their drink standing up in vast undivided bars, from Victorian times, there were tables and chairs in all bars.[87] However, 'perpendicular' or 'vertical drinking' never totally disappeared from public bars and tap rooms. It was also during Victorian times that bar counters with beer taps were first installed, making it much more efficient and faster to dispense beer. At the same time, bars became sub-divided into a number of different drinking spaces by either walls or screens. These were used by different social constituencies. Pubs, during this time, 'were in every way the antithesis to the clubs for which the middle classes had abandoned them. . . . it was all glare, glitter and rattle'—ornamental glass, brass, mirrors, and lamps glowed and sparkled all over London during this period.[88] Jennings adds that, during Victorian times, the pub acquired a homogeneity in appearance and in the sociability provided.[89]

No reliable census data are available about the proportion of the population that visited pubs at different times and with what frequency (licensing statistics do not distinguish pubs from other types of hostelries selling alcohol, such as hotels and restaurants). Girouard, writing about London,[90] reports that in 1896 London had a pub for every 345 persons. Although high, this number was much lower than in large northern towns where the industrial working class was concentrated. In the early 1800s, there are estimated to have been 58,000 alehouses—one for every 90 of the country's inhabitants—of which 44,000 brewed their own ale.[91] One house in every 41 was a licensed pub.[92] However, alcohol consumption declined continuously from the 1870s, when it had peaked. From the end of the nineteenth century, a numerical decline of pubs became noticeable.

During the Edwardian period, the pub lost some of its old significance as a facility for meetings of all sorts—it became more a place of leisure and drinking. The working class had become more affluent and had better homes, as well as access to a more diverse range of leisure activities. Working Men's Clubs became a competitor.[93] Increased suburbanization and dramatic slum clearance also contributed to the decline of the public house. The new estates built had far fewer pubs, and new towns, such as Letchworth Garden City, were built without making provision for any pubs.[94] Between 1905 and 1935, a significant reduction in pubs occurred, from 99,000 to 77,500[95]—the first of several waves of closure in the twentieth century. Selley, providing a rough estimate based on his extensive field work during the first half of 1920s, suggests that 'well over half the adult population visit public houses either occasionally or regularly'.[96]

During the early twentieth century, largely under the influence of the Temperance Movement, the movement for 'improved pubs' started with the foundation, in 1901, of the Public House Trust. The principle behind this recognized the public house as a social institution, but wanted to transform it, as far as possible, from a mere drinking place into a well-conducted club.[97] The Trust installed 'disinterested management' of the pubs to keep down the price of beer.[98] Their coherent philosophy for improvement included the following objectives: weaker drink, an improved physical environment, and more food—all to provide a better environment not only for the traditional drinkers, but also for their families.[99] The pubs were to be managed in the interest of the community and not for private profit.[100] Historians generally suggest that the reformed pubs were only a qualified success.[101] Publicans mostly lacked the skills and interest in providing food, and profits could not be made. Nevertheless, the adoption of the improved or reformed pub in many parts of the country provided for the first time the model which would be resurrected in the twenty-first century, when the food-led pub and eventually the gastro pub emerged. Its association with the Temperance movement, however, rules out any open recognition of such a forerunner.

The Pub Improvement movement picked up strength, particularly as a result of World War I. Pub life was transformed by drastic restrictions on the hours of drinking, increases in the prices of drink, and a considerable reduction of the alcoholic content of beer. Drunkenness declined significantly,[102] with alcohol consumption cut by half—this was fully reversed only during the 1990s.[103]

Selley, writing as a sympathizer of the Temperance Movement,[104] observes that 'the bad old swing-door types of pub', which are small, gloomy, and unpleasant, without adequate toilet facilities and beyond renovation, had by no means disappeared by that time. Such small back-street pubs nevertheless attracted large crowds at the weekend, so that much drinking occurred in alley-ways or on the pavement. Rather than providing social activities, this type of pub, Selley suggests,[105] was associated with a lot of obscene language and bad behaviour. A more sympathetic view of even back-street pubs or locals is provided by the Mass Observation study, carried out in the late 1930s.[106] While the vaults and taprooms of the Bolton pubs they studied were, indeed, very basic and sometimes dirty, they are not portrayed as gloomy and unpleasant. Instead, they are viewed as the setting for social interaction and often lively conviviality. Moreover, the 'best room' or parlour of these pubs was usually much more comfortable and cleaner, and more like these people's living rooms at home. Mass Observation states that, even with the ongoing slow decline of the pub in the late 1930s, the pub held its position of an eminent social institution: '[O]f the social institutions that mould men's lives between home and work in an industrial town, such as Worktown [Bolton], the pub has more buildings, holds more people, takes more of their time and money, than church, cinema, dance-hall, and political organizations put together.'[107]

Jennings views the years of World War II as something of a swan song for the central role pubs had performed in the past,[108] even though the pub had played a vital role as a social centre during the War. Heydon, too, reports a decline in the number of pubs and in drinking.[109] Other commentators, however, emphasize the continuing vitality of pubs. Tiptaft, writing in the late 1940s/early 1950s about notable pubs in and around Birmingham, gives a less pessimistic picture and portrays them as lively and many-sided social hubs of the community.[110] Thus, despite much lament about the decline of the pub's social functions, examples of traditional pubs that combined drinking with community functions were still found at this point in time. The decline clearly was proceeding in an uneven fashion, and, compared with contemporary pub closing, its scale was moderate.

Community studies carried out in the mid-1950s[111] also make clear that traditional pubs maintained their attraction and persisted in large numbers in old-established working-class areas, such as Bethnal Green, east London, or the small mining town of Ashley, Yorkshire. The suburban periphery of London, however, home to new housing developments for recently resettled Londoners, contained very few pubs. Moreover, they lost the allegiance of many of the re-housed people who had been avid pub goers in their old homes. Whereas in the tightly packed area of Bethnal Green there had been around 100 pubs—one pub for every 100 dwellings, in the new suburb, with its low-density housing development, there were merely two pubs. The new pubs' loss of popularity among the re-housed Londoners was due to a variety of factors: distances from home to the pub had greatly increased; a new pride in their much better homes diverted both interests and resources from the pub to a new home-centredness; the new pubs no longer offered an extension of either close work or neighbourhood relationships—it lacked a community feeling; and, last, the new pubs, although larger and cleaner and with better facilities, just did not have the ambience of the pubs they had lost. Willmott and Young comment:

> They [the new pubs] are not small cosy bars...filled with the cheerful jangle of a honky-tonk piano or a twanging juke box. They are often much larger places, with

carpeted lounges, furnished in pseudo-Jacobean style, where the landlords wear crested blazers and call their customers 'old boy' and where the drinks are more often pink gins or whiskies and soda.[112]

During the late twentieth century, very decisive changes occurred in the pub landscape when government action led to significant transformations of ownership. The Beer Orders Act of 1989 forced the big brewers (the Big Six) to divest themselves of some of the pubs they had owned since the late seventeenth century. (A detailed description of the Act's consequences is provided in Chapter 5.)

The transformation, following the 1989 Act, additionally encouraged the creation, from the late 1980s onwards, of a new breed of pubs, the branded mega pubs that usually operate very large chains.[113] Their emergence and growth also received a boost from the liberalization of the licensing laws at the beginning of the twenty-first century. These mega pubs or bars have come to dominate city centres, taking over former cinemas, banks, shops, and even churches. They are very different from traditional pubs both in appearance and in the way they are run. Their owners wanted to give customers a consistent formula and standard. They introduced a very streamlined food offer during the day, while at night time they became drinking and entertainment pubs. Each new outlet is developed in line with the brand template. They are epitomized 'by a standard approach to their signage and appearance, their method of operation and their customer base'.[114] Among them are names like J.D. Weatherspoon, All Bar One, Pitcher and Piano, Slug and Lettuce, and Harvester. They are mostly very large, and some, such as J.D. Weatherspoon, are massive, having nearly 1,000 branches in 2017.[115]

These mega pubs sell both drinks and unpretentious food at relatively low prices and are widely seen to offer good value. A look at Harvester, which comes fourth among top branded UK pub restaurants, well illustrates their scale and the challenge they pose to non-chain city centre pub restaurants. Although these chains became very popular among students, women, and families in the day time, and have revived pub-going among young men and women in the evenings, they have had a negative impact on the survival of small entrepreneurial pubs of the traditional kind—the community hubs or locals. Their impact may be likened to that of the supermarkets upon small owner-managed food shops. The closure of smaller traditional drinking pubs therefore continued into the twenty-first century, and both its scale and the various reasons for it will be discussed in detail in Chapter 5.

One reaction to this trend towards turning pubs into eating houses or closing them down was initiated by the Campaign for Real Ale (CAMRA), founded in the 1970s. CAMRA has sought to resuscitate the drinking side of pubs through the introduction of real ales and ciders. It has become a high-profile and successful campaigning body in the industry, engaged in trying to stem both the dying of pubs and their conversion into 'mere' restaurants, as well as lobbying government for the reduction of duty on beer. CAMRA view pubs as the hub of the community and declare in their manifesto:

> Well-run pubs play an invaluable role at the heart of their local communities. They provide a safe, regulated and sociable environment for people to enjoy a drink responsibly and meet people from different backgrounds.[116]

All these developments, together with the broadening out of the customer base to include women and families, and the diversification of both food and drink offerings, means that the pub has become a highly heterogeneous institution. Thornton suggests a broad, three-fold division of the pub landscape into mega pubs or bars, food-led pubs, and a minority of old-fashioned drinking pubs or boozers, each with their own identity.[117] This three-fold categorization is further refined according to location and customer base in the marketing segments used by the big pub companies. Thus, in the early 2000s, Punch Taverns divided its 9,200 plus pubs into four categories:

1. The basic local with a generally working-class customer base and relatively few women, largely dependent on sales of drink and of little food.

2. Mid-market locals—the traditional pub—in mid-market residential areas that mostly offer food and themed evenings, quizzes, darts, or pool.

3. City locals away from the night-time circuit, catering for local workers and shoppers by day and residents by night.

4. Upmarket locals that are still community pubs in low-density housing areas for white-collar workers and professionals, and with a higher proportion of women than other locals.

Together, these four types made up 78 per cent of their holdings.[118]

In conclusion, this chapter has provided a historical overview of the development of the three hospitality venues, underlining both the different commercial and social functions of each, as well as pointing out their overlaps during times of transition. Whereas the pub was always the lowest in the social hierarchy among the three, it has been the longest survivor and has gradually taken over some of the functions formerly performed by inns and taverns, including the provision of food. Pubs have also tried to cultivate some of the design features and, above all, the perceived social aura of the inn and tavern. The category 'pub', at the end of the twentieth century, inevitably has become more internally differentiated in terms of size and amenities offered, providing a variety of venues to consumers seeking a range of public house experiences. Where pubs are food-led, we find marked differences in the kind and quality of the food offered. At the top end of the resulting scale, from the late 1990s/early 2000s onwards, we find gastropubs.

Endnotes

1. Habermas, J. 1989, *The Structural Transformation of the Public Sphere. An inquiry into a category of bourgeois society*. Cambridge: Polity Press.
2. Kümin, B. and Tlusty, B.A. 2002, 'The world of the tavern: an introduction', B. Kümin and B.A. Tlusty eds, *The World of the Tavern*, 9. Aldershot, Hampshire: Ashgate.
3. Burke, T. 1947 [1930], *The English Inn*, 7. London: Herbert Jenkins Ltd.
4. Batchelor, D. 1963, *The English Inn*, 17. London: B.T. Batsford Ltd.
5. Batchelor, 1963; Chartres, J. 2002, 'The eighteenth-century inn: a transient golden age?', B. Kümin and B.A. Tlusty eds, *The World of the Tavern*, 205–26. Aldershot, Hampshire: Ashgate; Jennings, P. 2011, *The Local. A history of the English pub*, 2nd edition. Stroud: The History Press.
6. Parr-Maskell, H. 1927, *The Taverns of Old England*. London: Allan & Co. Ltd; Burke, 1947 [1930], 41.
7. Coysh, A.W. 1972, *Historic English Inns*, 11. Newton Abbott: David and Charles; Clark, P. 1983, *The English Alehouse. A social history 1200–1830*, 7. London and New York: Longman.
8. Burke, 1947 [1930].
9. Batchelor, 1963, 24.
10. Mass Observation 1987 [1943], *The Pub and the People. A Worktown study by Mass Observation*, 81. London: The Cresset Library.
11. Chartres, 2002, 207.
12. Coysh, 1972, 14.
13. Borsay, P. 1989, *The English Urban Renaissance. Culture and society in the provincial town*, 210–11. Oxford: Clarendon Press; Scarfe, N. 1995 [1785], *Innocent Espionage. The La Rochefoucauld brothers' tour of England in 1785*, 52, 143. Woodbridge: The Boydell Press.
14. Clark, 1983, 7; Burke, 1947 [1930], 65.
15. Chartres, 2002, 207, 208.
16. Borsay, 1989, 223.
17. Chartres, 2002, 219.
18. Scarfe, 1995 [1785], 22–3.
19. Everitt, A. 1985, 'The English urban inn', *Landscape and Community in England*, 155–208. London: Hambleton Press; Brandwood, G., Davison, A. and Slaughter, M. 2011, *Licensed to Sell. The history and heritage of the public house*. Swindon: English Heritage.
20. Chartres, 2002, 204.
21. Thompson, L.P. 1947, *Norwich Inns*, 15. Ipswich: W.E. Harrison & Sons Ltd.
22. Thompson, 1947, 5.
23. Borsay, 1989, 223; Brandwood et al., 2011.
24. Everitt, 1985; Borsay, 1989, 223.
25. Chartres, 2002, 206.
26. Burke, 1947 [1930]; Coysh, 1972; Everitt, 1985.
27. Burke, 1947 [1930], 7.

28. Thompson, 1947, 14, 49; Tiptaft, N. 1951, *Inns of the Midlands*, 21, 22, 154. Birmingham: Norman Tiptaft; Riddington Young, J. 1975, *The Inns and Taverns of Old Norwich*, 33. Norwich: Wensum Books.
29. Thompson, 1947, 19; Picard, L. 2001, *Dr Johnson's London. Everyday life in London 1740–1770*, 251. London: Phoenix.
30. Everitt, 1985, 165–6.
31. Chartres, 2002, 187.
32. Byng's Diaries, A Vision of Britain Through Time, at http://www.visionofbritain.org.uk/travellers/Byng.
33. Andrews, C.B. ed., 1954, *Torrington Diaries. Containing the tours through England and Wales of the Hon. John Byng between the years of 1881–1794*, 55. London: Eyre and Spottiswoode.
34. Cited by Batchelor, 1963, 122.
35. Grosley, M. 1772, *A Tour to England or, Observations on England and its Inhabitants. Volume I*, 20–1. Dublin: J. Exshaw et al.
36. Ratcliffe, B.M. and Chaloner, W.H. eds, 1977, *A French Sociologist Looks at England. Gustave d'Eichthal and British society in 1828*, 63. Manchester: Manchester University Press and Rowman and Littlefield.
37. Ratcliffe and Chaloner, 1977, 13.
38. Richardson, S. and Eberlein, H.D. 1925, *The English Inn, Past and Present*, 108. London: Batsford.
39. Chartres, 2002, 223.
40. Everitt, 1985, 156; Ing Freeman, J. ed. 2012, 'Introduction', *The Epicure's Almanack. Eating and drinking in Regency London*, xxxviii. London: The British Library. First published by Ralph Rylance under the title *Places of Alimentary Resort* in 1815.
41. Coysh, 1972, 16.
42. Tiptaft, 1951.
43. Fothergill J. 1931, *An Innkeeper's Diary*, 130. London: Chatto & Windus.
44. Mennell, S., Murcott, A. and van Otterloo, A.H. 1992, *The Sociology of Food: Eating, diet and culture*, 82. London: Sage Publications.
45. Clark, 1983, 13; Ing Freeman, 2012 [1815].
46. Brandwood et al., 2011, 10.
47. Earle, P. 1989, The *Making of the English Middle Class. Business, society, and family life in London, 1660–1730*, 52. London: Methuen.
48. Earle, 1989, 53.
49. Berry, G. 1978, *Taverns and Tokens of Pepys' London*, 40. London: Seaby Publications Ltd; Brandwood et al., 2011, 10.
50. Ing Freeman, 2012 [1815], 40.
51. Brewer, J. 1997, '"The most polite age and the most vicious": attitudes towards culture as a commodity, 1660–1800', J. Bermingham and J. Brewer eds, *The Consumption of Culture 1600–1800. Image, object, text*, 38. London and New York: Routledge.
52. Clark, 1983, 13; Brewer, 1997, 38.
53. Brewer, 1997, 182–3.
54. Stanley, L.T. 1957, *The Old Inns of London*, 11. London: Batsford; see also Brewer, 1997, 37.

55. Burke, 1947 [1930].
56. Ratcliffe and Chaloner, 1977, 28.
57. Boswell, J. 1953, *Boswell's Life of London*, 284. Oxford: Oxford University Press; Parr-Maskell, 1927, 96.
58. Tombs, R. 2015, *The English and their History*, 294. London: Penguin Books.
59. Brewer, 1997, 366.
60. Medcalf, S. 1988, 'Introduction', J. Farley, *The London Art of Cookery*, 2. London: Southover Press. (First published in 1783.)
61. Medcalf, 1988, 2–3.
62. Mennell, S. 1985, *All Manners of Food. Eating and taste in England and France from the Middle Ages to the present*, 99. Oxford: Basil Blackwell. https://en.wikipedia.org/wiki/The_English_Art_of_Cookery https://en.wikipedia.org/wiki/The_Universal_Cook.
63. Sims, G. 1917, *My Life. Sixty years' recollections of Bohemian London*, 95. London: Eveleigh Nash Company.
64. Shelley, H.C. 1909, *Inns and Taverns of Old London*, 154. London: Sir Isaac Pitman.
65. Grosley, 1772, 59.
66. Boswell, 1953, 697.
67. Shelley, 1909, 163.
68. Stanley, 1957, 14.
69. Burke, 1947 [1930], 143; Smith, M.A. 1984, *The Public House. Leisure and social control*, 17. Centre for Leisure Studies: University of Salford.
70. Jennings, 2011, 19.
71. Shelley, 1909; Burke, 1947 [1931].
72. Burnett, J. 2004, *England Eats Out: A social history of eating out in England from 1830 to the present*, 86. Harlow: Longman.
73. Burnett, 2004, 139.
74. Sims, 1917, 330.
75. Newnham-Davis N. 1901, *Dinners and Diners: Where and how to dine in London*. London: Grant Richards.
76. Clark, 1983, 5; Jennings, 2011, 15–16.
77. Clark, 1983, 34.
78. Brandwood, et al., 2011, 16.
79. Hailwood, M. 2014, *Ale Houses and Good Fellowship in Early Modern England*. Woodbridge: Boydell Press.
80. Clark, 1983, 4.
81. Wrightson, K. 1982, *English Society, 1580–1680*, 227. London: Hutchinson.
82. Clark, 1983, 195.
83. Clark, 1983, 3.
84. Clark, 1983, 273–4.
85. Clark, 1983, 275.
86. Clark, 1983, 1.
87. Girouard, M. 1984, *Victorian Pubs*, 4. New Haven and London: Yale University Press.
88. Girouard, 1984, 4.

89. Jennings, 2011, 219.
90. Girouard, 1984, 2.
91. Jennings, 2011, 22–3.
92. Wilson, B. 2007, *Decency and Disorder. The age of cant 1789–1837*, 255. London: Faber and Faber.
93. Jennings, 2011, 132.
94. Jennings, 2011, 195.
95. Haydon, P. 2001[1995], *Beer and Britannia*, 271. Stroud: Sutton Publishing.
96. Selley, E. 1927, *The English Public House as It Is*, 21. London: Longmans, Green and Co. Ltd.
97. Girouard, 1984, 219.
98. King, F.A. 1947, *Beer has a History*, 150. London: Hutchinson's Scientific and Technical Publications.
99. Selley, 1927, 69ff.
100. Selley, 1927, 74.
101. Selley, 1927, 75: Girouard, 1984, 219; Gutzke, D.W. 2004, *Pubs and Progressives. Reinventing the public house in England, 1896–1960*, 226. DeKalb, Illinois: Northern Illinois University Press.
102. Harrison, 1943, quoted in Hey, V. 1986, *Patriarchy and Pub Culture*, 39. London: Tavistock Publications.
103. Tombs, 2015, 628.
104. Selley, 1927, 57, 58.
105. Selley, 1927, 62.
106. Mass Observation 1987 [1943].
107. Mass Observation 1987 [1943], 17.
108. Jennings, 2011, 211.
109. Haydon, 2001[1995].
110. Tiptaft, 1951, 99.
111. Dennis, N., Henriques, F. and Slaughter, C. 1956, *Coal is our Life*. London: Eyre and Spottiswoode; Willmott, P. and Young, M. 1976 [1960], *Family and Class in a London Suburb*. London: The English Library; and Willmott, P. and Young, M. 2011 [1957], *Family and Kinship in East London*. London: Routledge Revivals.
112. Willmott and Young 1976 [1960], 85.
113. Jennings, 2011, 218; Thornton, T. 2014, *Brewers, Brands and the Pub in their Hands*, 61ff. Kibworth Beauchamps: Matador.
114. Thornton, 2014, 69.
115. *The Observer Magazine*, 06.08.2017: 22–4.
116. CAMRA 2015 at http://www.camra.org.uk/home.
117. Thornton, 2014, 219.
118. Reported in Jennings, 2011, 228–9.

2

The Social Identity of Hosts and Patrons

In Chapter 1, I provided a general historical outline of the activities of inns, taverns, and pubs. This chapter analyses these hostelries in their social context. It explores the organizational identity of the three types of venue and the social positions of tavernkeepers, innkeepers, and publicans. It additionally examines how their patrons express their class, gender, and national identity by their participation in different kinds of sociality.

Innkeepers, Tavernkeepers, and Publicans

Innkeepers

Innkeepers' considerable wealth and relatively high social status derived not merely from providing lodgings and refreshment for travellers but also from the many economic and social functions they were able to play beyond these, as described in Chapter 1. They could become influential economic middle men and even coaching magnates, exercising rudimentary banking functions as well as acting as cultural impresarios.[1] By the eighteenth century, most stage coach services were owned by wealthy innkeepers.[2] Because they hosted many important meetings and men of great social importance, innkeepers had to be of good standing. Among them were retired artists, schoolmasters, MPs, and former politicians. They developed a web of connections to local and even national men of status and power. The entrepreneurial among them used these opportunities to become men of substance who then assumed positions in the local power structure. In Norwich and Northampton, for example, it was not unusual for innkeepers to be mayors, sheriffs,[3] and aldermen.[4]

Such innkeepers needed a deep resource base, as well as social refinement and cultural competence. Hence, they usually came from the middling classes and had middle-class manners, and sometimes even behaved like gentry.[5] Borsay and Everitt place the elite of the inn-keeping fraternity among the wealthiest members of the bourgeoisie or at the lower levels of the 'urban gentry' of professional men.⁶ Examination of probates in eighteenth-century Northampton showed that the deceased keepers of the principal inns were able to amass considerable fortunes.⁷

Tavernkeepers

The literature is much more reticent on the social status of tavernkeepers. Tavernkeepers were quite similar to innkeepers in the functions performed, in the social and organizational competences they brought to their trade, and in their position in society. They were often hosts of large and splendid establishments and executed social and economic functions far exceeding the mere provision of food and drink. While they were not as influential and wealthy as innkeepers, they had to have considerable capital to acquire the, often large, stocks of wine they held in their vaults.⁸ Tavernkeepers acted as hosts to powerful organizations, such as guilds or City companies and Masonic lodges, and tavernkeepers often were active in the Church or in politics.⁹ Just as the patrons of taverns were generally of a higher social class than those frequenting public houses, tavernkeepers also were of higher status than publicans. In the nineteenth and early twentieth centuries, however—as the fortunes of taverns declined—the social origins and position of any remaining tavernkeepers came to resemble those of publicans.

Publicans

From alehouse keeper to publican, those who ran public houses are unanimously placed significantly lower in the social scale than the hosts of taverns and, even more so, in relation to innkeepers. Alehouse keepers, in earlier centuries, were from low social strata/the village poor,[10] selling ale in their dwelling house to supplement their meagre income from work in other fields. At the beginning of the seventeenth century, the majority had been husbandmen and labourers, with smaller groups coming from a variety of urban trades.[11] Alehouses were owned mainly by men, but women were often left in charge of much of the day-to-day running,[12] coining the term of ale-wife.

By the eighteenth century, people no longer became publicans just to survive, but to better themselves financially. By the middle of that century, poor alehouse keepers had been weeded out by magistrates and brewers. The new-found relative affluence of the pubkeeper was accompanied by small but significant improvements in his social position. Pub-keeping had the 'makings of a fully-fledged, respectable trade in its own right'.[13] By mid-century, the majority were able to make a good living, and their average personal wealth was significantly greater in real terms than it had been a century earlier.[14]

The Social Identity of Hosts and Patrons

Socially, publicans were situated between skilled workers and the lower middle class (small shopkeepers, tradesmen, and independent artisans). Sometimes they had previously served in an inn or in a household, but often they came from different, mainly skilled working-class or lower middle-class occupations, such as baker, tailor, carpenter, carver, auctioneer, and shoemaker.[15] It was common in the eighteenth century for publicans to be constables—then an unpaid position.[16] Many publicans also had a second occupation, leaving their wives in charge of the public house for long periods. Of these, being a farmer was by far the most frequent,[17] and publicans often were simultaneously bakers or millers. Figures from the mid-nineteenth century show that many of the larger pubs also employed a number of servants. Publicans have little opportunity to acquire significant wealth. Whereas the capital amassed by some London innkeepers and tavernkeepers at the end of their life, during the middle of the eighteenth century, could easily come to £1,000, most alehouse keepers were worth only £100, putting them below the level of many artisans.[18] However, despite the relatively modest income and the hard work and long hours required by pubkeepers, the occupation was sufficiently popular for successive generations of the same family to take it up, at least in rural areas, as shown by a history of pubs in the Cambridgeshire village of Balsham.[19]

Once the breweries had assumed control of a large number of pubs by the middle of the eighteenth century, one has to make the further distinction between owners and mere tenants whose opportunities for profit-making were strongly curtailed by the breweries. During Victorian times, there occurred a differentiation among publicans, with a significant group of entrepreneurial and wealthy men emerging. A large number of new pubs were being built by publicans themselves, who made their money not just from hospitality, but from rapid gains on their investments,[20] restlessly moving from one pub to another. Such publicans thus must be counted among the more prosperous entrepreneurial middle classes. Many owned a large number of pubs, giving rise to the phenomenon of pub chains. These men, Girouard notes,[21] were no longer the old-style genial 'mine host', but were often regarded as 'tough and flashy' men who set out to make money quickly. This entrepreneurial and higher social status group of publicans, however, was exceptional and relatively short-lived. It does not undermine the general impression of publicans' lower middle class status.

An analysis of trade journals at roughly the same time found among publicans a former tobacconist, sailor, courier, commercial traveller, hotel porter, a teacher of boxing, and an actor[22]—mostly occupations located between the lower middle and the working class. Equally, these men came to pub-keeping from occupations with limited duration, such as being in the forces, in the police, or in a sport such as boxing, as well as being retired jockeys and music hall artists.[23] The portrait of the publican emerging from the Mass

Observation Study of Bolton pubs in the late 1930s places them somewhat lower in the class structure.[24] It highlights the general similarity in local pubs between publicans and their customers—both are among the poorest.

The relatively low social status of publicans continued into the late twentieth century. They still entered the job after having first worked in a number of other occupations, which were predominantly skilled working class or lower non-manual. If anything, their economic position deteriorated when they had to meet the competition from the supermarket sale of drink. It was just as well that a large majority of publicans interviewed in 1970 liked the job for the opportunities of meeting people it gave and not for the income they could derive from it.[25] Indeed, in recent times, the economic position, particularly, of tied publicans, especially if their pubs are mainly drink-led, has become as precarious as that of semi- or unskilled workers. Their precarious economic situation is widely seen as one of the several causes of accelerated pub-dying in the twenty-first century.

Jennings provides a useful summary assessment of publicans' economic situation over the four centuries.[26] They enjoyed relatively low incomes during the seventeenth and eighteenth centuries. However, with the rising prosperity after the 1860s, the majority could again make a good living, as pubs were popular and occupied a central position in working-class life. From the turn of the century, however, a number of factors began to undermine the trading position of publicans, reflecting, among others, the gradual decline in drinking during the early twentieth century. Publicans' material well-being was not only determined by what they could raise from customers, but also by their dependence on brewers and the underwriting of this dependent relationship by the state, as well as the latter's demand for taxes on drink.

To sum up the differences between tavernkeepers, innkeepers, and publicans, publicans neither require deep resources and organizational skills to enter into business, nor does owning/leasing a pub present an avenue of social mobility into the bourgeoisie or a prominent position in local politics. In conclusion, the differing wealth and social status of tavernkeepers and innkeepers, as compared with publicans, has been closely aligned with the organizational identity of these different types of hostelry and the hierarchy between them. This identity, as the following section will show, has influenced the types of patrons attracted.

The Patrons of Inns, Taverns and Pubs: Social Mixing or Class Segregation?

There is a significant current in historical writing commenting on the easy social mixing in England of members of different social orders in public places,

The Social Identity of Hosts and Patrons

and this includes social mixing in public houses and taverns.[27] In the seventeenth century, according to Hailwood,[28] around 25 per cent of patrons came from the 'middling ranks'. Tombs also points to many examples of easy social mixing in taverns and cafés in this century, in both town and country.[29] Clark, too, identifies relatively harmonious relations between people of different rank, with conflicts between vertically differentiated social groups rarely erupting. He points out that, in the seventeenth century, such differences were still regarded as God-given.[30] Tombs, however, also recognizes the limits of affable social mixing, as well as its fairly superficial character.[31]

'Social distinctions, though certainly maintained, were probably looser then on much of the Continent.'[32] While they were not much remarked upon by the English themselves—they must have been taken for granted—foreign visitors from the more hierarchically ordered societies of France and Germany frequently commented on this 'egalitarian' feature of English society, particularly during the seventeenth and eighteenth centuries and much less during Victorian times. One foreign visitor is quoted by Tombs as remarking:[33]

> Nothing is more common than to see in a tavern or café, Milords and Artisans sitting at the same table, talking familiarly about the public news and the affairs of the government.

Any social mixing between the different ranks/classes during this period certainly was not due to a high degree of economic equality. There was no absence in England of stark differences of wealth, of standard of living, and of life style. Whereas, during the seventeenth century and the first half of the eighteenth century, disparities of wealth were mainly based on land ownership and, less so, commerce, from the middle of the eighteenth century onwards, manufacture became an additional source of economic and social inequality.

Borsay[34] and Langford[35] are more sceptical about social intercourse 'between milords and artisans'. They suggest that the social norm of 'politeness', which encourages social mixing, referred mainly to increased social intercourse in public places between members of the upper classes and those of the 'urban gentry', particularly the rising urban professionals and the larger merchants and manufacturers. The latter two groups were now granted gentility. The vague and ambiguous notion of politeness, Langford suggests, while being related to property-owning, primarily 'affected the everyday routine and rules of social life', including those around dining. They distinguished 'the innate gentleman's understanding of what made civilised conduct'.[36] The promotion of sociability had become a great preoccupation of urban culture. Cultural factors had played a particular role in the social acceptance of the middling ranks by those above them in the hierarchy,[37] who had acquired such gentility by birth and/or by the ownership of large amounts of land. This practice of social politeness also united the otherwise highly diverse group of the urban middling class and served to distinguish it from the lower orders. This is endorsed also by Wrightson.[38] Borsay summarizes this growing accommodation between the upper and the middling classes:[39]

> [T]he new urban culture...contributed to stability in practical ways by providing attractive contexts in which the traditional elite and the growing middle ranks could freely mix and acquire and exchange status and wealth.

That such clear collective identifications existed mainly in London and a few larger cities in the seventeenth and early eighteenth century, and were still absent in smaller provincial places, is suggested by French.[40]

Taverns and inns, as well as coffee houses, were among the public spaces where such a more liberal sociality could be practised. The existence of the 'common table' in taverns, where a newcomer might sit down next to a complete stranger, facilitated conversation that could promote sociability across class boundaries. In practice, such polite social intercourse mostly referred to a gentlemanly behaviour *within* classes that required their members not to let their party political or religious affiliations introduce conflict into social meetings. As one frequenter of coffee houses observes: 'A Tory does not stare and leer when a Whig comes in, nor a Whig look sour and whisper at the sight of a Tory.'[41]

Borsay is explicit also that social mixing did not extend to the popular masses. He points out that 'there were limits to sociability: the hand of friendship stretched [only] so far down the social ladder' and that the cultural gap between the higher echelons of society and the populace as a whole had widened.[42] He dates the process of withdrawal from traditional social leisure activities of the higher echelons from the end of the seventeenth century. Although the notion of 'politeness' claims an ethos of social equality, it is inclusive only of property holders and/or those possessing education and culture. It most definitely does not include women.

There is less ambiguity about the extent of social mixing during the nineteenth century. Class segregation had become the norm. Extensive suburbanization, among other processes, both expressed and reinforced segregation by class. Just as there was a clearer division between the classes in the political and general social realm, so it became expressed in visiting taverns and, more so, pubs. This pattern persisted into the first half of the twentieth century, when residential segregation between the classes had become even more pronounced.

From the early 1960s to the 1990s, class segregation became less marked again. The collapse of the basic industries from the late 1970s onwards drastically reduced the traditional working class—previously the mainstay of local pubs. Hence urban, male-dominated pubs, attracting men straight from work and often still in their work clothes, lost a large section of their clientele. This also obviated the continuation of a division between bar and lounge and made it possible to open up smaller, previously cramped premises into one large space where mixing between members of different classes again was facilitated, though by no means ensured.

To conclude, many instances of social integration between the different ranks are reported for the seventeenth and eighteenth centuries, and there are economic and political reasons to account for this. However, even in these centuries, such integration was fairly superficial and existed side by side with instances of social exclusion. Preservation of social exclusivity and even downright avoidance of the lower orders by the middling and upper classes was more frequently found in the nineteenth century, when it had become almost the rule. From World War II onwards, class segregation again became more relaxed, mirroring the more egalitarian ethos of society in general.

But did this pattern of social mixing or social segregation apply to all types of hostelries, or were there marked differences between them? I now move on to describe patterns of social mixing and avoidance in each particular type of hostelry.

Inns and Class Identity

Some writers view the inn very idealistically as giving sustenance and shelter to all groups of English society: 'Every rank of society from king to beggar, criminal to judge, has lodged...within their doors, and every aspect of English life has been and is reflected there.'[43] Lord Macaulay's portrayal of a seventeenth century inn, too, was one 'in which all classes, from the Lord of the Manor down to the labourers, were wont to gather...in friendly intercourse'.[44]

More historians, however, associate them with the higher social ranks. Clark, for example, refers to the inn as 'that elite establishment...the place for the upper classes to meet, trade, parade, politick and get drunk'.[45] Several travellers report with some dismay that those who arrived on foot were either turned away or, at best, were asked to eat in the kitchen at the common table. Journeying on foot from London to Oxford, a German minister of religion was repeatedly turned away from inns where he tried to stay and pay for the night. He comments with bitterness that 'if you come in a post-chaise you are treated with all possible respect,...even if you only buy two pots of beer'.[46] The English radical, Samuel Bamford, too, in 1820 complained about not being catered for in an inn for coming on foot.[47]

Inns may be viewed as almost the mirror image of public houses, in that they catered predominantly for the middling and upper ranks in society. The class composition of inn customers was very much determined by the many economic, social, and political functions inns fulfilled, in addition to providing bed and board to travellers. The presence of many well-to-do travellers made inns ideal places to provide various professional services, such as legal and medical ones, to sell all manner of goods, and to stage a variety of entertainments. Also, during the early eighteenth century, inns became social centres for the local elites. The assembly rooms of inns—found mainly in county towns, provincial capitals, and resorts[48]—hosted dinners for all sorts of celebratory occasions, as well as dances for the local rural and urban gentry. They additionally staged concerts, plays, and exhibitions, with appeal mainly to those classes possessing cultural capital (education and knowledge), i.e. the well-to-do urban and local landed gentry.[49] Everitt makes their class character very explicit when he relates that, in Hanoverian England (1740–1901), 'distinctions of class were inflexibly observed',[50] and great seasonal feasts in the inn were not accessible to other than country and town gentry.

After the importance of inns as transport nodes had declined with the development of the railways, inns gradually began to decline in gentility. However, they did not lose their somewhat glamorized social image in the popular historical imagination and retained the aura of upper-class gentility. This aura has been appropriated by licensees of many contemporary hostelries and even by pub chains to claim a superior position in a very overcrowded market.

The Social Rank of Tavern Patrons

The social profile of those who frequented taverns was very similar to that of guests of inns. Most accounts of tavern life connect them to men of the middling and upper orders. 'By the accession of James I the tavern was established as the drinking place of the upper classes.'[51] The customers of London taverns often had a somewhat bohemian character. They attracted many literary and professional men, journalists, political thinkers, and other members of the intelligentsia or, in the terms of the time, London wits. Politicians and, particularly, members of Parliament, too, often frequented taverns.

Wining and dining in taverns took two different forms that also encouraged different degrees of social mixing. First, there was drinking and eating by individuals and small groups at the common table, which, by facilitating conversation, might have brought together people from different social backgrounds in common sociality. Second, taverns had many private rooms of various sizes, which could be hired for special dinners that, by their spatial seclusion, simultaneously encouraged social exclusivity. Last, some taverns had very sizeable assembly rooms that provided lavish banquets for very large companies, usually composed of members of the upper and upper middle classes or of the 'gentlemen of London'. The visual splendour of these occasions and the lavishness of the entertainment was frequently remarked upon. People who attended these dinners did not simply take their food, they 'dined' with all the pomp and circumstance, including the obligatory evening wear. Such special social occasions hardly suggest a mixing of all social classes, but were attended mainly by the intellectual, political, and propertied elite.

Class segregation during the heyday of taverns, the seventeenth and eighteenth centuries, was not completely rigid, and aristocrats and well-established tradesmen were known to mix with, for example, boisterous apprentices. Sometimes the former went incognito, because 'it would never do to flaunt rank in front of the democratic London pleasure seekers'.[52] Burke talks about the Earl of Barrymore being taken to Jacob's Well Tavern to experience 'a scene of true conviviality'. He remained incognito. Clark speaks of 'debauched aristocrats [who] might carouse with dissolute tradesmen in the cellars of St Giles'.[53] The labelling of such tavern goers as 'debauched' hints at the fact that such mixing was not the normal practice, and the fact that aristocrats went incognito reinforces the impression that class integration was only skin-deep.

There existed also social and economic barriers to social mixing in taverns. As they served mainly wine, which was much more expensive than beer, they were affordable chiefly for members of the middle and upper ranks. Exclusivity could also be fostered very deliberately. Brewer cites the example of the Castle Society at the Castle Tavern on Paternoster Row,[54] where 'vintners, victuallers, keepers of coffee houses, tailors, peruke makers, barbers, journeymen and apprentices'—the independent tradesmen who often counted themselves as part of the middling orders—were not welcome. Brewer even claims that taverns [and coffee houses] 'fashioned themselves as communities of taste and knowledge' and were places 'involved in all the processes by which culture was shaped'.[55] It seems likely that such communities of taste were not crossing social class boundaries, but rather reinforced them.

Taverns, like inns, lost their social pre-eminence, when, towards the end of the eighteenth century, their high-class customers began to create a specialized institution that gave admittance only to their own kind, namely the Club. Social mixing was no longer desired and gave way to social exclusivity. Burke attributes it to the fact that this social group had grown in size to such an extent that there were sufficient numbers of like-minded people to set up their own institution and 'exclude the general public'. Burke concludes that 'when the better classes had what they wanted of it, it [the tavern] passed to the working classes',[56] and turned into a public house.

Notwithstanding some internal differentiation, it is fair to say that taverns, just like inns, were institutions attracting mainly the urban and rural gentry who had both a good income and a relatively large amount of cultural capital. These attributes and the activities they permitted, in turn, shaped the organizational identities of inns and taverns and gave them the genteel character often aped in future centuries.

The Social Identity of Public House Customers

The pub is often viewed as a British institution attracting patrons from all social classes.[57] This position is summed up in the following citation from Burke:[58]

> The man of ten thousand a year dines at the next table to the holidaying clerk of two hundred a year, both of them within ear-shot of the tap room labourers of twenty-five shillings a week; and in the bar, the peer ceases to be a peer and the peasant ceases to be a peasant.

At the same time, much of the literature portrays the pub as mainly a place where members of the working class or even the poor come to drink and socialize.[59]

Social mixing in public houses—one of the beloved stereotypes about the British—has varied considerably in degree, depending on the social historical context in which the public house existed. However, at the same time, 'from early times a hierarchy of premises existed catering for different social groups'.[60] In this hierarchy, the pub has always been placed at the bottom, below the inn and the tavern. Hence, the degree of actual social mixing—though allegedly greater than on the Continent—probably was not marked. It became less common over time, but, arguably, resurfaced again after World War II.

As already described in Chapter 1, in the seventeenth century and the first half of the eighteenth century, the alehouse/public house was not solely a place for drinking and socializing, but fulfilled many social and political functions. Hence, during this period, people—mostly men—from different social backgrounds frequented pubs in pursuit of economic activity, as well as seeking fellowship. In addition to common labourers, shopkeepers, and small tradesmen, some professional men and even members of the gentry sometimes socialized in public houses.

Pepys, in the late seventeenth century, often took upper-class acquaintances to drink in pubs. Nevertheless, the predominant section of customers of the alehouse after the Restoration belonged to 'the lower ranks of the social hierarchy',[61] including labourers, servants, husbandmen, and a number of urban craftsmen, as well as coachmen, carters, and petty traders.

During the first half of the eighteenth century, the public house was viewed as having become more respectable and was no longer seen as a threat to public order. Not only were the tramping poor less in evidence, but the public house started to attract 'visitors from higher social groups'.[62] Skilled workers

The Social Identity of Hosts and Patrons

and craftsmen formed clubs around a variety of common interests and based them in the public house. A significant number of men of the middling sort and even some gentry also frequented pubs.[63] Whig and Tory members of Parliament, during the eighteenth century, are said to have met in pubs and coffee houses to agree tactics and policies prior to parliamentary sessions.[64] Parson James Woodforde and John Byng, both of whom kept lively and informative diaries about this period, also note the presence of gentlemen in more humble drinking places. This degree of social mixing caught the attention of foreign visitors to London, who clearly thought it unusual. Thus, in 1791, a Prussian visitor called D'Archenholz remarked that in English ale houses 'all ranks are mixed and confounded together; it is not uncommon to meet with even persons of quality there'.[65]

However, as Beresford, the editor of Parson Woodforde's diary, points out, this apparent 'democracy of the public house' was fairly superficial.[66] During the eighteenth century, the notion that society was arranged hierarchically in separate social orders was still dominant, and social mixing in the home was very rare. However, it was the unquestioned acceptance of social inequality during this time that made short-lived fraternity within pub walls acceptable. It was not perceived as threatening to the established social order.

During the course of the eighteenth century, many towns developed purpose-built venues for the various activities previously conducted in hostelries. The ensuing contraction in the provision of services in public houses towards the end of the period also began 'to sever the connection between the middling and upper group in society and the world of the public house'.[67] Thereby 'public houses were becoming more exclusively social centres for those who had always formed the great mass of their customers—the lower orders in society'.[68] Thompson, too, implies more class segregation when he assigns 'gentlemen and the better sort of tradesmen' to Norwich's taverns.[69] In any case, the middling ranks were never more than a minority among the frequenters of ale/public houses.

This process of increased social differentiation and even strenuous avoidance of certain working men's milieus by the middling ranks accelerated in the second half of the eighteenth century. From the end of the eighteenth century, widespread drunkenness and an attendant coarse sociality lowered the reputation of the public house and hence further deterred the middling sort and the more respectable manual workers from visiting.

Thus, stigmatization of public houses by the reforming middling classes and by the state and its law enforcing agencies led to a deterioration of their reputation. Concern with the drunkenness and vice of the lower orders seems to have quickened in the 1770s and 1780s. In this context, a Royal Proclamation against Vice and Immorality, in 1787, sent to every magisterial bench, was regarded as an official nod to the justices that they were free to crack down on the alehouses as they saw fit. As Jennings observes, throughout the eighteenth century, 'all the concern was for misdemeanours of the lower orders connected with drinking in alehouses, branding many of them as "places of ill fame"'.[70]

The acceleration of industrialization at the end of the eighteenth century, it is claimed by historians, brought a recognition of class differences. In the nineteenth century 'coherent and consolidated classes were finally created'.[71] Furthermore, the enduring and pervasive influence of Malthus's (1798) writing created a perception of the poor as a danger.[72] Hence, all this rapid change evoked a less relaxed approach to the mixing of the social classes and even increased segregation of the lower and middle and upper classes. Such a divided picture of nineteenth-century society is painted also by Disraeli—the first One-Nation Tory. In his novel *Sybil or The Two Nations* (1845), he identified not only fundamental economic and social divisions, but also deep cultural differences, encompassing the food eaten by the rich and the poor:

> Two nations; between whom there is no intercourse and no sympathy; who are as ignorant of each other's habits, thoughts and feelings as if they were...inhabitants of different planets; who are formed by a different breeding, are fed by a different food, are ordered by different manners, and are not governed by the same laws....[73]

Over the course of the nineteenth century, the use of the public house by the middling classes and by artisans suffered further decline. Also, socio-spatial differentiation *within* public houses increased. By the late nineteenth century, many London pubs had two bars—one for superior artisans and one for labourers. Where there were few separate rooms, partitions and screens were used to segregate the different kinds of customers.[74] Thus, a London pub could have a Saloon Lounge, Saloon Bar, Private Bar, Public Bar, Jug-and-Bottle, a Ladies' Bar, and/or a snug, with the saloon or lounge now mainly used by the middle class.[75]

Semi- and unskilled workers formed the largest group of pub customers by then, and the greatest concentration of pubs was to be found in poorer working-class neighbourhoods.[76] As the nineteenth century progressed, successful tradesmen began to distance themselves from workers.[77] By 1830, certain groups of craftsmen were no longer frequent visitors of pubs. They, too, had new alternatives, such as coffee houses and Mechanics' Institutes. This situation applies particularly to the south of the country, whereas their northern equivalents continued to drink in public houses.[78]

Although middle-class people still used pubs, they would go much more infrequently than working-class drinkers, mainly to socialize with friends. The pub was not a major element in their social life.[79] Clark ascribes it to the many new opportunities for socializing they had, particularly in the club, to their more comfortable homes, as well as to campaigns against drinking by medical men.[80]

During the late nineteenth century, when many pubs had been renovated or newly built, and standards of comfort were much increased, the social class of drinkers may have been pushed up slightly. However, members of the upper classes who, in the past, had chosen pubs 'for deliberate slumming' had mostly deserted pubs, as had members of the professional and business classes and even most writers and artists. By the 1890s, the middle classes had abandoned pubs for clubs, the big new hotels, and the restaurants of the 1870s, 80s, and 90s. Only the tavern-style pubs 'that concentrated on the eating side kept up the social level of their clientele'.[81]

Nineteenth-century commentators on social integration and segregation, from both ends of the social spectrum, show clear awareness of social divisions. Girouard cites the Secretary of White's Club as saying in 1896: '...the class I deal with and the class I associate with and the class I know do not go into public houses'.[82] The working-class radical, Francis Place, when writing on educational segregation in his autobiography, makes this remark on class and hostelry frequented:

> [T]he children of the richer and prouder class immediately above the tradesmen, those who instead of frequenting the public house assembled at Coffee Houses and Taverns, were sent to boarding school.[83]

The observations by Selley and by Mass Observation on the 1920s and late 1930s respectively,[84] make clear that the working-class character of pubs had endured during the first few decades of the twentieth century. The lower orders remain the mainstay of pubs. Among the middle classes, a much smaller proportion visit pubs, still mainly because they have more alternatives for socializing. They are rarely seen in locals, but visit city centre pubs during weekends.[85] In the local pubs of Bolton, during the week, 'the vault is working class masculine'. When it comes to the highest-ranked people in Bolton, 'the "best class" of people in Worktown do not go into pubs'.[86] Segregation by class of pub customers, based on residential segregation, is still found in the 1950s, this time in Banbury, a small market town in Oxfordshire, and if they do drink in the same pub, they do not mix.[87]

Class identification is even obvious in the clothing of pub customers. The insignia of the class of vault drinkers are wearing a cap and a scarf around their neck, though at weekends, when they join their wives in the lounge, they would be better attired.[88] Gorham points out that social distancing between the classes is a two-way process in that, in some public bars, any patron not dressed as a labourer is regarded with distrust.[89]

The situation had not changed fundamentally by the end of the twentieth century. The pub devoted mainly to drinking, excepting some city centre pubs, remains a working-class institution. One new development is the differentiation by age, with younger people visiting much more regularly than older ones, and the second new development is the higher representation of women—a phenomenon to be discussed at length in the next section. Whereas in the past, young people had met the opposite sex in dance halls, the demise of the latter brought them back to the pub—particularly the branded mega pubs—in search of partners. Also, alcohol has become available at an increasingly younger age, and young people have more money to spend. But these visits occur mainly at night time during the weekend, and people often do the round of city centre pubs. This indicates some return to cross-class mixing, although well-educated upper middle-class people are less likely to be part of this night-time economy.

It would be fair to conclude that, despite variation during different periods of history, pub-going defined the social identity for members of the working class—it was the only or main place of leisure they attended. For men of the middle classes, in contrast, drinking in pubs never had this defining influence. From the nineteenth century onward, it was even avoidance of pubs which came to signify social respectability for both many artisans/craftsmen and for professional men.

Thus, class integration only went in one direction, and it occurred on the terms of middle- and upper-class visitors to pubs. Rules of social hierarchy would be temporarily suspended, and rules of egalitarian courtesy and politeness would be observed—'it is not done to draw attention to status differences'.[90] Yet even Fox recognizes the temporary character of this suspension and its lack of sincerity. She concludes: 'Our rules and codes of polite egalitarianism are a disguise, an elaborate charade, a severe collective case of what psychologists call "denial".'[91] However, there has been sufficient mixing in pubs between the social classes, all through the centuries, to sustain the belief that class boundaries may be ignored in pubs.

Division along lines of class hardened and social segregation increased in the nineteenth and twentieth centuries, up to World War II. In the post-War era, increased democratization of society at large also became reflected in an easier social mixing in pubs. Social divisions became less marked or were, at least, less overtly acknowledged, and the pub again attracted customers from across the social spectrum. But even then, pubs were often stratified either according to socio-geographical location, or, in the centres of large towns, maintained a social distinction between the bar and the lounge.

Despite this democratization since the World War II period, during the twentieth century the dominant image of the pub as a working-class institution persisted. This has been reflected also in the attitude towards pubs and drinking by the state, which has mainly connected pubs with social disorder. In Chapter 6, I will investigate to what extent and how the rise of the gastropub from the turn of the century has changed the image of the pub and the nature of social mixing within it.

Pubs and Taverns: A Male Bastion?

Although this section focuses mainly on pubs, much of what is said also applies to taverns, as isolated comments on the latter bear out. As inns offered hospitality to travellers, women could not be excluded. These mainly higher-rank women guests would be secluded within their rooms, where they would also take their meals.

Historians usually draw a line between the Middle Ages,[92] when female attendance appears perfectly common, and later periods, when women did not go to alehouses without a very good reason or, if they went, were accompanied by a man. However, the actual number of women found in pubs is often under-represented, and, depending on the circumstances, they often constituted a significant minority.[93] Nevertheless, for most of the time, they were more tolerated than welcomed. Jennings puts it very politely when he describes female drinkers as 'guests in a male world', bound by male-oriented conventions.[94] The degree of women's exclusion varied in different historical periods, culminating during the early Victorian period and falling off radically, though not totally disappearing, during the present time.

To understand the way women were long kept out of taverns and pubs or, when admitted, barely tolerated, must be viewed in the wider social context of gender relations in English society from the seventeenth to the late twentieth century. Women's position in Britain, in many ways, was relatively better than in Continental societies of the time. From the eighteenth century, they enjoyed many social rights and privileges, as well as remarkable social visibility in public affairs and in the literary arts.[95] At the same time, women had few political and economic rights. They were completely barred from 'high politics' during the nineteenth and most of the twentieth century.[96] The right to own and manage independently any property left to them was gained only in 1882 and 1893, and divorce on equal terms came not until 1923.[97] Working-class women, too, were effectively excluded from meetings of Chartists that took place mainly 'in the masculine world of the pub'.[98] Women were long barred from receiving the vote. James Mill, in his article *Essays on Government* (1820), justified their exclusion with the claim that women, like children, were clearly dependents of men, either of their husbands or their fathers.[99]

During Victorian times, the growth of both rapid urbanization and of the industrial working class had forced increasing contact of the social classes in public spaces. It had led, on the one side, to a greatly diminished willingness of the working classes to show respect for rank and status and a concomitant effort among the middle classes to re-establish class boundaries and to insulate themselves, and particularly their women, from too much contact with the lower classes. Davidoff suggests that,[100]

> by effectively preventing upper and middle-class women from playing a part in the market, any part of public life whatsoever, the Victorians believed that one section of the population would be able to provide a haven of stability, of exact social classification in the threatening anonymity of the surrounding economic and political upheaval.

Davidoff refers to the creation of two separate spheres—a public and a private sphere—for the Victorian middle classes. Women's sequestration at home, removed from any sexual temptation and protected against any sordid behaviour in public spaces, was meant to preserve social respectability.[101] Respectability and the social worth signalled by it did not remain confined to the middle classes, but was also cultivated by the more skilled and better educated segment of the working classes. This preoccupation led to both trade unions' demands for a family wage and efforts to keep women out of gainful employment. It resulted in attempts to insulate women in the home, away from social mixing in public spaces. For women, visiting a pub unaccompanied was either socially out of the question or, among the working classes, closely circumscribed and controlled. Despite some fluctuations through history in the presence of women in pubs, one can agree with Kümin and Tlusty that 'the overall trend in gender relations has been conceptualized as a gradual "masculinization" of the atmosphere'.[102]

Female drinkers were never legally barred from drinking in pubs, but until the Equal Opportunities legislation of the middle 1970s, landlords were free to designate a bar as 'for men only'. Additionally, strong informal exclusionary norms were probably more effective in keeping women out of bars. Even when women visited pubs, they did so in relatively small numbers and were usually marginalized *within* pubs, as well as being often stigmatized because of their presence. Single women were invariably suspected of sexual license. There were, of course, always token women among those serving in pubs, namely the landlord's wife and, more significantly, the bar maid. The latter was not merely tolerated, but was seen as providing a welcome sexual focus for many drinkers.

While gender norms were relaxed during World War I, 'after WWI the traditional family emerged more tightly-knit and more home-centred than it had before'.[103] The issue of voting was solved for women over thirty in 1916. In 1918, magistracy, jury service, and the legal profession was opened to women. However, women received the vote on same basis as men as late as 1928. After World War I, gender differences, in many spheres, were reaffirmed and women were returned to domesticity.

More radical changes in gender relations came only from the late 1960s onwards. Introduction of the contraceptive pill in 1961, giving women control over reproduction, received an immediate, big take-up. Women's economic independence received a slight boost with the passing of the Equal Pay Act in 1970. New ideas of femininity were developed that called the male-dominated and prudish culture into question.[104]

> All this amounted to a cultural, social and intellectual transformation—still in progress—of profound importance, creating a gulf separating modern experience of life from that of previous centuries.[105]

All these economic, political, and social developments had a marked impact on women's and men's attitudes towards frequenting pubs and towards men's willingness to accept women into one of the last remaining domains of aggressive masculinity.

Expressing Gender Identity in Taverns and Pubs

The evidence for women's tavern and pub visits is only sketchy, but during the seventeenth and eighteenth centuries more evidence points towards women's access to these hostelries, though mainly accompanied by a man except perhaps in some of London's less salubrious districts where working people lived.

For the seventeenth century, evidence comes from Pepys's diaries, covering the period of 1660 to 1669.[106] Pepys not only frequently took his wife out to dine in taverns, but also had sexual encounters in public houses and taverns with both women known to him and with prostitutes. Although Pepys himself gives no indication that it was unusual to take women to public houses or taverns, he relates one example showing that some women were reluctant to dine in a tavern. When, on 25 November 1660, a dinner had been arranged by him in the Fleece in Covent Garden, together with his wife and another friendly couple, the other wife was reluctant to stay, and the dinner had to be abandoned.[107] Also, most of Pepys' frequent visits to pubs and taverns occurred either alone or in the company of male friends and acquaintances.

During the early eighteenth century, according to Clark,[108] 'fewer eyebrows were now raised about respectable women drinking in pubs in company'. However, it is clear that 'respectable' referred to women accompanied by their husbands or 'young men'. D'Archenholz notes that, on Sundays, the alehouse 'is full of persons of both sexes'.[109]

Working women, particularly in London, frequented the popular gin palaces in significant numbers, both alone and in single-sex groups.[110] In Manchester spirit vaults, too, on Saturdays, nearly 50 per cent of drinkers were women.[111] During the second half of the eighteenth century, the number of women frequenting public houses is thought to have increased and the disgrace attached to this to have disappeared.[112] However, Clark opines that it remained uncommon for 'respectable' women to visit unaccompanied by men.[113]

The situation clearly differed between working-class women who earned their own living and women of the middling classes. However, working women's drunkenness caused much more consternation than that of working men. The shocked comment on women's drinking by a French upper-class visitor to Britain in the early nineteenth century expresses this latter sentiment, as well as indicating that this spectacle could not be seen in Paris. Thus, Gustave d'Eichthal reports on a large crowd of women in front of an alehouse in a poor area of London: '[T]hese women are a sight to be seen as they gulp down their glasses of gin, whisky, toddy and cheap brandy, and some of them smoke pipes.'[114]

A widespread exclusion of women from the public sphere applied not only to pubs, but also to taverns, although the picture is ambiguous. While Haydon claims that female participation in taverns in the eighteenth century was acceptable and commonplace,[115] few descriptions of tavern sociality bear out their widespread participation. A conversation between Dr Johnson and Boswell suggests that women were not frequent visitors, and that, if they did visit, they were usually accompanied by a man.[116]

In the London of 1814, reputable women would rarely be seen in chop houses, coffee houses, taverns, or public houses.[117] In 1851, the anonymous author of *London at Table* comments:

> [O]ne evil of long standing is the difficulty of finding an Hotel or Restaurant where strangers of the gentler sex may be taken to dine. To give a private dinner with women as guests you must go to the Albion or the London Tavern.[118]

Looking back nostalgically on the nineteenth century in 1917, the journalist George Sims celebrates the exclusion of women from taverns:

> Where will you find a 'song and supper room' with a dozen men... and listening to an entertainment in which no woman takes part, held in an establishment through the portals of which no petticoat is allowed to pass?[119]

During the nineteenth century, women's exclusion from hostelries became intensified, though it became less rigid towards the end of the century.[120] Girouard, studying London pubs in the late 1890s,[121] reports an increase in women drinkers attracted by the many private bars and the high standards of comfort and finish in pubs of the time. Women tended to be assigned to separate rooms within pubs, which their husbands contemptuously referred to as 'cow sheds' or 'duck pens'.[122] Thus, as in previous centuries, significant minorities of working women did frequent pubs.

Women's drinking in pubs probably also varied between London—which had a considerable pub culture—and provincial cities, particularly northern ones. One estimate, in 1875, by a temperance campaigner in the north, estimates the proportion of women in pubs on Saturdays to be 15 per cent.[123] Clark, in her comparative study of northern textile towns and London,[124] confirms that working women had a small but significant presence in pubs and, at certain hours of the day or days of the week, might even dominate.

During the first half of the twentieth century, a modest increase in women's pub visits may have occurred, particularly during World War I. The strength of beer fell during World War I, and women resorted to the pub in greater numbers. This greater degree of alcohol consumption was also facilitated by the fact that many more women were earning during the war years or received the Soldiers' Dependants' Allowance.[125] Selley, too, supports the idea that the war had broken down some of the exclusionary strategies. Nevertheless, he sees the increased women's presence mainly confined to the better-class public houses and among the more respectable types of women.[126] This modest increase in women's admission to pubs, however, may have been temporary, as data for the 1920s and 30s, particularly for non-London and working-class areas, do not confirm their increased presence in pubs. The authors of Mass Observation, writing on the eve of World War II, estimated the proportion of women in the locals of Bolton to be a mere 16 per cent, and 19 per cent in city centre pubs.[127] Hence, the evidence for this period between the wars is mixed, to say the least. Most of the issues covered for the preceding centuries prove remarkably persistent.

The above study and that by Selley also carefully document the forms taken by exclusion from, and segregation within, pubs. First, women only drank in pubs on Saturdays and special holidays, whereas their husbands drank also on week-days. Second, their presence was not tolerated in what were regarded as strictly male preserves—the vault and the tap room of the pub—and they were obliged to drink in the lounge.[128] Women were even more marginalized in the pubs in various provincial towns that Selley studied during the late 1920s. They were drinking in passages, in jug-and-bottle departments (places where take-away drinks are bought), alley-ways, yards, kitchens, and in the street.[129]

Mass Observation provide an informative description of the spatial gender segregation in Bolton's local pubs. Here, the equivalent to the public bar—the room where the beer engines are and working men mainly stand on a stone floor—is the vault. The social distinction between vault and tap room (where games are played), on the one side, and the lounge or parlour, on the other, is not in class terms, but in terms of sex. This segregation is extremely rigid, with the vault and tap room taboo for women, and men entering the lounge or best room only for the last hour of Saturday, when they join their wives.[130]

To sum up the situation during the first decades of the twentieth century, we can agree with Jennings that, generally, the trend of the war years continued, but the evidence is mixed, and the picture is ambiguous. The situation was also diverse, with some women never entering a pub, others only with husbands, and yet a third group going by themselves.[131] Middle-class women found it much harder than their working-class equivalents to visit pubs without male companions. Women's presence was most limited in small towns and rural public houses. But in large towns and where women's employment was developed, they frequented pubs more regularly and without being accompanied by men. Overall, women shunned pubs, whether by choice or, as is more frequently claimed, because of exclusionary strategies.[132] It would be no exaggeration to conclude that even in the early twentieth century, women were by no means accepted on equal terms in pubs, but remained a barely tolerated minority.

The Second World War brought a rise in female attendance again. In a London borough in 1943, 40 per cent of women under thirty years of age claimed to be frequenting pubs. The increased incidence of women's pub visiting was due to their greater spending power; and freedom from neighbourly surveillance and family control were also held to be contributory. But women's own beliefs had also changed in that many claimed a right to leisure as contributors to the war effort.[133]

Yet, there were exceptions, with very traditional gender relations continuing even after World War II in small, self-contained communities, such as mining towns and rural communities. A study of a highly traditional working-class community during the early 1950s,[134] a small Yorkshire mining town, finds a picture almost unchanged from the nineteenth century. In this town, with its economy based exclusively on mining, an extremely rigid role division by gender was observed. 'The notion that "women's place is in the home" is a very definite and firm principle in Ashton [a pseudonym]',[135] leading to women's exclusion not only from work, but also from the town's institutions of leisure. Working men's clubs and pubs were portrayed as 'exclusively male institutions'. As soon as the husbands feel clean and rested after finishing work 'they look for the company of their mates'.[136] Women, in most cases, are only found in pubs at weekends,[137] and then they must be accompanied by their husbands or fiancés. A study from the same time about Pentre, a rural, fairly isolated community in North Wales, comes to similar conclusions: 'Women and girls, with very rare exceptions, do not go to the public houses in Pentre.'[138] However, such communities with a heavily accented division of labour between the sexes had become exceptional by the 1950s. In the larger towns near to both Ashton and Pentre, women's situation had become much more equal.

Even in the early sixties, according to Thornton,[139] women rarely entered pubs on their own. To do so, he suggests, would invite questions about their moral rectitude. Pubs remained largely 'a male refuge'. A general survey of pub attendance established that, in 1970, 90 per cent of women stated that they would not enter a pub alone.[140] A study by Whitehouse of a small rural community in Herefordshire in the early 1970s discovers that, even when women were visiting the pub, their husbands found ways to limit their participation in the sociability around the bar.[141] Their mere toleration as customers found expression in their physical occupation of unobtrusive and marginal spaces. Jennings is therefore right to conclude that 'on the whole, the real movement of women, and young women in particular, into the world of the pub was still to come'.[142]

The definite arrival of women in pubs in greater numbers came only at the end of the twentieth century, when their number was probably greater than at any previous time.[143] Now women, particularly young unmarried ones, are a major group of participants in night-time culture. As the economically and socially founded bases of the traditional male-oriented pub were disappearing, and women no longer accepted any exclusionary or segregationist gender ideology, they finally entered pubs as equals. Women's respectability is no longer conditional on avoiding pub visits and/or alcoholic drink. This applies to all socio-geographical areas and all classes. Significantly, as will be shown, pubs themselves have changed dramatically, and the emergence of food-led pubs certainly eased women's integration into the social life of pubs.

Means of and Explanations for Women's Exclusion

How has it been possible to exclude the majority of women from pubs for several centuries and to persist in making those women who nevertheless came to drink thoroughly unwelcome? In the absence of few formal rules of exclusion, the informal rules of a well-entrenched gender ideology must have been at play to exert control over the space within pubs. What were they and how did they become so effective?

It has repeatedly been suggested that men do not frequent pubs merely to drink but also to socialize in a group of men who share their outlook on life and on the role of women within it. Conversation may be exclusively about either work or sport. Drinking in pubs serves to affirm masculinity, particularly among working men. This necessitates exerting control over those men see as threatening it, namely women and particularly wives and partners, who are viewed as trying to wrest this control from them. Maintaining control over one's wife not only heightens self-esteem, but also prestige within the male drinking group. The presence of women would disrupt the male bonding, as well as hamper the husbands' free spending on beer. As Clark suggests,[144] there rages a continual struggle for the breeches, and men try to assert their power and control by drinking in pubs, while, at the same time, excluding women from this privilege. Jennings cites a ditty,[145] sung in East Anglian pubs during the Edwardian period, that illustrates this aggressive masculinity:

> Oh, she makes me do the washing;
> She makes me scrub the floor,
> She makes me run all errands
> Until my feet are sore.
> But I'll be level with her;
> Oh, I'll be level with her.
> I'll cut her throat
> And away I'll sloap
> I will! So help me never!

Dominant women, it was held by men, created drunken, absent husbands.[146] Hence, an ideology that asserts that women's place is in the home—even if only during leisure time, as most lower-class women have always worked outside their home—was effective. This ideology was already present in the eighteenth century, but achieved its fullest development during the Victorian period. The Victorian middle-class wife 'was thought of as the perfect lady, ... completely leisured, ornamental and completely dependent....'.[147] Originating in the leisured and propertied classes, this ideology permeated other aspiring social strata, particularly the labour aristocracy, and the ability to keep a wife at home became one of the marks of respectability enjoined on the working classes.[148]

The ideology devised to justify women's exclusion, particularly during Victorian times, revolved around women's sexuality, the focus of both constant moral exhortation and publicly flaunted vice. Pubs, on the one side, provided men with opportunities for illicit sex and, on the other hand, caused them to wish to protect their wives from exposure to the sex trade. This was done to secure the family's respectability. The latter was a very prominent notion in which were entangled conflicting ideas of protecting women and, at the same time, restricting them. This notion of respectability was also a class ideology distinguishing the middle class and increasingly also some skilled workers from the lowest orders of society. As men's wages rose, working-class mothers increasingly stayed at home.

Women themselves internalized this ideology and, particularly those holding non-conformist beliefs, came to be prominent campaigners, involved in temperance movements and campaigns specifically targeted at prostitution. They called for the prosecution of obscenity and illicit sexuality. However, it is too simplistic to view this desire to protect women from less savoury pubs as a 'mere' ideology and to ignore the sordid and degrading conditions in some pubs, which were genuinely repellent to many women of the middling sort.

How is masculinity expressed and masculine identity reinforced? Answers to this question come from twentieth and twenty-first century studies, but it is likely that they applied also in earlier centuries. *First* and foremost, it is expressed in group conversation where jokes are frequently made at the expense of women and where hostile stereotypes about them are asserted in often obscene language.[149] *Second*, this masculinity is asserted aggressively in pub songs, which frequently adopt a very coarse and misogynistic tone towards women.[150] *Third*, the drinking of pints themselves is seen to demonstrate virility, as opposed to the supposedly more genteel drinks ordered for women in the lounge.[151] This distinction between male and female drinks even endures in the late twentieth century, with women far less likely to drink beer and more likely to drink cocktails and premium-packaged Bacardi Breezers and the like.[152] Moreover, whereas male drunkenness, particularly in the seventeenth and eighteenth century, was admired as drinking prowess, it was and still is much less tolerated in women. *Fourth*, masculinity may be expressed in actual violence against wives who are seen to challenge their husbands' dominance in front of their mates, ranging from hostile verbal to actual physical abuse.[153]

Women do not willingly endorse this gender ideology. Instead, it often leads to constant and bitter quarrels among the spouses, with women resenting both the partner's time away from the home and the squandering of family resources.[154] Women who have directly challenged their exclusion from pub sociability have usually been labelled as loose or unrespectable, often by groundless malicious rumour and assertion. Any women who used pubs without male escorts were seen as non-respectable and often as tarts.[155] They suggest that ideas of what a woman should and should not do persist very strongly and that no 'self-respecting' young woman will go into a public house unaccompanied by her husband or fiancé. Alternatively, as has been demonstrated with striking continuity across the centuries, women have been segregated away from men in a variety of separate rooms of public houses where they could not exercise their perceived threat to male solidarity. Additionally, their presence in pubs has been also temporally restricted and mainly confined to weekends.

How is it that this exclusionary ideology has been so effective for such a long time? It has been most effective when it was backed by superior male economic power and been more effectively challenged when women acquired independent economic resources through paid employment. Hence, working-class women challenged this ideology more often by visiting pubs, than did middle-class women. The ideology has additionally acquired effectiveness because the stigmatization of women who drank was a very invidious weapon against which there was little defence, and which could ruin women's chances of finding a marriage partner.

Once women, from the late 1960s onwards, began to visit pubs in greater numbers and more often without escorts, they made an impact on the physical and social environment pubs provided. Among these, a shift in demand for a greater balance between drink and food became one of the incentives to develop more food-led pubs. Women's wishes for a more civilized and comfortable environment within which to consume food instigated a separation between bar and dining room, often the former saloon. Both played a role in the appearance of the gastropub, although a general decrease in drinking was also a weighty factor.

The Sociality of Pub and Tavern Life

During the seventeenth and most of the eighteenth century, the nature of sociality in taverns and pubs in some ways did not differ greatly, despite their generally divergent class bases. In both types of establishment, heavy drinking and rowdiness were very common.[156] Indeed, drinking heavily was almost a social norm, with top eighteenth century politicians like James Fox, Sheridan Grey, and William Pitt all known for their bouts of drunkenness.[157] However, the serving of wine in taverns, as an accompaniment to food, as well as the lower alcohol content of wine, would have served to moderate drunkenness.

Yet, during the last few decades of the eighteenth century, a change in tavern sociality came about in that heavy drinking, swearing, and fighting were no longer regarded as compatible with the conduct of intellectual pursuits conducted in meetings within taverns. Clark attributes this significant change of tone to the influence exerted by the Evangelical and Non-Conformist Revival during this time.[158] From then onwards, a relaxed sociality, lubricated by drink and often associated with uncouth or indecent language and rowdy behaviour, became associated mainly with public houses. It led to the greater distancing themselves from pubs by the middle classes, who tried to cultivate a sociality compatible with their now more clearly articulated class identity.

Social and political censure of working-class boisterous or even coarse conviviality, however, was not universal. Many commentators, particularly at parish level, recognized that it was by no means a universal feature of alehouse/pub life and that, moreover, it was only one side of conviviality.[159] They focused also on the positive aspects of pub sociality or tried to understand why working men craved this kind of fellowship. The majority of pubs were not simply drinking houses, but, particularly during the earlier centuries, offered opportunities for social intercourse where nothing else existed. Hailwood's focus on 'good fellowship' offered by seventeenth century alehouses emphasizes the 'merriment, liberality and affectionate social bonds' implied by it.[160] During a time of social dislocation—in the seventeenth to nineteenth centuries—'the pub remained a centre of warmth, light and sociability for the urban poor as well as serving as a magnet for disoriented migrants into towns'.[161]

Working men spent a lot of time by waiting for work in so-called 'houses of call' where a publican would allocate jobs daily. Men's friendly societies met in pubs. Drink lubricated solidarity. Parr-Maskell points out that 'it was through these rudimentary forms of collective action that, in the early 19th century, wage earners first learnt the art of combination for the improvement of their conditions'.[162]

This eventually led the way to the trade unions. Other organizations that were connected with pubs are political parties and secret societies. Pubs also provided opportunities for collective organization for merely social activities, saving-up money for outings and picnics.[163] The pub even acted as a kind of people's university. Thus, it is said of Thomas Paine that 'public house conversations familiarized him with the scientific, political and religious assumptions of Enlightenment Europe'.[164]

In addition to facilitating occupational and political contacts, pubs provided all sorts of diversions, such as a large variety of games, music, and singing,[165] at a time when such diversions were not available elsewhere. Pub singing saloons eventually resulted in the establishment of music halls and variety theatres. Bayley, focusing on the period between 1830 and 1885, adds another set of diversions to the list: bowling, glee clubs and free and easies, amateur and professional dramatics, fruit and vegetable shows, and sweepstake clubs, as well as betting, dog shows, and pigeon flying. Bayley therefore justifiably calls the public house of this period 'the institutional hub of working class recreation'.[166]

Pubs were also important social venues beyond providing the above opportunities for formal organization and informal play. They provided fellowship, opportunity for conversation with like-minded men, and relaxation after a hard day's work. Selley, who describes pubs at the beginning of the twentieth century, refers to the pub that fulfils all these functions as a 'social house', in distinction to mere drinking houses.[167] Mass Observation, in contrast to Selley, deem *all* pubs outside the city centre to be 'social houses'.[168]

The authors of Mass Observation well define the sociality found in ordinary local pubs and identify the ties that bind individual drinkers into the community.[169] Drinking, they say, is primarily social: '[I]t is a motive that seeks the breaking down of barriers between men, the release from the strain of everyday life in the feeling of identification with a group.'

Even the temperance lobby recognized that drink was not always the main or even only attraction the pub offered. They realized that,

> persons in the humbler walks and occupations of life...were often compelled to frequent the public house, because in this class of establishment alone were supplied the ordinary and natural cravings for society, the news of the day, and a place where they could pass a sociable hour.[170]

Although drinkers in local pubs were usually well known to each other, it is notable that strangers would usually be made very welcome,[171] and clustering around the bar assisted the easy integration of newcomers into the group. Going up to the bar to order a drink provides a valuable opportunity for social contact and promotes sociability. The anthropologist Kate Fox describes the bar area as a 'liminal zone' in which one finds a degree of 'cultural remission', that is a temporal relaxation or lifting of normal social controls. 'Normal rules of privacy and reserve would be suspended'.[172]

In many locations, particularly in rural and settled working-class areas, pubs became the 'hub of the community'—the local[173]—and the sociability provided was valued for its own sake. Writing about the early post-World War II period, Thompson describes one pub 'as a place where men have talked, and formed opinions and put the world to rights and then gone home to bed',[174] and this description of what one pub offered may be generalized to a large number of other pubs. In pubs of a small mining town during the early 1950s, too, drinking and talking—almost exclusively about work and sport—is the main interest.[175] Pubs thus enabled men to express and reinforce not only their working-class identity and their masculinity, but also to satisfy their search for convivial company and community.

Kate Fox, an observer of present-day pub culture, throws further light on the type of sociality men cultivate in pubs. Conversation and banter among drinkers crowding around the bar is regulated by informal rules that prescribe equality, reciprocity (relating to 'round' buying) and the pursuit of intimacy, all of which facilitate social bonding.[176] It is, however, notable that the intimacy sought remains at a very superficial level. Although jokes about personal or work problems are acceptable, 'earnest outpourings' of one's heart are frowned upon,[177] presumably because the cultivation of masculinity proscribes it. We would do well to remember the integrative function of the pub, and the creation of a community spirit it may foster, when we confront the dismay of some sections of contemporary society, in the face of the current transformation of what were mainly drinking pubs into dining or gastro pubs.

It is notable that throughout the above discussion of sociality the talk is only about the cultivation of sociability among men, reflecting the exclusion or marginalization of women until the end of the twentieth century. Even when women were accepted as drinkers, this bantering kind of conversation, often focused on sport, and the shying away from real intimacy between drinkers, does not appeal to women in the same way as it does to men. Differences between the sexes on the permissibility of making feelings public have endured to the present day.

However, this positive and sometimes sentimental view of pub culture prevalent in the literature presents only one side of its functions and reputation. Many social commentators during the early eighteenth century, when drunkenness was very widespread, condemned pubs in harsh words, attributing all sorts of social evils to their influence. Tobias Smollett, the Scottish poet and author—in his 1790 *History of England*—made the following comments on the 'incredible number of publick houses which continually resounded with the noise of riot and intemperance; they were the haunts of idleness, fraud and rapine, and the seminaries of drunkenness, debauchery and extravagance; and every vice incident to human nature'.[178] A little later, the Victorian middle classes, in particular, were said to find the amusements offered by pubs 'crude and offensive to their sense of station and social order'.[179] For them, and for later generations, the pub not only fostered conviviality, entertainment, common purpose, and community, many were solely drinking houses that were 'shabby, ill-kempt, offensive alike to eyes and nostrils'. They invited drunkenness, and excited violence and other disorderly and obnoxious social behaviour.[180] London's Victorian pubs of the 1890s, according to Girouard,[181] 'had a particular combination of toughness, squalor, drunkenness and glitter'. Selley, a temperance sympathizer, estimates that, during the early decades of the twentieth century, such mere drink shops sometimes amounted to 80 per cent of houses in large industrial centres.[182]

But did the search for sociality remain an important motivator for pub visits into the late twentieth century? The pub's role as a place where economic and political business could also be transacted had already steeply declined all through the nineteenth and twentieth centuries as alternative institutions developed. The pub's perceived function of offering release to working men who laboured in physically exhausting jobs in the heavy industries had also become largely redundant. The pub's loss of function was less pronounced in the purely social realm, although even here many alternatives to the pub had developed. Leisure time could now be profitably spent in the much-improved home, both with the family and in extending hospitality to friends. Television watching in particular became an important evening leisure activity. The search for leisure activity also found many new specialized outlets, from sports clubs to cinemas.

However, many of these alternative venues do not offer the same possibilities to cultivate conviviality and fellowship over a pint or two, with either friends or strangers. Hence, the pub has remained attractive for many people in search of such impromptu and informal sociality. Even with the availability of many alternative venues for spending leisure time in the twenty-first century, in many places, particularly in villages, the pub remains the only venue to unite the local community. Moreover, the local community now also includes women. It is this function which has motivated recent efforts to have pubs preserved as 'community assets'.

At the same time, the pub itself changed after the Beer Orders Act of 1989, with implications for sociality. Smaller local pubs that had been foci for community activities increasingly gave way to the foundation of large, corporately-owned and styled city centre mega pubs. These attracted, particularly at night time, mainly the younger population in search of a combination of alcohol-enhanced mood elevation, dancing, and sexual partners. It has been suggested that the 'chain' model of this type of pub did little to revive pub sociability, being described by one author as 'dispiriting, homogenised and soulless'.[183] However, these mega pubs are only one section of today's pubs.

The nature of pub-going has also changed in that there are far fewer people who visit regularly, whereas the number of occasional visitors has increased—a fact that must impede the development of a spirit of community. Last, the nature of pub sociality has changed itself in that heavy drinking as a lubricant of conviviality has become much rarer. Hence, the relaxation of inhibitions to break down social barriers between men also has become harder to achieve. Nevertheless, the craving for a release from the strain of everyday life in the feeling of identification with a group has remained a constant, and the convivial atmosphere of the pub keeps it exceptionally well equipped to satisfy such craving.

The sociality provided by both taverns and pubs has not been solely facilitated by drink, but also by the provision of meals. As Mennell, Murcott and van Otterloo observe,[184] meals are 'the very stuff of sociality'. Warde and Martens agree that 'eating out is a major and expanding conduit for sociable interaction'.[185] Eating together at the same table creates equally strong, if not stronger, social bonds, as it is usually a temporarily more extended activity, of which relaxed conversation constitutes an integral and much valued part.

Eating out in taverns in earlier centuries took place at the 'common table' and thus could bring even strangers into close social contact and thereby create new social bonds or facilitate access to new social networks. In alehouses and public houses of the seventeenth to the nineteenth centuries, eating always took a poor second place to drinking and comprised consuming snacks rather than meals. It therefore played no significant role in promoting sociality, which firmly developed around drink. As will be shown later, this imbalance in favour of drink has fundamentally changed in later centuries—only hesitantly and selectively in the twentieth century, but more radically in the twenty-first century, with the arrival of the pub restaurant or gastropub.

To sum up this section, my investigation of whether pubs and other hostelries encouraged social mixing yielded different findings at different points in history. Whereas a social mixing between lords and labourers has always been more of a social myth than a reality, hostelries in the seventeenth and eighteenth centuries afforded more opportunities for cross-class sociability than they did in later centuries. This was partly due to the fact that lines of social division were not yet as rigidly drawn in society more generally.

Additionally, social mixing was facilitated because pubs, taverns, and inns fulfilled multiple economic, social, and political functions and thereby provided room for social interaction apart from drinking and eating communally. Yet, even in these earlier centuries, each type of hostelry already had a distinctive class character, shaping its organizational identity. The pubs/alehouses were more strongly associated with the drinking and socializing of the lower orders, than were taverns and inns. As inns and taverns had lost their special social and economic functions, the middle and upper classes generally either retreated into their homes, or sought out new types of more select establishments, such as clubs and, from the last quarter of the nineteenth century, restaurants.

Division along lines of class hardened and social segregation increased in the nineteenth and twentieth centuries, up to World War II. In the post-War era, increased democratization of society at large also became reflected in an easier social mixing in pubs. Social divisions became less marked or were at least less overtly acknowledged, and the pub again attracted customers from across the social spectrum. But even then, pubs were often stratified either according to socio-geographical location, or, in the centres of large towns, maintained a social distinction between the bar and the lounge. Despite this democratization since the World War II period, during the twentieth century the dominant image of the pub as a working-class institution persisted. This has been reflected also in the attitude towards pubs and drinking by the state, which has mainly connected pubs with social disorder.

Even though pubs now rarely bring together drinkers in games, communal sing-song, and more formalized activities connected with employment and work, they still offer opportunities for conviviality within groups of friends, neighbours, and complete strangers. The informal and relaxed atmosphere in which conviviality is fostered and community reaffirmed is found in few other places in contemporary society, and it is this feature of the pub which continues to make it a valued institution. Whether or not the contemporary gastropub will still be able to fulfil these functions is an important question to be addressed in Chapters 6 and 7.

Endnotes

1. Everitt, A. 1985, 'The English urban inn', *Landscape and Community in England*, 155–208. London: Hambleton Press; Borsay, P. 1989, *The English Urban Renaissance. Culture and society in the provincial town*. Oxford: Clarendon Press; Chartres, J. 2002, 'The eighteenth century inn: a transient golden age?', B. Kümin and B.A. Tlusty eds, *The World of the Tavern*. Aldershot, Hampshire: Ashgate.
2. Chartres, 2002, 18.

3. Thompson, L.P. 1947, *Norwich Inns*, 10. Ipswich: W.E. Harrison & Sons Ltd.
4. Everitt, 1985, 167, 189.
5. Jennings, P. 2011, *The Local. A history of the English pub*, 2nd edition,105. Stroud: The History Press.
6. Borsay, 1989; Everitt, 1985.
7. Everitt, 1985.
8. Earle, P. 1989, *The Making of the English Middle Class. Business, society and family life in London, 1660–1730*, 53. London: Methuen.
9. Berry, G. 1978, *Taverns and Tokens of Pepys' London*, 48. London: Seaby Publications Ltd.
10. Wrightson, K. 1982, *English Society, 1580–1680*, 168. London: Hutchinson.
11. Clark, P. 1983, *The English Alehouse. A social history 1200–1830*, 76. London and New York: Longman.
12. Clark, 1983, 82.
13. Clark, 1983, 202–5.
14. Jennings, 2011, 107; Clark, 1983, 284.
15. Jennings, 2011, 90–6.
16. George, D. 1925, *London Life in the XVIIIth Century*, 301. London: Kegan Paul, Trench, Trubner & Co.
17. Jennings, 2011, 91.
18. Jennings, 2011, 106.
19. Robinson, A. 2010, *Public Houses of Balsham*. Privately published. Available in Cambridge University Library's Rare Book Room.
20. Girouard, M. 1984, *Victorian Pubs*. New Haven and London: Yale University Press.
21. Girouard, 1984.
22. Girouard, 1984, 13.
23. Stanley, L.T. 1957, *The Old Inns of London*. London: Batsford; Riddington Young, J. 1975, *The Inns and Taverns of Old Norwich*, 33. Norwich: Wensum Books; Girouard, 1984, 7–8.
24. Mass Observation 1987 [1943], T*he Pub and the People. A Worktown study by Mass Observation*, 66. London: Cresset Library.
25. Jennings, 2011, 222.
26. Jennings, 2011, 107–8.
27. Burke, T. 1947 [1930], *The English Inn*. London: Herbert Jenkins Ltd; Clark, 1983; Picard, L. 2004, *Dr Johnson's London. Everyday life in London 1740–1770*. London: Phoenix; Tombs, R. 2015, *The English and their History*. London: Penguin Books.
28. Hailwood, M. 2014, *Alehouses and Good Fellowship in Early Modern England*, 179. Woodbridge: Boydell Press.
29. Tombs, 2015, 295.
30. Clark, 1983, 166.
31. Borsay, 1989; Tombs, 2015.
32. Tombs, 2015, 296.
33. Tombs, 2015, 295.
34. Borsay, 1989, 230ff.

35. Langford, P. 1998, *A Polite and Commercial People: England 1727–1783*, 59–63, 71–3. Oxford: Clarendon Press.
36. Langford, 1998, 71.
37. Borsay, 1989, 278, 231.
38. Wrightson, 1982, 226ff.
39. Borsay, 1989, 282.
40. French, H. 2007, *The Middle Sort of People in Provincial England 1600–1750*. Oxford: Oxford University Press.
41. Cited by Borsay, 1989, 280.
42. Borsay, 1989, 283, 284.
43. Burke, 1947 [1930], 9.
44. Gutzke, D.W. 2004, *Pubs and Progressives. Reinventing the public house in England 1896–1960*, 187. Illinois: DeKalb.
45. Clark, 1983, 4.
46. Moritz, C.-P. 1965, *Journeys of a German in England in 1782*, 124. London: Jonathan Cape.
47. Jennings, 2011, 42.
48. Borsay, 1989, 29.
49. Everitt, 1985; Jennings, 2011.
50. Everitt, 1985, 181.
51. Haydon, P. 2001, *Beer and Britannia*, 160. Stroud: Sutton Publishing.
52. Burke, 1947 [1930], 58.
53. Clark, A. 1995, *The Struggle for the Breeches. Gender and the making of the British working class*, 31. London: Rivers Oram Press.
54. Brewer, J. 1997, *The Pleasures of the Imagination*, 366. London: Harper Collins.
55. Brewer, 1997, 366.
56. Burke, 1947 [1930], 142, 143.
57. Selley, E. 1927, *The English Public House as It Is*, 3. London: Longmans, Green and Co. Ltd.
58. Burke, 1947 [1930]. 36.
59. Mass Observation 1987 [1943].
60. Clark, 1983, 3.
61. Clark, 1983, 226–7.
62. Clark, 1983, 222–7.
63. Clark, 1983, 226.
64. Tombs, 2015, 302.
65. D'Archenholz, M. 1790, *A Picture of England*, 203. Dublin: P. Byrne.
66. Beresford, J. ed. 1968, *The Diary of a Country Parson. The Reverend James Woodforde. Volume I—1758–1781*, 29, 31. Oxford: Clarendon Press.
67. Jennings, 2011, 47–8.
68. Jennings, 2011, 48.
69. Thompson, 1947, 13.
70. Jennings, 2011, 52.
71. Hewitt, M. 2004, 'Class and classes', C. Williams ed., *Companion to Nineteenth Century Britain*, 315. Oxford: Blackwell Publishing.

72. Tombs, 2015, 428.
73. Disraeli, B. 1998 [1845], *Sybil, or The Two Nations*. Oxford: Oxford University Press.
74. Girouard, 1984, 4.
75. Girouard, 1984.
76. Jennings, 2011, 110; Smith, M.A. 1984, *The Public House. Leisure and social control*, 20. Birmingham, UK: University of Salford, Centre for Leisure Studies.
77. Clark, 1995, 7.
78. Clark, 1983, 308–9.
79. Smith, 1984, 53; Clark, 1983, 307.
80. Clark, 1983, 307.
81. Girouard, 1984, 5–6.
82. Girouard, 1984, 5.
83. Francis Place, cited by Picard 2004: 178.
84. Selley, 1927; Mass Observation 1987 [1943].
85. Selley, 1927, 21; Mass Observation 1987 [1943], 148.
86. Mass Observation, 1987 [1943], 136, 155, 259.
87. Stacey, M. 1960, *Tradition and Change. A study of Banbury*, 171. Oxford: Oxford University Press.
88. Mass Observation 1987 [1943], 141.
89. Gorham, M. 1939, *The Local*, 1. London: Cassell & Co. Ltd.
90. Fox, K. 2004, *Watching the English*, 95. London: Hodder & Stoughton.
91. Fox, 2004, 97.
92. Kümin, B. and Tlusty, B.A. 2002, 'The world of the tavern: an introduction', B. Kümin and B.A. Tlusty eds, *The World of the Tavern*, 45. Aldershot, Hampshire: Ashgate.
93. Hailwood, 2014, 154ff on the seventeenth century; Jennings, 2011; Selley, 1927; Mass Observation 1987 [1943] on the twentieth century.
94. Jennings, 2011, 225.
95. Tombs, 2015, 528; Richardson, S. 2004, 'Politics and gender', C. Williams ed., *A Companion to Nineteenth Century Britain*, 175. Oxford: Blackwell Publishing.
96. Richardson, 2004, 180.
97. Perkin, H. 1969, *The Origins of Modern English Society*, 160. London: Routledge, Keegan Paul.
98. Richardson, 2004, 183.
99. Cited by Clarke, N. 2000, *Dr Johnson's Women*, 180. London, New York: Hambledon.
100. Davidoff, L. 1973, *The Best Circles. Society, etiquette and The Season*, 16. London: Croom Helm.
101. Davidoff, 1973, 13.
102. Kümin and Tlusty, 2002, 45.
103. Tombs, 2015, 750.
104. Tombs, 2015, 787, 788.
105. Tombs, 2015, 788.
106. Pepys, S. 2011, *The Joys of Excess*. London: Penguin Books.
107. Pepys, 2011.
108. Clark, 1983, 225.

109. D'Archenholz, 1790, 208.
110. Jennings, 2011, 112.
111. Jennings, 2011, 113.
112. Jennings, 2011, 112.
113. Clark, 1983.
114. Ratcliffe, B.M. and Chaloner, W.H. eds, 1977, *A French Sociologist Looks at Britain. Gustave d'Eichthal and British society in 1828*, 27–8. Manchester: Manchester University Press and Rowman and Littlefield.
115. Haydon, 2001, 156.
116. Boswell, J. 1953, *Boswell's Life of London*, 123–4. Oxford: Oxford University Press.
117. Clark, 1995, 39, 40.
118. Anonymous 1858, Review of the antiquarian copy of John Farley's 1783 *The London Art of Cookery*, at http://www.oldcooksbooks.com/master_book_by_let_search.php?passed_book_id=11035.
119. Sims, G. 1917, *My Life. Sixty years' recollections of Bohemian London*, 330. London: Eveleigh Nash Company.
120. Jennings, 2011, 117.
121. Girouard, 1984, 5, 80.
122. Jennings, 2011, 117; Girouard, 1984, 4.
123. Jennings, 2011, 116.
124. Clark, 1995, 39, 40.
125. Jennings, 2011, 183, 190.
126. Selley, 1927, 127, 129.
127. Mass Observation, 1987 [1943], 38.
128. Mass Observation, 1987[1943], 134–5.
129. Selley, 1927, 125.
130. Mass Observation, 1987 [1943], 93–105.
131. Jennings, 2011, 205–6.
132. Jennings, 2011, 117.
133. Jennings, 2011, 206.
134. Dennis, N., Henrique, F. and Slaughter, C. 1956, *Coal is our Life*. London: Eyre and Spottiswoode.
135. Dennis et al., 1956, 174.
136. Dennis et al., 1956, 183, 181.
137. Dennis et al., 1956, 154.
138. Frankenberg, R.F. 1957, *Village on the Border*, 52. London: Cohen & West.
139. Thornton, T. 2014, *Brewers, Brands and the Pub in their Hands*, 3. Kibworth Beauchamps: Matador.
140. Jennings, 2011, 225.
141. Whitehead, A. 1976, 'Sexual antagonisms in Herefordshire', D. Leonhard Barker and S. Allen eds, *Dependence and Exploitation in Work and Marriage*, 169–203. London: Longman.
142. Jennings, 2011, 207.
143. Jennings, 2011, 230.
144. Clark, 1995.

145. Jennings, 2011, 128.
146. Hey, V. 1986, *Patriarchy and Pub Culture*, 19. London: Tavistock Publications.
147. Perkin, 1969, 159.
148. Davidoff, 1973; Hey, 1986, 32.
149. Whitehead, 1976.
150. Clark, 1995, 34; Jennings, 2011, 128.
151. Hey, 1986; Selley, 1927, 123.
152. Heydon, 2001, 305.
153. Whitehead, 1976.
154. Dennis et al., 1956; Clark, 1995; Whitehead, 1976; Hey, 1986.
155. Hey, 1986; Dennis et al., 1956.
156. Clark, P. 1986, *Sociability and Urbanity: Clubs and Societies in the Eighteenth Century City*, 20.
157. Haydon, 2001, 156.
158. Clark, 1986, 21. Eighth H. J. Dyos Memorial Lecture. University of Leicester.
159. Hailwood, 2014, 109.
160. Hailwood, 2014, 113.
161. Bayley, P. 1978, *Leisure and Class in Victorian England. Rational recreation and the contest for control, 1830–1885*, 10. London: Routledge, Keegan Paul.
162. Parr-Maskell, H. 1927, *The Taverns of Old England*, 119. London: Allan & Co. Ltd.
163. Mass Observation, 1987 [1943], 20.
164. Kuklick, B. ed. 1989, *Thomas Paine,* Political Writings, vii–viii. Cambridge: Cambridge University Press.
165. Selley, 1927; Mass Observation, 1987 [1943]; Dennis et al., 1956.
166. Bayley, 1978, 9.
167. Selley, 1927, 35, 45.
168. Mass Observation, 1987 [1943], 256–98.
169. Mass Observation, 1987 [1943], 312.
170. Girouard, 1984, 200.
171. Fox, 2004.
172. Fox, 2004, 89.
173. Jennings, 2011, 14.
174. Thompson, 1947, 28.
175. Dennis et al., 1956, 155.
176. Fox, 2004, 102.
177. Fox, 2004, 106.
178. Cited by George, 1925, 304.
179. Bayley, 1978, 22.
180. Selley, 1927, 44, 47.
181. Girouard, 1984, 4.
182. Selley, 1927, 46.
183. *Guardian 2*, 28.01.2016: 12.
184. Mennell, S., Murcott, A. and van Otterloo, A.H. 1992, *The Sociology of Food: Eating, diet and culture*, 116. London: Sage Publications.
185. Warde, A. and Martens, L. 2000, *Eating Out. Social differentiation, consumption and pleasure*, 227. Cambridge: Cambridge University Press.

3

Eating Out in the Seventeenth and Eighteenth Centuries: The Contest between English and French Food

This chapter examines the food eaten in these centuries both at home and, more extensively, in taverns, inns, and pubs. It analyses not only the material factors of eating out, but also its symbolic aspects. While the identification of certain culinary styles with either national belonging or cosmopolitanism is an important theme, food consumption is often simultaneously connected with, and expresses, class and/or gender identity.

It is a difficult undertaking to write about the food served in past centuries in taverns, inns, and pubs. Even in the more detailed accounts of tavern hospitality, food is rarely at the centre, and most descriptions of meals do not go beyond a list of the main dishes. What the food looked like, how it had been prepared, and, above all, how it *tasted* rarely receive coverage. While accounts of inn and tavern life usually report with enthusiasm on the elegance of the physical environment and on the splendour of the dinner conversation and/or of the speeches made, little excitement is expressed about tavern or inn meals, let alone food consumed in pubs. Meals are rarely perceived as a gastronomic experience about which delight or dismay may be expressed. Compared with the rapturous accounts of dishes consumed found on today's food blogs, with the detailed descriptions of ingredients, appearance, and tastes of various dishes, the analyst of historical accounts of food consumption is faced with impoverished culinary information.

How can one account for this? Is it that people cared little for culinary pleasures in past centuries, or was it socially unacceptable to express judgements of taste? Was the food so plain and unvaried that it evoked few judgements of taste? Or, is it simply too difficult to express sensory perception and culinary judgements of taste? The answers to these questions must remain tentative. From a look at the admittedly scant evidence available, the last three explanations seem more plausible than the first. Customers certainly cared greatly about the drink consumed, hence one cannot claim that English people in past centuries cared less about physical pleasures. Moreover, the huge quantities of food eaten at the tavern table and at home do not point towards ascetic abstinence. Last, meals served in bygone centuries, by and large, were fairly plain and did not warrant a long rapturous disquisition. They were less conducive to elaborate judgements of taste.

Meals served in taverns receive by far the most and the most extended mentions, while food consumed in pubs merits relatively few and only brief comments. Hence, my analysis will distinguish eating in pubs from dining in taverns and inns. The very different habits of the upper, middling, and labouring classes in eating both at home and in hostelries requires a study of dining/eating and the food served filtered through the lens of class, used as a concept which takes into account both economic and cultural capital (knowledge and education). Additionally, an understanding of dining out has to consider the economic and social context in which it took place.

Between the late seventeenth and the early eighteenth century, England underwent dramatic commercial and population expansion, the market economy became ever more integrated, and London emerged at its head as an international metropolis.[1] After the Restoration in 1660, the country became more settled, and agricultural and commercial capitalist development began. The greater security of property made possible the further development of a monetized economy, with price stability, sophisticated means of exchange and credit, mobility of labour, and increasingly efficient transport by road and canals. Food could now be brought from all parts of the country to London.[2] This period is marked also by a new wave of the setting up of great country estates, financed from the profits of the great trading ventures of this time. These new landowners were not merely seeking social prestige from ownership, but also brought an entrepreneurial spirit and new agricultural methods to the cultivation of their estates. This increased appreciably both the quantity and quality of grain cultivated, as well as the quantity of meat produced.

Another new development was the popularity gained by gardens among the rural gentry, including cultivation in glass houses. This provided them with a much greater variety of vegetables and fruit, including more exotic ones like grapes, peaches, and nectarines and even oranges and lemons. However, the variety and quantity of vegetables grown remained surprisingly small, as vegetables were not yet accepted as tasty food stuffs and were even regarded as harmful to digestion.[3]

Post-Restoration London was the hub of a growing empire and 'began to think of the world as its larder'. The establishment of trading posts in North America, the Caribbean, Africa, and the East led to the appearance of many more exotic food stuffs, such as oranges, soy sauce and tea, coffee and spices.[4]

It is, however, difficult to discern much impact on food served in eating-out venues, although cookery books began to feature recipes for curry in the second half of the eighteenth century.[5] London was also the nucleus of all domestic trading, holding 'a virtual monopoly on all exports and imports'.[6] The better sorts had greater opportunities and the ability to seek out 'expensive and rare dainties' as food from many parts of the world became available.[7] Tavern life became seriously circumscribed, however, during two catastrophic events during the 1660s: the plague of 1665 that killed tavernkeepers and customers alike, and the great fire of London of 1666, which destroyed many taverns.[8]

The expanding commercialization of entertainment from the Restoration, including that of dining out, indicated the growth of a significant middling class. It encouraged a greater focus on consumption, particularly of food and drink. 'It points to an affluent and growing middle class which was willing to spend for the sake, not only of prestige, but also for enjoyment.'[9] The seventeenth century saw the beginning of the London season, in which dining played a prominent part. Dining out and an appreciation of good food by the better sorts spread gradually from London back to the provinces.[10]

The nobility, gentry, and the emerging urban bourgeoisie and professionals lived well during this period. The conditions of the lower orders also improved during the second half of the century, although poverty remained widespread. Food supply became much more varied and secure, and the gulf in consumption patterns between the better sorts and the lower orders became less marked.[11] The common estimation of the standard of living of the lower orders by the amount of meat eaten indicates that, after 1660, meat could be afforded by most people, even if the quality and the amount consumed differed.[12] Towards the end of the century, reliable observers judged that the English lived far better than their counterparts in other European countries.[13]

Compared with later centuries, however, food supply often lacked in hygienic standard and quality. Lack of any refrigeration and extremely widespread adulteration of food and drink (including milk)[14] meant that, by current standards, food was not always very tasty, let alone healthy, except for that enjoyed by the small elite of landowners who fed themselves almost entirely from food stuffs raised on their own estates, including much game.

Dining out in taverns and inns was, of course, mainly confined to the higher social ranks, including 'an expanding bourgeoisie'.[15] The early development of taverns as dining destinations, as compared with dining-out opportunities in France, is evident in their profusion in seventeenth-century London. In addition to individual or small group consumption, a lot of provision of food in this century was associated with corporate institutions such as the East India Company, guilds and craft companies, and Inns of Court, as well as the Church and parochial feasts.[16] It is, therefore, unsurprising that, when restaurants finally appeared in France in the last quarter of the eighteenth century, one of them was named *La Grande Taverne de Londres*.

The Contest between English and French Cuisine

One theme which constantly appears in the literature on dining out in the seventeenth century and, more so, the eighteenth century, are the opposed claims on diners' allegiance to English and French cuisine. The strong disapproval of French cuisine in these centuries by some sections of English society has to be viewed not only in culinary terms. It represents an attempt to link consumption of English dishes to national identity and belonging and make indulgence in French meals appear unpatriotic. This should be placed in the context of the prolonged and often bitter enmity between the two countries, and the waging of five costly wars against the French between 1689 and 1815.

Among various English dishes, beef was often singled out. While beef has been consumed by members of many other European nations, it is widely assumed that both the superior quality and the quantity of beef consumed in England (Britain) has been due to the country's specific geographic and agricultural conditions. In other words, English beef was seen to have 'the taste of place' that sets it apart from the beef eaten in other countries.

Preferring good English meat, particularly beef, has been linked not only to national allegiance, but, in turn, must be studied in a complex intertwining of the latter with both class affiliation and gender identity. Masculinity was expressed when beef eating was linked to prowess on the battle field. Consumption of beef became partly a political statement and became closely linked to cultural production in both literary and visual media, particularly in posters and the theatre.

The craze for French food was given a strong impetus by the many aristocrats and politicians who had an association with Stuart royalty and Roman Catholicism, and who returned from a more or less extended exile in France where they had come to favour French cuisine.[17] Foremost among these returnees was, of course, the future King Charles II. The liking of French food by him and his courtiers sparked off a wave of enthusiasm among the aristocracy for refined French cuisine, as well as for fashion and dancing.[18] Although the English aristocracy was not nearly as Court-centred as the French,[19] aping the king and his inner circle nevertheless was widespread. La Varenne's book of cookery, published in France in 1651 and prefaced with the nationalistic sentiment that 'of all Cookes in the World, the French are Esteem'd the best', appeared in an English translation by 1653.[20]

While different food is generally consumed by the different social ranks, food can also unite them when faced with foreign cuisines, tastes, and cultural identity expressed through them. Even English servants in grand houses regarded vegetables with some contempt, believing their own meat-focused consumption patterns to be far superior to that of their French equivalents, who greatly relied on vegetables and pottages.[21] Aping their superiors in food preferences must have been seen to raise their own social status.

Dining in the Seventeenth Century

When turning to descriptions of food and dining, both domestic dining and dining out in taverns and, less so, inns are considered. Sources on dining in the seventeenth century are not plentiful. Food is considered a neglected aspect of this age.[22]

Despite all the new colonial influences on the availability of more exotic food stuffs, taverns have been mainly associated with plain English fare. In the late seventeenth century, taverns became connected with the provision of fixed-price Ordinaries.[23] First introduced in 1560 by the comedian Richard Tarleton in his tavern near St Paul's, they carried their popularity into the nineteenth century.[24] The term 'Ordinary' came to be applied both to the meal and, very often, to the tavern serving such a meal. The Ordinary consisted of several dishes, of which one took as much as one pleased at a fixed price. The menu was arranged in terms of separate courses, similar to the *table d'hôte* in later restaurants, although our current idea of three courses was not yet prevalent. The Ordinary was served by the landlord at the common table, and conversation was general. While most of these dining taverns were known for their solid English food, and particularly their beef, even at this early date there were a few serving French meals. The most outstanding—and the most expensive among them—was Pontack's.

Samuel Pepys's diaries, of 1660–69,[25] are generally held to give the best account of dining during this period, both at home and in taverns. Pepys, a high-level employee of the Navy Board, may be regarded as a member of the rising bourgeoisie who frequently socialised with members of the aristocracy, parliamentarians, and even members of the Royal Court.[26] His diaries give an impression of both the wide diversity and the huge quantities of the food consumed by him and his guests from middling and upper-class backgrounds. Unlike many later accounts, Pepys' writing at least expresses appreciation of the preparation and quality of the food, as well as conveying enjoyment of meals consumed. But even he comes across as more of a glutton than a gourmet.

Pepys provides the greatest detail when describing domestic dinner parties, showing some pride in the richness of what his household could offer. It invites an interpretation of 'conspicuous consumption'[27] for the rising bourgeoisie of England at this comparatively early time. At a dinner given at his home on 13 January 1662, he offered his guests oysters, a hash of rabbits and lamb, a rare 'chine' of beef, a great dish of roasted fowl, a tart, and fruit and cheese; and a dinner on 4 April 1662 consisted of a 'fricassée of rabbets [sic] and chicken', a boiled leg of mutton, three carps in a dish, a dish of a side of lamb, a dish of roasted pigeons, a dish of four lobsters, three tarts, a lamprey (a kind of eel) pie, and a dish of anchovies. Apart from the richness of these meals, they also show a use of ingredients—lampreys, anchovies, carp, and roasted pigeons—that had fallen out of use by the twentieth century, to return (with the exception of lampreys and carp) as something novel only in the 1990s. The popularity of anchovies was due to the influence of the Portuguese-born queen Catherine of Braganza.[28]

Pepys's home-cooked dinners additionally showed some evidence of French influences, particularly in the mode of preparation—a 'fricassée of rabetts [sic] and chicken', daubes and bisques. Vegetables and fresh fruit are rarely mentioned. Vegetables were regarded as less tasty and less potent, fit only for consumption by women.[29] The virtual absence of fish eaten at home at this time resulted from the lack of refrigerated transport. However, Pepys often brings home oysters and lobster (kept alive in tanks), which were plentiful and relatively cheap at that time.[30]

Pepys, like many higher-class Londoners of his day, loved to eat out. Berry lists ninety different taverns that he frequented,[31] while Spencer talks of visits to 'over one hundred taverns in Westminster and London alone'.[32] Visiting taverns, for Pepys and other middling sorts, was, however, not solely motivated by the food and drink served, but was equally about seeking companionship and picking up the latest news at a time when newspapers hardly existed.

Although Pepys at first mildly derides the appointment of a French cook by his aristocratic patron, the Earl of Sandwich, he became quite partial to French food himself. This is evident from his report on a visit, in May 1667, to a simple French Ordinary in Covent Garden, owned by a Monsieur Robins. He and his wife enjoyed 'a mess of potage, a couple of pigeons a l'esteuvé, a piece of beef a la mode, all exceedingly well seasoned and to our liking'. He also expresses pleasure at 'the pleasant and ready attendance that we had, and all things so desirous to please and ingenious in the people [despite the location in then unfashionable Soho], did please me mightily'.[33] For all this he paid six shillings, which is more than he would have paid in most English taverns, but less than in the more fashionable taverns serving French food.

Other French Ordinaries mentioned in the literature are Lockett's and Chatelaine's. Pepys, who refers to the latter as the 'French House', also liked to dine in this very expensive and upmarket Ordinary.[34] Such French meals were invariably accompanied by expensive imported wine. The following little verse pokes gentle fun at men who ate in expensive French restaurants in preference to the consumption of solid English food:

> At Lockett's, Brown's and at Pontack's enquire,
> What modish kick shaws [*quelque choses*] the beaux Desire,
> What fam'd ragouts, what new invented sallat,
> Has best pretensions to regale the palate.[35]

Spending freely on good French food is satirized when it is said that Lockett's was the resort of those who thought quite as much of spending money as of eating.[36]

Who, then, consumed French food in the late seventeenth century? It was idolized by a section of the aristocracy and the gentry, who often employed top French chefs at home and dined in French taverns/Ordinaries. They were said to be of Whig political persuasion, less tradition-minded, less loyal to the king, and not close to the Established Church. In other words, French food was embraced by the cosmopolitan elites with a less developed national identity that allowed them to develop and display wider horizons in food consumption.

Many of the upper and some of the middling sorts had travelled to France repeatedly. The existence of many hotels in Calais catering for the English[37] suggests that a liking of French food was not confined to a few aristocrats. Some members of the bourgeoisie—merchants, members of the creative and liberal professions—particularly in London, who were in contact with those above them in the social hierarchy, like Pepys, also developed some fondness for French dining. According to Tombs, writers, artists, politicians, and many members of the aristocracy were 'determinedly cosmopolitan'.[38] In contrast, English culinary nationalism was avidly embraced by other sections of the upper and upper middle social groups, who tended to be Tories.

Most of the food served in taverns and homes of the middling sorts did not show this French influence, and meals were deemed to be plain and typically English. Whereas English food had only been gradually adapted from what it was in the Middle Ages, the French had been more innovative. The range of spices used in English cooking was much smaller than in earlier centuries, being confined to mace, cloves, nutmeg, and ginger.[39] There was a great emphasis on meat, which was tougher and more sinuous than it is today.[40] Potatoes had not yet been introduced. Vegetables were rarely eaten as accompaniments to meat and became mentioned only towards the end of the seventeenth century[41]—they consisted mainly of carrots, turnips, and cabbage. Fruit was more widely available in markets, though exotic fruits were usually gifts from aristocratic households with hothouses.

A meal had by Pepys at The Bell in King Street, Westminster, for example, consisted of a leg of veal, bacon, two capons, sausages, and fritters, and at The Dog in King Street, near the Thames, he ate ham with lobster, oysters, anchovies, and olives.[42] If he wanted a fish meal, he usually travelled down the Thames to Greenwich, as fish, in the absence of refrigeration, travelled badly. When Pepys wanted to eat in a tavern, he usually made a reservation.[43]

It is more difficult to decide where the other great diarist of the seventeenth century, John Evelyn (1620–1706), stood in the controversy around food and nationalism/patriotism. Evelyn had a more intellectual and aesthetically informed approach that treated food as a cultural good. He was in some ways well in advance of his time, but in others shared its preoccupations around plain and ample meat. His outlook on food was strongly informed by considerations of health, rather than the simple and often greedy delight communicated by Pepys. On the one side, he worked tirelessly for king and country,[44] on the other, he had spent much time in France and admired a lot about its culture, including its cuisine. The French people, he noted 'ate like Princes, and far exceeded our tables'.[45] He also collected a lot of recipes on his travels abroad. His critical comments on a dinner given by the Portuguese ambassador to England, however, betray more of a liking for ample meat and a disdain for sauce: 'The dishes were not at all fit for an English stomac [sic], which is for solid meate [sic].'[46]

Food in taverns and inns of this period was comparatively varied in the basic ingredients used and offered many varieties of meat, fowl, game, and fish which have since disappeared from most menus. Stanley, commenting on a special occasion,[47] describes a 'plentiful table' as bearing 'capon, brawn, venison, neats' [calves] tongue, goose, hare, kid, snipe, larks, sturgeon, carp, pike, elvers [young eels], lampreys, crayfish, rook pie and pigeon pie, as well as various sweetmeats'. This great diversity is also emphasized by Burke, who, moreover, contrasts it favourably with the food served by hostelries in the first half of the twentieth century:

> The kitchens of inns and dining rooms have held the odours of all sorts of pies – e.g. pigeon pies and humble pies, and eel pies, many kinds of fish, such as carp pike, eel and sprats; all manner of wild birds; ox cheek, boar's head, neats' tongues, and suckling pig; tansy cakes, hasty pudding; frumenty, syllabub and cheese cakes; and now hold the eternal soup, chops, steaks and cutlets, plaice, joint, fruit and cheese.[48]

Meals consisted of ample portions of meat, cooked in a fairly homogenous manner—either boiled or roasted in very large pieces on what were called smoke jacks. It was void of refinements in terms of stock-based sauces with a vegetable foundation (onions, mushrooms, etc.). Instead, gravy and pungent, often vinegar-intensive, accompanying condiments, such as mustard, horseradish, or mint sauce, were well liked.[49] Meat and venison pies also were popular. Puddings tended to be heavy or, in more negative terms, stodgy, but existed in an astonishing variety. If you merely wanted a snack with your drink, there were dishes of anchovies or neats' tongues. Misson, a self-declared Anglophile who travelled and lived in England for several years early in the eighteenth century, showed himself very impressed by the quantity of meat sold by cook shops.[50] Meat was mainly the staple diet of the middling and upper classes. However, the widespread existence of cook shops in London, providing snack meals of various cuts of meat, indicates that these were affordable also for the lower stratum of the middling classes, such as skilled workmen of various kinds.

The nature of English food and its comparative plainness even in this period was often remarked upon by visitors to England from France. Thus, Henri Misson comments in his memoirs on the food of the 'middling sort' of English people as follows:

> Generally speaking, the English Tables are not delicately served... Among the middling Sort of people they have ten or twelve common sorts of Meats, which infallibly take their Turns at their Tables, and two dishes are their Dinners: a Pudding, for instance, and a piece of roast beef; another time they will have a piece of boiled beef, and then they salt it some days beforehand, and besiege it with five or six heaps of cabbage, Carrots, Turnips or some other Herbs or Roots, well pepper'd and salted and swimming in butter: a Leg of Mutton, dished up with same dainties....[51]

The quantity of meat consumed by the English, for Misson, therefore did not translate into quality. He draws an unfavourable comparison with the French: 'The English dress their meat much plainer than we do. We eat abundantly more delicately than they do.'[52] Whereas French food, during the seventeenth century, became increasingly refined, the English cuisine remained comparatively 'backward',[53] or, in some eyes, 'honest'.

Misson was, however, very appreciative of English savoury and sweet puddings—'Ah, what an excellent thing is an English pudding!'[54]—of which a much greater variety existed than is presently the case. Plum pudding appeared more often than any other, and in any season. According to Misson, fruit, unlike in France, 'is only brought to the Tables of the Great, and of a small number even among them'.[55]

During the seventeenth century, meat—particularly beef—consumption is said to have greatly increased.[56] Both foreign visitors, e.g. Misson, and domestic commentators, e.g. Fynes Moryson, a Lincolnshire gentleman and Cambridge graduate who travelled in Europe at the end of the sixteenth century, have pronounced the English to be much better supplied with meat than their European neighbours, and particularly the French.[57] This is most likely due to the leap in agricultural methods in this century. Those members of the aristocracy, gentry, and the middling class who agitated against French cuisine and extolled plain English food, particularly English lamb and, more so, beef, had the additional benefit of counting as loyal patriots. During times of war, they were able to pose as sturdy and courageous defenders of their country, due to their ample consumption of beef.

The aristocratic defenders of English cooking were usually Tories. One such aristocrat was the Earl of Rochester—a wit at the Restoration Court of Charles II—who, at London's Bull Inn, praises English roast beef dinner in verse:

> Our own plain fare, and the best terse the Bull
> Affords, I'll give you and your bellies full.
> As for French kickshaws, sillery and champaigne,
> Ragouts and fricassees, in throth, w'have none.
> Here's a good dinner towards, thought I, when straight,
> Up comes a piece of beef, full horseman's weight.[58]

(The term kickshaws (*quelque choses*) for light French dishes had been introduced by the playwright Thomas Dekker at the beginning of the seventeenth century and by the middle of that century had become a term to deride French cuisine.)

Most members of the upper classes prided themselves on their plain, unaffected taste and their liking for country fare. They extolled their virtues by contrasting themselves to the French who, they claimed, were more prone to use cooking to signal and entrench class distinctions.[59] This, however, exaggerates the simplicity of upper class food and, more so, its similarity to that of lower classes. The food of the better sorts, particularly in the country, was more varied—game and fruit, for example, played a big role—and, above all, more plentiful in the amount of meat consumed.

Meat was also enjoyed by the urban lower bourgeoisie, such as artisans, skilled craftsmen, and traders, and, more so, by wealthy squires and yeomen farmers in the countryside. Members of the lower classes in both town and country, although generally on a poor diet, could join in the prodigious consumption of beef on special feast days, and, in the country, also at the end of the harvest, at the expense of their employers or their political overlords. Soldiers and sailors, too, were entitled to generous rations of meat.

The middling and upper classes were able to enjoy a comparatively wide variety of food stuff—both at home and in taverns. The lower orders frequenting ale houses were not so lucky. Alehouses sold very little food and where they did, it was either to stave off hunger or to serve it merely as a basis for alcoholic consumption. Not surprisingly, it was as or even more monotonous than patrons' domestic consumption. The staple fare was buns and cakes, which might stretch to apple pie and cheese cake or herring and salt fish, but it mainly consisted of bread and cheese,[60] our current ploughman's lunch. Generally, when a man wanted a more substantial meal he brought his own food.[61] However, a few pubs combined the functions of an alehouse and a cook-shop,[62] and in this way were the fairly basic forerunners of our twentieth and twenty-first century pub restaurants.

Moving from food to drink, drinking in excess was common among Englishmen of all classes in the seventeenth century: 'There seems to be little doubt that drinking, often to excess, was the main entertainment of contemporary [late seventeenth to early eighteenth centuries] Londoners.'[63] Among the beverages that accompanied meals, beer or ale was by far most commonly drunk everywhere. In the towns, home-brewed beer had largely disappeared, and innkeepers had become their own brewers. Farmers, in contrast, continued home-brewing. This led to a bewilderingly large number of different beers being drunk.

In taverns, however, wine was the predominant drink. In the first half of the seventeenth century, canary and claret were the most popular wines. However, the Navigation Act of 1651, reducing the admission to English ports of foreign goods, substantially increased the price of French wine. Even after the end of the wars with Holland (whose merchants handled much of the shipping), the Wine Act of 1688, levying new taxes, kept the price of French wine unaffordable for all but the rich. Stronger and sweeter wines from Portugal, Madeira, and Spain took their place.[64] Tavernkeepers, however, continued to stock some French wines even during times of prohibition. The English taste for claret, according to Earle,[65] was not easily eradicated.

When we move to the eighteenth century, a glance at England's varying economic fortunes in the first and the second half of that century must provide the context for an examination of the food consumed. The English supremacy on the seas and their dominance of foreign trade meant that, for the first half of the eighteenth century, 'fortune smiled on most of the people of England'.[66] A series of good harvests and the relatively low price of grain meant that the cost of living in relation to wages was favourable to a steady rise in the standard of living during this period. In the towns, too, where the new industries had increased employment and wages, the conditions of living had improved.[67] During the second half of the century, however, times became harder again, and there was much grumbling among the poorer working people in the towns who had become used to plenty of butter, cheese, and the good butcher's meat they had been able to eat during earlier decades.[68]

Further improvement of transport meant that all kinds of regional food stuffs were easily transported around the country to satisfy the continuously growing demand, particularly of Londoners. The expansion of the empire and of overseas trade during the eighteenth century was accompanied by an even more intense commercialization of the supply of goods and leisure, to the extent that historians date the beginning of the consumer society in this century, including the prevalence of conspicuous consumption.[69] Although the latter have much to say about the commercialization of leisure, dining out in taverns and inns surprisingly receives no coverage.

Food and Nationalism in the Eighteenth Century

The link between embracing English food and cooking and cultural nationalism, elaborated above for the seventeenth century, became even more pronounced during the eighteenth century.[70] The wars with France continued, and invasion by the French became perceived as an acute danger during the period of 1798–1815.[71] French cultural conquest became portrayed 'as part of a larger and more sinister scheme to paralyze native resistance and virtue'.[72] D'Archenholz observes that 'the English in general have the greatest hatred that can be imagined to the whole French nation'.[73] 'Beef and Liberty' became a rallying cry for Britons worried about the military threat from France abroad, and about the spread of Gallic luxury and alleged corruption at home.[74] The following extract, from a patriotic drinking song from the *Literary Magazine* of c. 1757,[75] expresses this link between traditional English food and nationalism:

> Should the French dare to invade us, thus armed with our poles,
> We'll bang their bare ribs, make their lanthorn [sic] jaws ring:
> For you beef-eating Britons are valiant souls
> Who will shed their last drop for their country and King.

Following the wars, many higher-class Englishmen formed themselves into beef-eating or beefsteak clubs to proclaim that beef and liberty were synonymous. The first of these, the Sublime Society of Beefsteaks, was founded in London in 1736 and revolved around a Covent Garden theatre. It had many prominent members, who were part of what one would call today the intelligentsia (artists, actors, poets, and journalists) rather than the aristocracy.

Until the French Revolution, the English upper classes were in thrall to all things French—valets, dancing masters, and cooks.[76] The opposition to French food, in many quarters, gave expression to a disapproval of the Whig grandees around Robert Walpole, who, between 1721 and 1742, completely dominated the government and the country. They had amassed great wealth and were seen by the middling ranks to live in immoral luxury. According to Newman, 'there was a sense that the dominant culture was far too much under the spell of France, and simultaneously, too much the bastion of an overbearing and selfish oligarchy, a Fashionable World excessively contaminated by corrupting spiritual influences originating...in France'.[77] Besides Walpole himself, the Dukes of Richmond and Bedford and Lord Albemarle all employed French chefs. The dominance of French *haute cuisine* in the highest circles was confirmed by the fact that Vincent La Chapelle's cook book appeared in England in 1733, two years before it was published in France.[78] Most aristocrats kept both a French and an English cook, and the former had to be paid double the amount of the latter.[79]

Conspicuous consumption at the higher levels of society evoked disapproval and resentment at the middle levels, which often became expressed as cultural nationalism, that is, opposition to French cultural influence, among others of the culinary kind. The resentment of this cultivation by the Whig-affiliated upper ranks of 'all things French' and particularly of French food was expressed by a variety of social groups. It came from patriotically minded English small merchants and traders. It was additionally articulated from the 1740s, by 'a broad and expanding generational cohort of sensitive and "socially conscious intellectuals"',[80] including literary men, such as Fielding, Shenstone, Goldsmith, and Smollet, as well as artists and journalists, such as William Hogarth, Samuel Johnson, and David Garrick, who articulated their disdain in their writing and art. Newman therefore views the mid-1740s to the mid-1780s as 'the crucial years for the launching of English nationalism'.[81]

These intellectuals, who were often Tory sympathizers, attacked the consumption of lavish French food, as they saw it, of their political opponents, the Whigs, whom they liked to portray as Frenchified aristocratic fops. In Hogarth's *A Rake's Progress*, for instance, they were portrayed as snobbish and mincing little men who could only come to a sticky end. Samuel Johnson, also a Tory, after having been shown a French menu, is supposed to have asserted his love of traditional plain English food thus: 'I prithee bid your knaves bring me a dish of hog's pudding, a slice or two from the upper cut of a well-roasted sirloin, and two apple dumplings.'[82] Influential journalists, like Richard Steele and Joseph Addison, also railed against 'over-refined' French food, and contributed greatly to putting 'food chauvinism' on the map. Steele, in the *Tatler*, 'pleaded for a return to the diet of our forefathers, the beef and mutton on which we had won the battles of Crécy and Agincourt'.[83] Some of these patriotic Englishmen pronounced French food not only as extremely expensive and extravagant, but also as unhealthy. They claimed that such made-up dishes held 'the Seeds of Diseases both cronick [sic] and acute'.[84] Paradoxically, patriotic critics of French cuisine often suggested that, in contrast to the English, the French subsisted on *soupe maigre*.

One of the most effective of the literary critics was the writer Henry Fielding, who, in one of his plays, *The Grub-Street Opera* (first performed in 1731), created a song, the refrain of which may be said to have become Britain's culinary anthem, namely:

> Oh the roast beef of England
> And Old England's roast beef.

The song became a popular hit and later provided the title for a 1748 print by William Hogarth, *Oh the Roast Beef of Old England*, also referred to as *The Gate of Calais*, which became a best-selling print. It features both a sturdy Englishman carrying a big round of beef and a skinny Frenchman with a pot of *soupe maigre*. No wonder the French subsequently came to refer to all Englishmen as 'roast beefs'.

An even stronger predilection for dining out than in the previous century was part of a new pattern of spending. Much of this activity was centred on London, which, by 1750, was the biggest and among the most splendid cities in the world. However, to many rural gentlemen and provincial 'traders', London, and particularly its West End, was also 'a place where courtiers and placemen, pimps and fops, pastry cooks and hairdressers united to drain the country of its wealth'.[85] London became portrayed as 'a cultural colony of Paris'.[86] This resentment was shared also by smaller merchants and tradesmen from the eastern parts of London. There arose then what we now regard as a rather contemporary sentiment, namely one that wanted to give priority to native produce. This nativism was closely linked to cultural, and sometimes even political, nationalism.

The hostility towards the French was not only expressed by men of the 'better sort'. The prejudices held against the French and their way of life, expressed widely on the stage,[87] seems to have been eagerly lapped up by the lower orders on London's streets.[88] Newman goes as far as detecting a 'tradition of xenophobic and anti-French feeling, particularly at the bottom of society'.[89] Grosley, an Anglophile visitor to England in 1765, recounts many instances of verbal abuse, such as 'French dog', as well as physical assault, met by him and some of his compatriots in the street. Muralt, a Swiss visitor at the beginning of the eighteenth century, also suffered being called 'A French dog'.[90]

Dining in the Eighteenth Century

Detailed information on domestic meals is conveyed by the diaries of the Reverend James Woodforde (1740–1803), resident in the village of Weston, near Norwich in Norfolk.[91] The meals Woodforde ate at home were mainly plain English, with only a very occasional mention of a fricassée. Thus, for a dinner (eaten at midday) on 15 May 1779, he gave his guests 'a dish of Maccerel [sic], 3 young Chicken boiled and some Bacon, a neck of Pork roasted and a Gooseberry Pye hot'.[92] On another occasion, in 1782, he served his dinner guests 'a Leg of Mutton boiled and Capers, a Calfs [sic] Head boiled and a Piggs [sic] Face, a fat Turkey rosted [sic], a Currant Pudding and Mince Pies'.[93] In 1798, a dinner consisted of 'a fine large eel stewed & a small turkey rosted', and in 1799, they dined on a 'boiled rabbit and onion sauce and a very fine Goose rosted'.[94] The parson also ate a good lot of beef, and his last diary entry before his death, on 17 October 1802, closed with 'dinner today, Roast Beef'.

The Reverend Woodforde entertained very frequently, and the range of foods served is quite large. Although boiled mutton with capers crops up in a large number of the dinner menus, many other meats and fowl, as well as fish, are served. He grew his own vegetables and fruit, kept bees and brewed beer, and had a small farm attached to his living where cows and pigs were kept. Nevertheless, vegetables do not feature very frequently in the menus he records. He often went fishing and hare coursing, hence river fish and hares were served. Woodforde received many presents of game birds from his squire and other gentry neighbours.[95] He and his companions and guests also ate a lot of puddings, with plum pudding being frequently on the menu. His diet tended towards the stodgy, and he was not unusual in this. 'Overeating, obesity and gout were afflictions of the age.'[96]

Woodforde frequently dined at his squire's house, where the dinner was more elaborate and with some French influence. His squire served vegetables such as asparagus and artichokes. They enjoyed a variety of game, which was shot locally, as well as a greater range of sweet water fish than is common today, such as pike and tench. Vegetables are more rarely mentioned, but a good variety of fresh fruit is eaten, though usually for dessert, rather than as a pudding where 'tarts, fruit pyes [sic], jelly, custard and plumb [sic] pudding' are served. Some of the more exotic fruit, like oranges and grapes, were probably grown in the squire's own hothouse—a common occurrence among the gentry of this time. Expensive parmesan cheese was also offered at the end of the meal.[97] The general impression is that, in this rural Norfolk area, the middling and upper classes lived extremely well, in terms of both quantity and variety of food eaten. However, there is never any extended comment on the taste of a particular dish.

That the household of Woodforde's squire was not exceptional is borne out by a lengthy description of the meals enjoyed at Brambleton Hall, provided by Drummond and Wilbraham.[98] This account confirms country gentlemen's self-sufficiency in food and, therefore, its much greater freshness and superior quality. It is this country-house cooking which is usually remembered when sociologists of dining and food, e.g. Stephen Mennell,[99] make a case for a great farmhouse tradition of good English cooking. It certainly was characterized by freshness and a variety of ingredients, but its mode of preparation even then appears to be basic. French cooking does not appear, except in the name of a very few dishes, such as fricassée.

Diary accounts from this period do not portray a dire situation, as far as villagers' diet in the lower classes were concerned. The Reverend Woodforde invited his tenants once a year for a veritable feast, with both ample beef and other meat and plenty of alcoholic drink. A French aristocratic visitor in the late eighteenth century, Francois Rochefoucauld, who visited many farms all around Suffolk, notes that meat consumption existed right down the social scale. He reports on harvest labourers receiving meat three times a day, and even the inhabitants of poor houses 'are well-nourished and eat meat three times a week'.[100]

More indirect information on the quality of the food consumed either domestically or in taverns and inns comes from the valuable study of food hygiene and adulteration conducted by Drummond and Wilbraham.[101]

During the first half of the eighteenth century, with the coincidence of rapid urbanization, growing commercialization of the food trade, enduring poor communication routes between the countryside and the towns and between the coast and inland towns, food quality often was gravely impaired. Cattle were still being driven by road to London over great distances, negatively affecting the texture and flavour of meat. Astonishingly, chickens were already fattened in coops, in conditions not so different from today's battery-rearing. The condition of fish and milk, too, remained severely impaired by unrefrigerated road transport. Additionally, the increasing homogenization of food began to impair its quality. The adulteration of food, already noted for the seventeenth century, continued apace, affecting almost every foodstuff.[102]

More vegetables and fruit came to the markets of towns from the countryside, even if frequently in very unsanitary conditions. London markets now could also rely on the increased import of foreign exotic fruit. Grosley, a visiting Frenchman, was not impressed with the quality and variety of English vegetables: 'All that grow in the country about London, cabbage, radishes and spinnage [sic], being impregnated with the smoke of sea-coal...have a very disagreeable taste...I ate nothing good of this sort, but some asparagus.'[103] Butter had become more plentiful and was consumed in far greater quantity, while a much wider range of cheese became available, from various English regions, including some from the villages of 'Chedder [sic]' and Stilton.[104]

Most of the writing on dining out in the eighteenth century refers to taverns. Overall, in comparison with the seventeenth century, continuity in ingredients and mode of preparation is quite striking, except for one significant change. The use of vegetables and fruits became more common than in the seventeenth century. The fixed-price Ordinary continues to be available. Well-to-do Londoners are still able to get a break from the 'plain English fare' served by going to a tavern offering French or Italian meals.[105] Both Earle and Shelley comment on the comparatively high and even outrageous prices of a French Ordinary.[106] Earle remarks that 'London was full of fops with small fortunes and the French Ordinaries prospered'.[107] The French Ordinary most frequently mentioned is Pontack's in Abchurch Lane. A meal there could cost between one and two guineas per head during the early years of the century, compared with only a few shillings in English establishments. Customers were said to be noblemen, merchants, and 'other affluent folk'.[108] At Pontack's you could have stewed snails, baby chicks, and 'all the best French dishes of the time'.[109] Patronage of these French Ordinaries was particularly pronounced among members of the aristocracy, and their dining habits again became likened to a cosmopolitanism that undermined English strength in the fight with France. The 'devils in the west end' of London were said to be assisting 'the devils in France'.[110]

Roast beef nevertheless continued to be much loved, being a favourite dish 'as well at the King's table as at a Trademan's'.[111] Georges Rochefoucauld notes: 'Sauces are never used in English kitchens... All the dishes are based on various joints of meat, either boiled or roast, the roast weighing as much as twenty to thirty pounds.'[112] Muralt, a Swiss visitor, is also astonished by the enormous size of the joints roasted. He recognizes beef as a symbol of national identity when he comments that beef is regarded as 'the Emblem of the Prosperity and Plenty of the English'.[113] D'Archenholz, a German visitor, comments on the simplicity of English ways of preparing meat positively: 'The English are for what is simple and natural.'[114] In contrast, Grosley, a French visitor, was not impressed by English meat and judged it much inferior to French meat: '... after having used it [meat] in all the different shapes in which it is served up to tables, that is to say both roast and boiled, I could find in it neither the consistence, the juice, nor the exquisiteness, of that of France.'[115] An English commentator, Count Romford, the inventor of the cooking stove in the late eighteenth century, opines that, because the English had focused all their energy on roasting meat, their cooks had neglected the art of making nourishing soups and broths.[116] D'Archenholz confirms that 'soup never appears on any table in England'.[117]

Much information about dishes prepared in high-end taverns at the end of this century can be gleaned from the cookery book first published in 1783 by the chef of the celebrated London Tavern, John Farley. Apart from the wealth of recipes supplied, we get some comments on the food's provenance and on the eating habits implied, from both Farley himself and his contemporary editor, Medcalf.[118] Farley pronounces his recipes to be for the use of 'all ranks' when he asserts that his dishes may 'decorate the Table of either the Peer or the Mechanic'. In reality, however, they are too elaborate and labour-intensive for working people, who, moreover, would not usually have the stove required for their preparation. Farley's experience comes from cooking in a very high-end tavern, where he is used to preparing feasts for groups of aristocratic and upper middle-class customers. The London Tavern regularly prepared meals, for example, for the directors of the East India Company[119] and for many other high-level societies and associations.

Medcalf points out that comments on the Tavern's grand dinners are mainly on the magnificent surroundings and the illustrious guests and very rarely contain appreciations of the cook, the quality of the food, or judgements of its taste. Wine, however, attracts appreciative comment, as does the large tank of live turtles in the tavern cellar. He cites the journalists of an article on the tavern as it being more concerned with 'class and cost' than with cookery. They say that the Tavern is 'not a place in which a man will have his dinner but one at which he will dine'. Medcalf concludes:

> I am inclined to guess that although the Tavern retained magnificence and geniality...the quest for splendour had rather driven the soul out of its cookery long before its owners sacrificed it, in 1876, in favour of their other tavern, the Albion in Aldersgate Street.[120]

Medcalf places Farley in 'the great tradition of English cookery which was well established by the early part of the eighteenth century; a tradition that...was much admired by visitors from the Continent'. Farley's recipes show influence both of regional English and of French sophisticated cooking, and a great many of them were plagiarized from Hannah Glasse's famous cookery book, first published in 1747.[121] While the quality and quantity of English meat, and particularly of beef, served was certainly commented upon in a favourable manner by foreign travellers, I have not encountered much praise for any 'great English tradition of cookery'.

Nevertheless, there is a tradition, rooted in the country cooking of the manor house and the parsonage, that Medcalf characterizes very well. He contrasts it with other cuisines and identifies both its positive and negative distinguishing features. As such a precise characterization is very rare in the literature, it deserves a full reproduction. Eighteenth century high-level cuisine as practised by Farley, Medcalf suggests, may be described as follows:

> There is nothing in Farley of the modern urge to preserve the native flavours of the raw foods. His notion of cooking involves a fairly elaborate art of mixture of ingredients, rather than an impregnation with sauces. His notion of a sauce remains an added ingredient, an extra vegetable, rather than something pervasively altering the whole nature of the dish...John Farley's then is a cookery neither contrastive, like the medieval, nor rich like the Elizabethans, not seeking essences, like the moderns, nor using impregnations like the French but rather combination. It is very much English.[122]

Farley's introductions of his recipes are not expansive on the aesthetics of food presentation, nor does he express much concern with taste. The recipes concentrate particularly on meat and on pies and pastry. The section on fresh vegetables amounts to only six pages, including a single dish for potatoes, whereas that on meat (including also a few on fish) takes up nearly 100 pages. Dishes tend to be on the rich side (much butter and cream). They are also stodgy—with savoury and sweet pies and puddings receiving much emphasis. Few desserts contain mainly fruit. Farley employed a large variety of ingredients. Many of these fell into oblivion in industrialized Britain until the fairly recent revival of interest in *haute cuisine*, such as artichokes, anchovies, olive oil, etc., and the use of a wide range of spices. Farley also introduces far more soups than had been common in eighteenth century household and tavern cooking.

The book contains a 'Bill of Fare' for each month, divided into 'First and Second Course', reflecting a different conception from our contemporary notion of courses. These Bills of Fare show some attention to seasonality, as well as some French influence on mode of preparation and choice of terms, but, on the whole, they mainly show an English influence. Thus, for June he suggests the following:

First Courses:
Fish; soup; ducks a la mode; fricasseed chicken; pigeons compote; Florentine Rabbits.

Second courses:
Larded turkey; Rocky Island [maybe a fish dish containing some lobster]; roasted duck; mushrooms; Transparent Pudding [baked pudding containing eggs, butter and sugar, plus a little nutmeg]; Cherry Tart; Macaroni; Stew'd Chardoon [cardoons are a variety of artichokes]; Moonshine [a recipe for a dessert plagiarized from Hannah Glasse, containing blancmange and jelly]; Omilot' [perhaps omelette].

In addition to the food to be enjoyed at taverns, we also learn about the quality of service. 'One is also astonished at the politeness and promptness with which he [sic] is attended at taverns....' While this at first comes as a surprise to D'Archenholz from a people who value their independence and who are relatively well-off, it is soon explained. Waiters expect a gratification which 'in principal houses amounts to a great sum'.[123]

For meals consumed at inns, we can draw on a little information from The Reverend Woodforde's diary for the late eighteenth century. He usually stayed at the King's Head, Norwich. During most of his stays at the inn he does not comment on the meals consumed, even though he never fails to do so for meals eaten at home or at friends' houses in Norfolk. On 17 February 1780, for example, after a visit to the theatre, he supped at the inn with some friends on 'a couple of rost [sic] Fowls, a barrel of Colchester Oysters, some cold Meats and Tarts', and on 15 March 1781, he and his friend dined 'on some fresh Salmon'.[124]

Woodforde arrived at his favourite inn by horse, accompanied by his servant, and his experience is very different from that of the German parson, Moritz, who arrived on foot. Moritz usually received only very basic meals. His lunches were mostly cold—a piece of cold meat, or eggs and salad, or, once, just bread and butter—and for evening meals, too, he was rarely served something warm. A high point on his journey occurred when he was offered hot 'cheese on toast'.[125] Another description of meals offered by inns comes from John Byng's diary, a minor aristocrat who travelled much in the provinces. Byng comments both on the wide range of dishes available at dinner and supper and on their lack of variability between inns: 'The food was standard fare, with recipes that were fairly identical in whichever part of the country I happened to be.'[126] The quality of food, however, varied enormously between inns and ranged from a delicious pigeon pie to a sub-standard damson tart. His summary comment is 'Inn cookery, in general, is wretched work'.[127] The French visitor Georges Rochefoucauld also bemoans the quality of food in inns. About an inn in Burnham Market, Norfolk, he writes: 'I arrived dying of hunger and scarcely managed to appease my appetite.'[128]

An entirely different take on foods prepared by an inn comes from the 1759 cook book, *A Complete System of Cookery*, by William Verral. Verral was the master of the White Hart Inn in Lewes, Sussex. He had learnt his craft under Monsieur de St Clouet, then cook at the Duke of Newcastle's residence—one of the eighteenth-century Whig grandees. His cook book provides almost entirely French recipes. Verral not only cooked at his coaching inn, but also hired himself out to gentry households that required a 'special occasion' meal. He would sometimes take all of his own equipment to cater for them. While it is unlikely that his cook book contained only recipes he had prepared at his inn, the book nevertheless must give a broad impression of what dinners could be enjoyed by high-ranking travellers or what dishes would be prepared for special occasion dinners for local elites' annual dinners, such as those for local MPs or justices. Recipes are for soups, fish, meat, game and chicken, desserts and savouries, with lots of made-up dishes, i.e. ragouts and fricassées.

The editor of Verral's cook book, R.L. Mégroz,[129] claims that 'so much of his cookery resembles what we have come to think of as good old English fare', but such English influences were scarcely visible to me. The English elements discerned may be the few pies, such as 'Pigeon pye', or the 'Piece of beef of a scarlet colour, with a Cabbage or Savoy sauce', but, despite their names, they bear little relation to English modes of preparation. Meat is usually stewed or braised and served with a sauce rather than a gravy, and even pies have lots of flavouring ingredients—shallots, parsley, and lemon or wine—not usually found in English cooking. Verral points to the use of roots and other vegetables for flavouring stock and emphasizes that no amount of meat can make up for these flavouring vegetables. He instructs how to make a coulis, or 'cullis'—the base for many sauces.

Verral was certainly not typical of his time. Nevertheless, his book shows that, if part of the social elite, one could eat extremely well in eighteenth-century England. It additionally suggests that dishes were not that dissimilar from those currently enjoyed in the more traditional French restaurants in England, such as those of Michel or Alain Roux. A remarkable feature of this edition of Verral's book is that it had been annotated by the eighteenth-century poet and Cambridge academic, Thomas Gray. Gray not only prepared some of the recipes himself, but also sent advice on them to his friends, many of whom were reverends, including even the Master of a Cambridge College.[130] Gray's annotations show that then, as now, French *haute cuisine* is not only liked by the moneyed elite, but also by men of the middling classes with more cultural than money capital. Gray was the only surviving son of a London scrivener and a milliner, although his mother's relatives had enabled him to go to Eton. To conclude, comments on food served in inns thus vary, but the meals served at most were not greeted with enthusiasm.

When we turn to the food available in eighteenth century public houses, a very different picture emerges. 'Serving food was never regarded as one of the principal duties of the alehouse keeper, as it was for the innkeeper.'[131] Most of the premises were not set up for providing food. Bread, buns, and cheese continued to be the staple fare. A typical meal was toasted bread and cheese steeped in ale. Pies were another favourite. Customers who wanted to eat something more elaborate took their own meat to be dressed and cooked or came to an agreement with the landlord.

The reasons why public houses did not develop a food trade were similar to those already rehearsed for the seventeenth century. They were connected with both supply and demand factors. There was an absence of adequate cooking facilities in pubs and of an aptitude by landlords for cooking. But there was also a lack of demand from customers who valued drink much more than food and only looked for something to still their hunger. When men were drinking in pubs, they cared little for what the food tasted like, brought to them by hawkers. Costermongers (itinerant providers of various basic foods such as cockles, whelks, or baked potatoes) found a lucrative trade in public house customers. One of them comments: 'Whelks is all the same, good, bad, or middling, when a man's drinking, if they are well seasoned with pepper and vinegar.'[132] This quote illustrates the often-mentioned propensity of the English to resort to strong condiments to spice up food that lacks any taste of its own, due to poor preparation. The eighteenth-century pub thus was far removed from the pub restaurant of today, and eating out by the higher ranks focused on the tavern.

However, there were exceptions. Larger establishments in urban areas specialized in serving proper meals to better-off customers, but most smaller landlords found it too much trouble. Rylance singles out two licensed London public houses—the Red Lion and the Dover Castle—as houses 'of a superior class' which serve with their ale 'Chops, kidneys, Welsh-rabbits and other titbits, in the way of a relish to the potent beverage'.[133]

Turning now to drinking outside the home, several foreign commentators remark on the large amount of drink consumed by all classes and the habitual nature of drunkenness encountered among all classes. Francois Rochefoucauld, writing about a country-house dinner he attended in 1784, comments: 'You can have no idea of the speed with which they emptied their bottles... After a few hours three quarters of the guests were very drunk... and everyone had had rather too much to drink.'[134] It was mainly porter—a slightly fortified kind of beer—they drank. In London, porter was enjoyed by all ranks.[135] Gin consumption, originating from the crowning of the Dutch William of Orange in 1689, assumed catastrophic proportions between the 1720s and 1740s. Its unregulated and cheap production in gin shops and back alleys, made gin the favourite drink of the lower orders. It evoked widespread fears about its effect on health, particularly maternal health, and on disorder and crime. Only after legislation in 1751 did the 'gin crisis' abate, and ale/beer again attain ascendancy. It remained the main drink of the ordinary Englishman. Sales of beer even rose after the introduction of the Beer House Act of 1830 and sustained a large number of sizeable breweries. Frequent complaints about the quality of ale at this time—about a reduction of malt, and other ways of tampering with its taste—show adulteration to be rife in this industry also.[136]

Wealthy upper-class people drank chiefly claret, burgundy, or Rhenish with their dinner, and port, Madeira, or another sweet wine with their dessert. As wine drinking was extremely expensive—due to high excise duty—drinking of port, though also quite expensive, became very popular. It was a lighter 'quaffing' wine than the port we know today. D'Archenholz notes that despite 'exceedingly dear Burgundy and champaign [sic], notwithstanding this, the consumption of these is very great in London'.[137] Then, as now, London had some exceedingly rich inhabitants who were able to indulge their expensive tastes. Spirit, such as brandy, was also widely consumed. In contrast, cider was drunk 'only in distant counties'.[138] Regarding non-alcoholic beverages, more tea was consumed in England than anywhere else in Europe, and the new availability of coffee led to the rise and brief flourishing of coffee houses. Drinking of both tea and coffee—products of the empire—became part of the routine of virtually every home, regardless of class.[139] In a rare negative comment, D'Archenholz notes that the coffee sold in English coffee houses was so weak and bad that not even the most simple German porter would have drunk it like this.[140]

In conclusion, in the seventeenth and eighteenth centuries, dining out in taverns and inns was already well established for the higher social orders. Meals enjoyed were predominantly traditionally English, with a strong prevalence of cooked and roast meat, pies, and stodgy puddings, while vegetables were either absent or indifferent accompaniments to the meat. The ingredients were very varied and did not yet display the homogenizing impact that came with industrialization.

Food consumed in and out of the home signalled both gender and class identity, as well as expressing national identification. Enjoying very large portions of beef was connected with masculinity and prowess in battle. Nothing is said in the literature about food specific to women.

There existed a strong identification of beef eating with English nationalism in both centuries, but particularly in the eighteenth century. That century also witnessed cultural and political conflict between social groups indulging in French food and groups expressing their patriotism through the love of English food. This conflict between cosmopolitan lovers of French dinners and patriotically minded consumers of English food constitutes, at the same time, an emerging class conflict. It was a conflict between, on the one side, typically members of the aristocracy, and, on the other, bourgeois intellectuals and artists, as well as yeomen farmers and urban merchants and larger craftsmen. Predilection for French food by a cosmopolitan social elite was seen to demonstrate a love of luxury and a squandering of resources, undermining national strength. The class-based nationalist conflict therefore had clear political overtones. It became manifested in many cultural creations of the time, ranging from novels to theatre plays and poster art. While patriotic sentiment thus was given expression mainly by the cultural professions, it appealed to other sections of the middling classes and even found resonance among the lower classes. The latter were found to express their xenophobic sentiments in direct confrontation with French visitors to London. These conflicts around culinary tastes and identities pose a challenge to those who assert the absence in English history of any nationalism, as well as to the historians who doubt the emergence of any class identity before the nineteenth century.

Endnotes

1. Fox, A. 2013, 'Drink and social distinction in early modern England', S. Hindle, A. Shepard and J. Walter eds, *Remaking English Society. Social relations and social change in Early Modern England*, 186. Woodbridge: Boydell.
2. Paston-Williams, S., 1993, *The Art of Dining. A history of cooking and eating*, 143. London: The National Trust.

3. Drummond, J. and Wilbraham, A. 1939, *The Englishman's Food. A history of five centuries of English diet*, 117, 134. London: Jonathan Cape.
4. Paston-Williams, 1993, 143; Bickham, T. 2008, 'Eating the Empire: intersections of food, cookery and imperialism in eighteenth-century Britain', *Past and Present*, 198, February: 85.
5. Bickham, 2008, 102, 99.
6. Spencer, C. 2002, *British Food. An extraordinary thousand years of history*, 157. London: Grub Street.
7. Fox, 2013, 184; see also Pennell, S. 2000, '"Great quantities of gooseberry pie and baked clod of beef": victualling and eating out in London', P. Griffiths and M.S.R. Jenner eds, *Londinopolis. Essays in the cultural and social history of early modern London*, 228. Manchester and New York: Manchester University Press.
8. Tomalin, C. 2002, *Samuel Pepys. The unequalled self.* New York: Alfred A. Knopf.
9. McKendrick, N. Brewer, J. and Plumb, J.H. 1982, *The Birth of the Consumer Society. The commercialization of eighteenth century England*, 285. Bloomington: Indiana University Press.
10. Paston-Williams, 1993, 143.
11. Fox, 2013.
12. Paston-Williams, 1993, 145.
13. Davenant 1698, cited by Drummond and Wilbraham, 1939, 123.
14. Drummond and Wilbraham, 1939.
15. Spencer, 2002, 154.
16. Withington, P. 2014, 'Food, drink and popular culture', A. Hadfield ed., *Popular Culture in Early Modern England*. Aldershot: Ashgate.
17. Spencer, 2002, 148.
18. Saunders, B. 1970, *John Evelyn and his Times*, 57. Oxford: Pergamon Press; Paston-Williams, 1993, 143.
19. Mennell, S. 1985, *All Manners of Food. Eating and taste in England and France from the Middle Ages to the present*. Oxford: Basil Blackwell.
20. Spencer, 2002, 166.
21. Drummond and Wilbraham, 1939, 124.
22. Driver, C. and Berriedale-Johnson, M. 1984, *Pepys at Table*, 7. London: Bell & Hyman.
23. Earle, P. 1989, *The Making of the English Middle Class. Business, society and family life in London, 1660–1730*, 52. London: Methuen.
24. Burke, T. 1947 [1930], *The English Inn*, 140. London: Herbert Jenkins Ltd.
25. Pepys, S. 2011, *The Joys of Excess*. London: Penguin Books.
26. Tomalin, 2002.
27. See Veblen, T. 1899, *Theory of the Leisure Class*, on the consumption of the nouveau riche in the USA of the late nineteenth century, at https://www.gutenberg.org/files/833/833-h/833-h.htm.
28. Paston-Williams, 1993, 149.
29. Driver and Berriedale-Johnson, 1984, 24.
30. Driver and Berriedale-Johnson, 1984, 24.

31. Berry, G. 1978, *Taverns and Tokens of Pepys' London*, 10. London: Seaby Publications.
32. Spencer, 2002, 148.
33. Pepys, 2011, 70.
34. Shelley, H. 1909, *Inns and Taverns of Old England*, 125. London: Sir Isaac Pitman.
35. Cited by Shelley, 1909, 113.
36. Shelley, 1909, 126.
37. Tombs, R. 2015, *The English and their History*, 296. London: Penguin Books.
38. Tombs, 2015, 298.
39. Spencer, 2002, 139.
40. Driver and Berriedale-Johnson, 1984, 23; Rogers, B. 2003, *Beef and Liberty*, 23. London: Chatto and Windus.
41. Drummond and Wilbraham, 1939, 133.
42. Berry, 1978, 25.
43. Berry, 1978, 25.
44. Bowle, J. 1981, *John Evelyn and his World*. London: Routledge, Keegan, Paul; Saunders, 1970.
45. Saunders, 1970, 37.
46. Spencer, 2002, 155.
47. Stanley, L.T. 1957, *The Old Inns of London*, 10. London: Batsford.
48. Burke, 1947 [1930], 12.
49. Rogers, 2003, 24.
50. Misson, M. 1719, *Memoirs and Observations in his Travels over England*, 145. London.
51. Misson, 1719, 314.
52. Misson, 1719, 316.
53. Rogers, 2003, 31.
54. Misson, 1719, 315.
55. Misson, 1719, 315.
56. Rogers, 2003, 7.
57. Misson, 1719, 313.
58. Goody, J. 1982, *Cooking, Cuisine and Class. A study in comparative sociology*, 134. Cambridge: Cambridge University Press.
59. Rogers, 2003, 34.
60. Earle, 1989, 55.
61. Clark, P. 1983, *The English Alehouse. A social history 1200–1830*, 132–3. London and New York: Longman.
62. Earle, 1989, 55.
63. Earle, 1989, 56.
64. Drummond and Wilbraham, 1939, 136–7; Earle, 1989, 53.
65. Earle, 1989, 53.
66. Drummond and Wilbraham, 1939, 205.
67. Drummond and Wilbraham, 1939, 206.
68. Drummond and Wilbraham, 1939, 261.
69. McKendrick et al., 1982.

70. Newman, G. 1987, *The Rise of English Nationalism. A cultural history 1740–1830*. London: Weidenfeld and Nicholson; Rogers, 2003, 56.
71. Tombs, 2015, 397ff.
72. Newman, 1987, 72.
73. D'Archenholz M. 1790, *A Picture of England*, 203. Dublin: P. Byrne.
74. Newman, 1987, 47; Rogers, 2003, 2.
75. King, F.A. 1947, *Beer has a History*, V. London: Hutchinson's Scientific and Technical University.
76. Rogers, 2003, 51.
77. Newman, 1987, 50–1.
78. Rogers, 2003, 43.
79. Paston-Williams, 1993, 231.
80. Newman, 1987, 63.
81. Newman, 1987, 63.
82. Spencer, 2002, 71.
83. *The Tatler*, 21 March 1710, cited by Drummond and Wilbraham, 1939, 254.
84. Campbell, 1747, author of the *Tradesman*, cited by Rogers, 2003, 40.
85. Rogers, 2003, 52.
86. Newman, 1987, 38.
87. Scarfe, N. ed. 1995 [1785], *Innocent Espionage. The La Rochefoucauld brothers' tour of England in 1785*, 206. Woodbridge: Boydell.
88. Grosley, M. 1772, *A Tour to England or, Observations on England and its Inhabitants. Volume I*, 78, 106. Dublin: J. Exshaw et al.
89. Newman, 1987, 37.
90. Muralt, B.L. de 1726, *Letter Describing the Character and Customs of the English and French*, 2nd edition, 40. London: Thomas Edlin.
91. The diaries were edited by Beresford in five volumes.
92. Beresford, J. ed.1967, *The Diary of a Country Parson. Volume I*, 252. Oxford: Clarendon Press.
93. Beresford, J. ed. 1968, *The Diary of a Country Parson, Volume II*, 1. Oxford: Clarendon Press.
94. Beresford, J. ed. 1968, *The Diary of a Country Parson. Volume V*, 117. Oxford: Clarendon Press.
95. Beresford, 1968, *Volume V*.
96. Spencer, 2002, 242.
97. Beresford, 1967 and 1968, *Volume II*.
98. Drummond and Wilbraham, 1939, 250.
99. Mennell, 1985, 135.
100. Scarfe, 1995 [1785], 152, 175, 207.
101. Drummond and Wilbraham, 1939.
102. Drummond and Wilbraham, 1939, 228–34.
103. Grosley, 1772, 78.
104. Drummond and Wilbraham, 1939, 232.
105. Earle, 1989, 52; Drummond and Wilbraham, 1939, 253.
106. Earle, 1989; Shelley, 1909.

107. Earle, 1989, 53.
108. Clark, 1983, 13.
109. Burke, 1947 [1930], 142.
110. Newman, 1987, 76.
111. Muralt, 1726, 39.
112. Scarfe, 1995, 22.
113. Muralt, 1726, 39–40.
114. D'Archenholz, 1790, 201.
115. Grosley, 1772, 75.
116. Wilson, B. 2012, *Consider the Fork. A history of how we cook and eat*, 13. London: Particular.
117. D'Archenholz, 1790, 201.
118. Medcalf, S.1988 [1783], 'Introduction', J. Farley, *The London Art of Cookery*. London: Southover Press.
119. Medcalf, 1988 [1783], 4.
120. Medcalf, 1988 [1783], 10.
121. Medcalf, 1988 [1783], 10.
122. Medcalf, 1988 [1783], 11, 12.
123. D'Archenholz, 1790, 207.
124. Beresford, 1967.
125. Moritz, C.-P. 1965, *Journeys of a German in England in 1782*, 175, 176. London: Jonathan Cape.
126. Andrews, F. ed. 1954, *The Torrington Diaries 1954 [1792]. A Selection from the Tours of the Hon. John Byng (later fifth Viscount of Torrington) between the Years of 1781 and 1794*. London: Eyre and Spottiswood.
127. Andrews, 1954, 390.
128. Scarfe, N. ed. 1988, *A Frenchman's Year in Suffolk. French impressions of Suffolk life in 1784*, 179. Woodbridge: Suffolk Records Society with Boydell Press.
129. Mégroz, R.L. ed. 1948, 'Introduction', *The Cook's Paradise, being William Verral's Complete System of Cookery*, 9. London: Sylvan Press. First published in 1759.
130. Megroz, 1948, 8ff.
131. Clark, 1983, 312.
132. Clair, C. 1964, *Kitchen and Table*, 154. London, New York, Toronto: Abelard-Schuman.
133. Ing Freeman, J. ed. 2012, 'Introduction', *The Epicure's Almanack. Eating and drinking in Regency London*. London: The British Library. First published by Ralph Rylance under the title *Places of Alimentary Resort* in 1815.
134. Scarfe, 1988 [1784], 24.
135. Grosley, 1772, 182; D'Archenholz, 1790, 203.
136. Drummond and Wilbraham, 1939, 238.
137. D'Archenholz, 1790.
138. D'Archenholz, 1790, 202–3.
139. Bickham, 2008, 107.
140. D'Archenholz, 1790, 203.

4

Eating Out in the Nineteenth and Twentieth Centuries: Changes in Food and in Social Identities

This chapter covers two topics. First, it will examine the growing standardization and degradation of food, together with the greater differentiation of eating-out venues. The nineteenth century was a period of great transformation in the eating-out sphere, with old hostelries becoming displaced by new ones and distinctions between the various dining venues becoming more blurred. The second theme revolves around the changes in class and national identity of diners and how they are expressed in visiting a range of eating-out venues. While in the nineteenth and early twentieth centuries a hardening of class differences is accompanied by a weakening of nationalist sentiment, from World War I onwards, both class division and food nationalism become de-emphasized.

While there were many similarities in the food consumed in the seventeenth and eighteenth centuries, the nineteenth century brought a lot of change, reflecting the tremendous economic transformation, accompanied by uneven social development. Total industrial production grew about fourteenfold, exports rose sevenfold, imports even more, and the population more than trebled, but per capita production and real income quadrupled.[1] During the second half of the nineteenth century the amazing development of commercial and industrial enterprises incited large-scale migration into the towns. The social benefits flowing from this unprecedented growth differed at different times of the century, and they were not distributed evenly.

Industrialization had brought greater wealth to the middle classes during the early decades of the nineteenth century, but workers' wages (particularly in the countryside) touched the lowest level of the century,[2] while prices for food staples were rising. 'In little over a generation, the rural population passed from a beef, bread and ale standard to one of potato and tea.'[3] In 1803, one in nine of the population was in receipt of poor relief.[4] With the passing of the Corn Law in 1815, discontent even spread to the newly expanded middle class.[5] The 1840s were referred to as 'the hungry forties', and political troubles and military engagements during the forties and fifties also undermined general prosperity.[6]

Several authors comment on the huge discrepancy in the standard of living and in the food consumed between the wealthy and comfortable classes and the large stratum of urban poor. 'During the first half of the century the diet of the poor people in the towns was terribly bad. The greater part of their nourishment came from bread, potatoes and strong tea.'[7] But at the top of the social hierarchy, wealth expanded spectacularly, and expenditure on consumer goods, including food, increased dramatically.[8] Some cooks of the rich with a social conscience, such as Francatelli and Soyer, disseminated recipes for cheap soups for the growing number of the poor.[9]

The second half of the century, in contrast, is regarded as an era of economic expansion. The cessation of hostilities with France had given an impetus to economic development and population growth. Living standards rose markedly for most people, including manual workers. For the first time, they achieved some margin of income over necessary expenditure. The years of 1850 to 1873 in particular were regarded as the golden age of Victorian prosperity.[10] The Victorian age, in addition to economic and social transformation, was distinguished also by greatly accelerated technological change and by new cultural developments and preoccupations.

The expansion of the railway net in the 1830s and 40s led to a greater homogenization of food supply over the country. People were able to consume more, notably by eating more meat.[11] Gladstone, in the 1860s, considered Britain to be 'the centre of the moral, social and political power of the world'. Although the Great Depression of 1873 to 1896 brought a deterioration for capitalists, the working classes continued to thrive.[12]

During the period from 1896 to World War I, the economic position of the Edwardian middle and upper middle classes improved again, enabling them to live lavishly, while that of the working classes deteriorated. Up to World War I, there existed great disparities of wealth—now mainly derived from manufacturing and commerce—with 92 per cent of wealth owned by 10 per cent of the population.[13]

The aristocracy, although diminished in wealth and influence, remained the undisputed social leaders until 1914.[14] Social differentiation increased greatly, with marked differences *within* the burgeoning working class and the expanding middle class. In the latter, the great manufacturers and merchants were at the top, the professions in the middle, and the petty tradesmen and clerks in the bottom tier.[15] In the working class, an upper section, greatly preoccupied with respectability, became influential.

The industrial revolution and the rapid urbanization of the population caused some deterioration in both home cooking and in what was offered in the various eateries. Mennell comments that the great farmhouse tradition of the previous century had declined, and cuisine had become coarsened.[16] While, on the one hand, industrialization of the food-processing industries improved food supply as well as its security and convenience, and thereby reduced mortality rates, on the other hand, it increased morbidity rates and, above all, it reduced both the freshness and, even more so, the taste of food.[17] With the increasing reliance on purchased food and the greatly improved food distribution system, it tended to become uniform in town and country, in the south and the north.[18] Easier access to this great variety of foodstuffs meant that 'everything can be had in London almost on the same day'.[19]

Added to this increased standardization of food was the enduring adulteration of both food and drink. The complete separation of the producer from the consumer, coupled to the lack of any governmental standards and supervision, encouraged its rampant practice. Although highly damning reports on adulterated and even diseased food were being published from the 1820s onwards, it was not until the 1870s that legislation caused the practices to gradually recede.[20] On the positive side, the continuing expansion of the empire meant that the British were more globally connected than any of their European neighbours, but it is not obvious that this led to vastly increased cosmopolitanism in eating-out practices.

Despite the greater national homogenization of food, eating-out venues, reflecting greater class differentiation, became more diversified. Taverns and inns had lost their pre-eminence and, with it, a lot of their distinctiveness. New places for dining, such as chop houses, gentlemen's clubs, and, in the second half of the century, also the first restaurants (outside hotels), had become competitors.[21] It is no longer clear in the literature whether a place is a tavern, an inn, or even a public house, and frequently a hostelry has several designations. The only continuity was enjoyed by pubs, even though some internal differentiation even in this category occurred. Nevertheless, eating in taverns and inns still features in the literature.

The French Influence on Gastronomy

The juxtaposition of English and French cooking continues, but French cuisine now receives as many favourable as dismissive comments. This is partly due to the fact that France was no longer England's political enemy—the assertion of culinary nationalism is no longer strident. Although anti-French feeling prevailed in the early nineteenth century, there now had developed a resistance to narrow nationalism and advocacy of cosmopolitanism.[22] This greater acceptance of the French and their cuisine reflects also the fact that the middle classes had acquired greater familiarity with French cuisine. To an extent, it had become integrated into otherwise English cookery books and menus, often without common awareness of this integration. Eliza Acton's *The Elegant Economist*,[23] published to great acclaim in 1845, freely mixes dishes from English and French traditions. She even melded the two different traditions within a recipe, such as 'Cauliflower A La Francaise' and 'Mushrooms au Beure'. Mrs Beeton, without acknowledgment, draws on the cookery books of the French-born chefs Soyer and Ude.[24] 'A la mode' beef, wedged between pieces of bread, had become a widely available evening snack meal. Moreover, the Reform Club—the haunt of the upper classes, particularly under its famous French chef Soyer—and other clubs had already introduced French food to a wider section of the gentry and the London upper middle classes at the beginning of the nineteenth century.[25]

French cooking remained extremely popular among the upper classes,[26] and sections of the wealthy middle class tried to emulate upper-class culinary style.[27] In fashionable circles, French cookery and having a French chef had by now become *de rigueur*.[28] Menus of dinners at court featured mainly French dishes and were written out in French, endowing even English dishes, such as turtle soup, with a French name.[29] In contrast, 'among country squires and parsons, doctors and attorneys, there was the utmost suspicion of the "fancy French dishes" which were appearing on the tables of the rich'.[30] Cosmopolitanism had not engulfed all sections of the middle classes, and the symbolization of a social gulf by culinary taste, evident in the previous century, endured to some extent.

Beef eating retained its popularity and, due to the positive impact of rail transport, even vaster quantities of beef were consumed. As much of it came from Scotland—Aberdeen Angus and Galloway breeds—it was now British, rather than English beef.[31] Beef, with lashings of mustard and horseradish sauce, was 'an integral part of the food of chop houses, inns and taverns all over Britain'.[32] Thus, a Dutch visitor to a Harwich Inn in 1815 exclaims on the plenitude of beef and other meat at dinner that 'there was an immense joint of roast beef at one end of the table [set for ten], and a leg of mutton of equal bulk at the bottom ... but there was no soup'.[33] Whether Elizabeth Acton's cookery book of 1845,[34] containing a valiant effort to persuade housewives to cook more soup, was successful, must remain doubtful, given the paucity of an English tradition of soup-making in the twentieth and twenty-first centuries.[35]

Beef remained the undisputed national dish for public holidays, available to all classes, even if more rarely to the poor.[36] Thus, during celebrations of the abdication of Napoleon in April 1814 at Yarmouth, 8,000 people feasted on nearly half a ton of roast beef, 1,800 plum puddings, and eighty barrels of beer.[37] Burnett, too, observes that, at the end of the century, 'cheaper meat allowed the Englishman to indulge his liking for a joint at every meal'.[38] Even gentlemen's clubs with a French chef were obliged to keep roast beef on the menu.[39] In this context, it is difficult to accept Rogers's claim that beef had now lost its symbolic power in asserting national identity.[40]

In addition to beef, what has become another typically British dish made its first appearance: fish 'n' chips. Starting as fish sold separately from chips in the form of mainly working-class fast snack food sold in the street, in 1864 the two became combined in the first proper fish-and-chips restaurant.[41]

Examining the food of this period, let us first consider some brief characterizations of domestic cooking. The author of *Memoirs of a Stomach* describes English domestic cooking in a very uncomplimentary way:

> When I think of that round of parboiled ox flesh, with sodden dumplings, floating in a saline, greasy mixture, surrounded by carrots looking red with disgust, and turnips pale with dismay, I cannot help a sort of inward shudder.[42]

This low estimation of English domestically prepared food is confirmed in a book published by Alexis Soyer—the celebrated chef of the Reform Club—in 1847. He comments on 'the poor state of cooking in England' in the middle of nineteenth century: '... the majority of people in England have only roast and boil, after a fashion; and there the culinary acquirements of the multitude find their extreme limit.'[43] Cookery books of this time, among them Mrs Beeton's, are judged by Mennell as being 'rather monotonous and, above all lacking any sense of the enjoyment of food'.[44] Quantity took precedence over the quality of food, and the new wealth often found expression in the consumption of 'gargantuan meals'.[45]

A completely different picture emerges when the tables of the well-to-do are described. Food served at their dinner parties was not only very ample, but also very varied and highly refined, usually prepared by French chefs. Burnett concludes:

> [T]he Victorian upper classes, who denounced gluttony almost as vehemently as they did immorality... came to be as fond of good food as they were of other sins of the flesh. Probably no civilization since the Roman ate as well as they did.[46]

Eating Out in the Nineteenth Century

When turning to the food of taverns, inns, and public houses, we are able to draw on more detailed sources than in previous centuries. Several guides to dining out were published by then, including that of Ralph Rylance in 1815, Arthur Hayward in 1899, and Colonel Newnham Davies in 1901.[47] With increasing expansion of the affluent middle classes, eating out was becoming quite common for members of the upper middle and upper classes. Newnham Davies's guide is surely an indication that hostelries catering for them in London had multiplied to the point where they could no longer be evaluated by personal experience alone.

One of the most wide-ranging accounts of where one may dine in early nineteenth-century London is provided by *The Gourmet's Almanack*. Written by Rylance in 1815 and re-edited in 2012, it was designed 'to assist a man [sic] to readily regale himself, according to the relative state of his appetite and his purse'.[48] Rylance unwittingly illustrates how eating houses no longer have a clear identity as either tavern, inn, coffee house, or even public house. They play safe by adopting more than one label and often add the new designation of 'chop house' or 'eating house' to the older ones. He thus directs men to such places as: Dolly's Eating House and Tavern; the Horse-Shoe Tavern, referred to as a superior licensed public house; the King's Head Tavern, a celebrated steak and chop house in Newgate Street; and the Struggler Tavern and Chop House.[49]

The London Tavern is still going strong in the nineteenth century, catering mainly for large-scale, high-level corporate events such as lavish monthly dinners for members of the Whig Party, in the mid-Victorian period, and annual banquets for the officers of many regiments, for city companies, and for charities,[50] where all men would be in evening dress. The food, however, is not singled out for comment. Private dinners built and confirmed men's social prominence, rather than pleased the palate.

Much emphasis in the *Almanack* is on dinner in the middle of the day, but evening snacks, like the extremely popular 'beef Alamode' [sic], a 'Welsh Rabbit' or a roast potato, are also mentioned. Victorians knew fast food of a kind, referred to by Rylance as a 'hasty dinner'.[51] Regarding the format of menus, the 'Ordinary', or fixed menu of courses at a set price, continues to be available. Eating houses might even offer something akin to today's *'amuse-bouche'*. Before a big beef steak, the waiter may put on the table 'a delicate trifle, or "bonne bouche", to serve until the steak was ready'.[52] In many taverns, inns, and chop houses prices were charged per head, rather than per dish.[53]

In common with food writers during earlier centuries, Rylance describes the substance of a meal only infrequently and refrains from any judgements of taste. He indicates only rough and unhelpful distinctions between eating places when he describes their larders as 'sumptuous, admirable, or merely good'. Rylance is so enamoured with the magnificence and size of the buildings of both the London Tavern and the City of London Tavern that food receives no mention at all. Very occasionally, he becomes slightly more expansive. Referring to the Spreadeagle Inn and Tavern in Gracechurch Street, he comments: 'Here is a good larder, containing everything of the best in season.'[54] Mr Smith's Eating-House in Mary-le-Bone Lane receives an even more enthusiastic endorsement—it is 'perhaps, the very best in London.... Every dish is composed of the best meat and cooked in the most scientific manner'. Smith offers 'collared beef, veal, pig, larded beef, and veal cakes... as well as an excellent raised pie of large dimensions, built with alternate strata or layers of ham and veal, the interstices being filled with a highly flavoured, well-seasoned jelly'.[55]

As in previous centuries, what strikes the reader about the dishes described is the strong emphasis on meat, whereas vegetables and fruit are regarded as only minor accompaniments. According to Rylance, 'it is one of the heaviest charges made against John Bull that when he intends to fare well, he cannot help crying out "roast beef"'.[56] And indeed, mentions of beef heavily outweigh the mentions of other types of meat. Beef comes either boiled, roasted, or *a la mode*. This consumption of vast quantities of meat and the generally plain nature of food is also commented on by the food historian, Burnett, referring to the later nineteenth century: '[T]avern meals continued to find favour among men who liked plentiful servings of good meat, fish and game undisguised by fancy sauces.'[57] However, slightly more exotic foods, such as turtles (which were imported live and lived in tanks) and venison, were also considered very desirable foods at the time.[58] Only once does Rylance mention vegetables, when he introduces the Nun's Head Tavern near (the then rural) Peckham, 'where a rural dinner, with vegetables fresh from the garden may be had in summer'.[59]

Fish as a main course is mainly mentioned in connection with specialized fish restaurants situated on or near the Thames, and whitebait was particularly popular. Renowned for their whitebait were the Ship Hotel and the Trafalgar Tavern by the waterside at Greenwich,[60] and at Blackwall/Woolwich 'one may indulge in the luxury of Whitebait'.[61] These were very large taverns. The Ship Hotel, for instance, accommodated individual diners on the ground floor, company dinners for up to 300 persons on the first floor, and smaller rooms for private diners on the top floor. The Trafalgar Tavern was the venue for the annual 'whitebait dinner' at the end of the parliamentary season in July.[62] Another popular fish dish at the time was of eel, which was then still plentiful in the Thames. In Twickenham, on an island in the Thames, one could eat 'eel pyes' [sic], with the eel caught by the husband and the pies made by the wife. The White Lion in Putney also served a good dinner of stewed eel or fried flounder from fish kept fresh in near-by moored boats.[63] In the second half of the nineteenth century, however, fish was consumed in greater quantities. This was made possible by technological innovation, namely steam trawlers where fish was packed on ice.[64] Nevertheless, all these exceptional places where the Victorians consumed either vegetables or fish only serve to confirm the rule of a very meat-heavy diet.

Rylance is very hesitant to express any sensual appreciation of the food he describes. Whether his reluctance to make aesthetic judgements is due to the fear of shocking his Victorian readers who, according to Spencer,[65] have a great nervousness of showing pleasure, is impossible to judge. There is, however, one notable exception to the lack of aesthetic discrimination and sensory awareness among diners during the early nineteenth century. It is the barrister Thomas Walker, son of a wealthy Whig politician and landowner. In his book, *The Art of Dining*, he sets out 'to please the palate'.[66] Unusually, he insists on the simplicity and high quality, rather than the quantity, of ingredients and on due attention to the seasons. He is exceptional in singling out well-cooked vegetables as one of the delights of dining: 'One of the greatest luxuries.... in dining is to command plenty of good vegetables, well served up.'[67] When he details one of the simple meals he has ordered at the Athenaeum gentlemen's club, it includes grouse served with a plate of French beans.[68] Walker, in this as in other ways, appears to be distinctly in advance of his time.

Menus of the period are not easy to come by. Only twice does Rylance provide one.[69] For the Telegraph Eating-House, it is (in shillings and pence):

Boiled beef, per plate	0.9
Roast beef	0.10
Roast mutton	0.10
Roast pork	0.11
Roast veal	0.11
Pork chop	0.6
Mutton chop	0.5
Rump steak	1.2
Mock turtle, per basin	1.10
Giblet soup	0.10
Gravy or pea soup	0.6

Although the British were said to have the primest raw ingredients of all kinds (if they were not adulterated or diseased!), in Rylance's opinion they were 'comparatively novices in cookery'. He believed that 'the whole system of English cookery is much inferior in economy and variety of resources to either the French or the Germans'.[70] Rylance's low opinion of English cooking is paralleled by his fascination with foreign eateries. He recommends a large number of eating houses serving French, Italian, and even German dishes. These were in both very expensive top hotels and more modest houses run by continentals mainly for their resident countrymen. The latter were mostly in Soho and in the Leicester Square area. Among them were the Saulieu, Pagliano's, and the Sabloniere (all considered restaurants), or the Prince of Wales Coffee House and Tavern, and Brunet's Hotel and Tavern in Duke Street.[71]

Although foreign cuisine, other than French, was already known in previous centuries, foreign-owned restaurants now became more prevalent, particularly in London. Judging from Rylance's guide, such restaurants are particularly of Italian origin. Whereas many cater mainly for resident foreigners, some aim to attract British customers as well. It seems as if, in the nineteenth century, we get the beginnings of a more cosmopolitan dining scene, albeit one still chiefly oriented to Europe and not yet globally. (Only one Indian restaurant is mentioned.) Also, dining out remains restricted mainly to the gentry and the upper middle class.

Rylance is particularly enthusiastic about a French establishment called Mollard's Old Drury Lane Tavern. It was run by what can only be described as an early celebrity chef, Monsieur John Mollard. He published *The Art of Cookery made Easy and Refined* that went through four editions. Rylance comments: 'As an author he is eminently distinguished and as a practical artist he is without rival.'[72] Another French eating house is Morin's Hotel, which Rylance contrasts favourably with English houses where dinners 'are often overdone or underdone'.[73] The Four Nations Tavern in Soho, run by Monsieur Barron, offers not only French fare, but also Italian, English, and German food served up to members of these four nations.[74] Rylance also mentions what must have been the first Indian restaurant in London, the Hindostanee Coffee House in George Street, run by Deen Mohamed or Mohamet who advertised his 'unequalled curries' for a short period.[75] The venues cannot easily be identified to be of a certain type and were often a mixture of tavern, inn, public house, and hotel. Only in the last quarter of the nineteenth century, did restaurants become securely established as distinct establishments.

While Rylance welcomes the spread of French restaurants in London, traditional diners, like the writer and journalist Edward Spencer Mott (his pseudonym was Nathaniel Gubbins), writing later in the nineteenth century, very much begrudge their conquest of the London restaurant landscape. He decries 'the grease-and-garlic shops' where the natural flavour of ingredients is destroyed. Spencer Mott regrets the disappearance of old English dishes, like tripe and onions or Irish stew, and bemoans the multiplication of new Parisian diners, threatening 'to throttle the roast beef of old England'.[76] Thus, even in the nineteenth century, culinary nationalism is still asserted by some sections of society.

Dickens, who often visits taverns and is inclined to enthuse about them in some of his novels, is nevertheless happy to point out their failings when annoyed by their offerings. During his travels as a young journalist, in his *The Uncommercial Traveller*, Dickens describes a dinner as an 'ill-served, ill-appointed, ill-cooked, nasty little dinner'.[77] Burnett confirms that 'the inns and eating houses...of this period had a generally poor reputation, and were used from necessity rather than for pleasure'.[78] Provision was particularly poor in many regions outside of London and other great cities. Old country inns of coaching days were described as 'miserable, comfortless and [having] a menu consisting invariably of "Chop, sir, steak, broiled fowl"'. It seems that the poor quality of food we knew in English hostelries prior to the 1980s had first set in in the nineteenth century.

Although the Victorians were already familiar with catering for very large numbers, systematically organized mass catering began in a moderate way only at the turn from the nineteenth to the twentieth century, between 1880 and 1914, to develop more fully after World War I.[79] Eating out for pleasure among working men and women was still unusual, and canteens in work places also did not come until after 1914.[80] But, as already mentioned several times, there were many affordable options for eating away-from-home commercially, such as buying pies, puddings, and other savouries from cook shops, as well as fish from virtually universal fish shops. Street sellers of all kinds of food were plentiful. Some specialized in offering soup, others sold whelks, eels, or sheeps' trotters. Sellers of pies, hot potatoes, and ham sandwiches were slightly less ubiquitous. Skilled workers and journeymen, according to Clark, eat in cook shops, and for those below them in the social hierarchy there were oyster, tripe, and chop shops.[81] A few commercially-run chains of coffee and tea houses, that also provided some snack meals, came on the scene in the 1880s and 90s, as did cafés in department stores that catered also for the upper working and lower middle classes.[82]

With shorter working days (the nine-hour day), breaks in the working day, and more days off, manual and lower white-collar workers provided a ready market for cheaper cafés and tea houses. This gap in the market was skilfully exploited by Joe Lyons. He rose to prominence when providing catering for the many at the Great Exhibitions in the 1880s, in honour of the Golden Jubilee. The first tea room offering snacks with its tea and coffee was opened in 1894 in Piccadilly, and its success led to replication of the model in many other locations. In 1904, he opened the huge Popular Café (catering for 2,000), which started to serve luncheons, then the Trocadero, and after that, in 1909, the Lyons Corner Houses. Lyons is credited with transforming the catering trade, though mainly in standards of cleanliness, decorum, and speed of service. At the same time, he is held responsible for debasing food in mass catering. According to Burnett, Lyons developed a formula by cooking all the food centrally and then warming it up on hotplates *in situ*, making the 'chain' model viable.[83] According to Spencer, the food was basically British and cooked without care, but dishes were often given French names.[84] The vast influence of Lyons' formula in twentieth and twenty-first century catering, including that in pubs, requires no elaboration.

Although eating houses, and, later in the century, fish-and-chips shops and restaurants, proliferated, pubs continued to serve some food. In the late Victorian and Edwardian periods, some pubs offered also coffee, hot dinners like hot-pot, or the traditional set Ordinary.[85] By then many pubs had luncheon counters and grill rooms and were offering various non-alcoholic drinks as well. 'Even so, food seldom provided more than a small percentage of the total sales and tended to be aimed at better-off customers.'[86] As pubs grew smarter, publicans became less prepared to heat up chops brought in by workmen for their midday dinner.

The culinary skill of the average pub landlord was not very high at this time.[87] Yet, a small number of pubs, aiming to attract the better class of customer, began to provide food in a more serious way. Thus, Rylance, writing at the beginning of the nineteenth century,[88] mentions two licensed London public houses—the Red Lion and the Dover Castle—as houses of 'a superior class' which serve their ale 'with chops, kidneys, Welsh-rabbits and other titbits, in the way of a relish to the potent beverage'. Girouard, too, points out that a few pubs began to sell hot luncheons, such as midday-joints or sausages and mustard.[89]

The first pronounced shift from sales of solely drink to include also some food came towards the middle of the century and was very much a result of the pressure brought by the temperance movement, rather than being due to initiatives developed by publicans or brewers. The first alternative to the drink-led pub was the 'coffee public house', which provided no alcohol but instead concentrated on non-alcoholic drinks and good cheap food—something that pubs had provided inadequately or not at all. Starting in the 1850s, by 1884 there existed 1,500 such coffee public houses in the British Isles,[90] but working men, generally, were not taken in by them, and this type of public house did not catch on in the long run. However, they provided a model for the 'improved pubs', which came early in the twentieth century when a movement towards providing food took hold in a larger number of public houses. However, the majority of pubs were not primarily eating houses and, if they provided food, it was mostly very basic.

Drink consumed in hostelries of the nineteenth century continued to indicate social differences. Gin was drunk by the poor all over London by 1820, and the amount drunk was widely seen as having reached crisis proportions. By the late 1860s, several Acts had got the gin craze finally under control, and the rising consumption of ale/beer took its place. The main varieties drunk were stout (porter), bitter, and mild, and, compared with today's beer, they were strong.[91] There was considerable variation in taste between regions. Gross consumption of beer in the UK rose steadily from the early 1800s until 1839 (a time of population increase), but per head consumption, measured in gallons, showed a gradual but steady decline from the 1840s onwards.[92] After 1870, taste in beer began to change, with sales of porter declining and that of mild, sweet beer increasing.

While 80 per cent of wines drunk during the first half of the nineteenth century were sherry, port, and hock,[93] the fashion in wine changed after 1861.

The taxes imposed on alcoholic beverages by Gladstone in 1861 helped to bring wine back into favour. Lower duties were paid on lighter table wine than on heavier port, but wine—due to its relatively high cost—was widely adulterated, with brewers adding noxious substances on a considerable scale.[94] Punch, both hot and cold, was also very popular, and the cold version appears to be similar to what we call cocktails today.[95]

Eating Out in the Twentieth Century

When we turn to food and dining in the twentieth century, the two world wars acted as watersheds. This was particularly true for the lower classes, but it also affected the middle classes, and some levelling between the classes, particularly after World War I, is discernible. Class differences in consumption patterns nevertheless continued. Rising health consciousness also began to moderate eating and dining habits for the first time.

In the early twentieth century, public dinners became shorter and less elaborate. Joints of meat continued to figure prominently, but excessive consumption of meat saw a reduction.[96] The Edwardian middle and upper classes nevertheless continued to live in splendour. Menus now featured a mixture of French and English culinary terms, such as Fillets of Salmon a la Belle-Ile or Cutlets of Pigeons a la Duc de Cambridge.[97]

During World War I, the British government was able to shield its people from the worst effects of the War. Food continued to be imported until 1917.[98] World War I alerted the establishment to the poor nourishment of a large part of the population. It revealed the enduring marked social inequality between the upper and middle classes, on the one side, and the rest of the population, on the other. It made evident the alarming extent of poverty and ill health which prevailed in a large section of the urban population at the height of Britain's wealth and prestige. For millions of soldiers and civilians, war-time rations represented a higher standard of nourishment than they had ever known before.[99]

War restrictions on drinking were lifted in 1921, but it took a while to return to the heights of Edwardian good living. As late as 1929, André Simon, a food and wine writer, comments that, although the recovery in food and eating out had advanced a lot, it had not yet returned to the pre-war level, especially for the wealthier classes. The middle classes, which had greatly expanded in size, were relatively poorer than before World War I, but matters had improved for the lower middle and working classes.[100] 'By the eve of the Second World War, the working classes... were better fed... than their parents had been a generation earlier.'[101]

Eating out in newly diversified venues (cafés, milk bars, snack bars, etc.) was, in the early twentieth century, a pastime enjoyed among all social classes, except the very lowest.[102] The gradual adoption of the motor car enabled people to drive out into the country to visit the so-called 'road houses', mock Tudor pubs with higher levels of comfort than urban ones, that were dotted along most arterial roads. Eating out had come to be more affordable, due to the development of 'popular' catering by entrepreneurs such as Lyons.[103] These new venues became competitors to traditional pubs offering food, and probably retarded the emergence of food-led pubs.

Another great social transformation occurred after World War II, particularly from the mid-1950s onwards. Average expenditure on food continued to rise, and the gap between the expenditure of the richest and the poorest had continued to close. With very few exceptions, the whole population was economically able to afford an adequate diet, and the nutritional standards between different classes varied less than before World War II.[104] Examining household expenditure data for 1960, it is notable that, for the first time since the seventeenth century, proportional spending on meat had decreased, and the whole diet had become lighter. Thus, steamed puddings had been largely replaced by lighter, milk- or fruit-based ones.

It is notable that beef continued as the most popular meat when it came to the traditional joint, although it gradually ceded first place in the popularity stakes to poultry. In 1960, 32 per cent of families still ate roast beef on Sundays.[105] Beef eating thus remained an enduring feature of national identification, even if it had become habitual, rather than demonstratively patriotic as in the eighteenth century.

The results of a 1962 Gallup Poll reveal that British people adhered to a marked conservatism in their food habits. When asked to detail their perfect meal, with eight choices from aperitif via beverages to cheese and biscuits, a lot of historical continuity was revealed. A comparison of responses with some obtained in 1947 shows that only one course had changed, namely trifle and cream had become fruit salad and cream. People may have been very keen on fish-and-chips and curry by then, but they did not qualify for the perfect meal.

By the 1960s, eating out at various levels had noticeably increased, and this trend included also the less wealthy salary- and wage-earners. Indian, Chinese, and Cypriot restaurants proliferated.[106] Catering had become a very large and growing industry. The partiality to other European cuisines came only a few decades later and, even then, only for a section of the population.

During the twentieth century, taverns had all but disappeared. In the late 1920s, the Ordinary survived in only a few exceptional places.[107] Inns—which survived longer, though in small numbers—became difficult to distinguish from hotels, restaurants, and better-class public houses. The general run of inns offered very mediocre food. The degradation of standards, noted earlier for the nineteenth century, had further intensified.

Burke comments with some scorn on what he views as a high tolerance for mediocrity on the part of English customers of inns and probably also pubs in the late 1920s:[108]

> You may see in the dining-room of many an inn a whole crowd of sturdy Englishmen, tamely eating, and paying smartly for, a dinner that would be approved only by a starving peasant... You will see them eating cheese fit only for a mouse trap. You will see them waiting meekly under bad service. Wine is poor quality and over-priced, and coffee is often unspeakable. They will even tip the waitress for the insult of the meal and the scornful service.

Burke bemoans the absence of knowledge of recipes by chefs, who serve the same six dishes all the year round. He suggests that the most used kitchen tool is the tin opener. The nameless cheese served and the totally unimaginative and repetitive manner of serving a salad also attract his ire.[109]

However, in this sea of mediocrity, a very small number of inns stood out that offered excellent hospitality. The literature, e.g. Batchelor,[110] singles out the following: the Spreadeagle at Thame, Oxfordshire, the Lygon Arms at Broadway, Cotswolds, The Bell at Aston Clinton, Warwickshire, and Barry Neames's Hind's Head at Bray. Batchelor attributes their excellence to the exceptional personalities of the people who kept these inns, and others endorse this judgement. These hostelries, in some ways, may be regarded as forerunners of today's gastropubs and therefore merit closer attention. The Hind's Head, for example, started life as a pub in the sixteenth century, before turning into a restaurant in the 1920s. Today, it is a famous gastropub, owned by Heston Blumenthal.

John Fothergill, the landlord of the Spreadeagle, published his diary in book form in 1931. As he provides an interesting account of how the Spreadeagle managed to stand out by providing good food and an appealing ambience, his diary deserves a detailed rendering. This inn was famous all over Britain, and the innkeeper's eccentric personality even endowed it with notoriety. Fothergill himself explains his dedication to providing good food and his method of sourcing the ingredients for it, in the following terms:

> Real food is a surprise, and simply because the gastric juices fly out to it, whilst they hold back aching at the aromalessness of synthetic, poor or adulterated products... Surely this is better, than buying everything from a hotel purveyor... it is better and more difficult than having one specialité gastronomique?[111]

He describes the inn's kitchen as 'our kitchen where the food is food, tastes of it, and tastes good' and contrasts it with that of the English hotel 'where the food, when even it is food, doesn't taste of anything, or tastes badly' and the French 'where the food doesn't taste of what it is, or ought to be, but tastes good'.[112]

Before Fothergill's assumption of ownership in 1922, the Spreadeagle had served the local farmers and masons as a pub, as well as catering for parties arriving by charabanc. Fothergill, however, thought the title 'inn' more becoming for an establishment selling upmarket food and wine, as well as offering some accommodation. He furnished the place with elegant antiques, obliterating any pub-style qualities. The beauty of the china dishes on which food was served was as important to him as the food itself. His insistence on good manners among his guests completely sets his establishment apart from the casual ambience of today's gastropub and brings it closer to the social formality of eighteenth and nineteenth century hostelries.

The dishes prepared and served in his inn, unfortunately, are very infrequently mentioned in his book and, where they are, they are not described in any detail. Fothergill outlines no menu, but his several incidental remarks about dishes suggest that his food was mainly English. He serves both the traditional English roasts, steaks, cottage pie, omelettes, trifles (but without using pre-packed jelly), and jam tarts, as well as more unusual dishes such as jugged hare and lemon flummery, for which he used an old eighteenth century recipe.

He is more informative when it comes to sourcing, where his method was highly unusual for the time and reminds us more of the practices of contemporary chefs: 'When I took this shop, I thought round for all the things I had found best and sent for them.' He regularly receives produce from 'Athens, France, Norway, Jaffa and Italy... And of English things we have daily from three bakers three different kinds of bread made from flours I have forced upon them, besides the bread we make ourselves, cheese from East Harptree, salt from Malden, mustard from Leighton Buzzard, sausages, after a search all over England, from a local butcher.'[113]

Cultivating his own garden, where he grows herbs and some vegetables, is also highly unusual for the time. In sum, Fothergill may be regarded as one of the first landlords expressing a strong concern with taste, and his care for quality and singularity of ingredients likens him to current-day chefs of the best gastropubs. The food served still leaned strongly towards the tradition of an English inn or tavern. The ambience of his inn, however, was more that of an upmarket restaurant.

Like many of today's owners of gastropubs, he came from an upper middle-class background and was university-educated. The guests that survived his selection process were from the same or an even higher class.[114] Personal interaction with such customers was one of the most important satisfactions Fothergill derived from running his inn.

Fothergill provides an insight into the difficulties of running his inn at such a high level of all round excellence. He worked long hours and rarely took a day off.[115] While he was never much interested in making a profit, he did have to break even and that, in the end, was not achievable and the inn had to close.[116]

In contrast to the paucity of literature on taverns and inns during the twentieth century, one can draw on more information regarding pubs, and particularly on the gradually accelerating shift from being drink-led to becoming food-led.

In the late nineteenth and early twentieth centuries, a hesitant movement towards a greater focus on pub food developed. It partly gained impetus from the various reform efforts, inspired by the temperance movement. It was additionally helped along by government intervention during World War I and by a few individual or chains of pubs recognizing the business opportunity entailed in moving towards the provision of food. Some of these initiatives were overlapping in intent and in the organizations involved, and it is difficult to disentangle them. These developments, however, encompassed only a minority of pubs, and the small scale and unevenness of change did not yet amount to a significant shift to food-led pubs.

During World War I, the government set up a Central Control Board, with a number of objectives to preserve sobriety, particularly of troops. As part of this initiative, it encouraged the provision of food in pubs, particularly in urban areas. The establishments resulting from this initiative were called 'food taverns', resurrecting the old name to lend the new type of pub respectability, as well as appealing to nostalgia. A food tavern, although having a licence to sell wine, sets out to provide meals, i.e. more than a snack. The largest number of them were in large towns such as London, Birmingham, Leeds, and Newcastle, and they provided mainly for luncheons.[117] Additionally, a few operated in market towns which catered for farmers. Food taverns still served Ordinaries on certain days of the week, but by now hotels rivalled them in the provision of meals.

The 'reformed pubs', established by voluntary associations with temperance concerns at the turn from the nineteenth to the twentieth century, also tried to counter 'excessive drinking' by offering food and non-alcoholic beverages. They were usually purpose-built to offer more and better-furnished space, with many indoor and outdoor amenities for recreation to make them attractive also to women and families.[118] According to Gutzke, the 'reformed pubs' did not prove economically viable in the competition with old-style pubs and the restaurants and cafés that proliferated by then.[119]

Selley's wider survey of all types of pubs concludes that 'these houses [food taverns and/or reformed or improved pubs] are the least common of all'. He explains their failure to catch on in a big way by singling out characteristics of pubs and publicans already familiar to us from past centuries:

> The ordinary public house has not the space or the domestic convenience for catering for meals, and the average publican will not engage in such difficult business, when he can make enough from drink alone.[120]

Selley furthermore suggests that the really good food taverns he found 'obviously cater for the middle classes'.[121] Gutzke largely agrees with Selley on the low rate of success of food taverns and reformed pubs: 'Pub reform, "good service plus sobriety" proved unobtainable as a uniform concept over the country.'[122]

However, some individual pubs and even pub entrepreneurs, outside the reform movement, also offered good food attracting the attention of those studying pubs. Their licensees overcame the limitations of the reformed or improved pubs singled out above. For Gutzke,[123] the return of the licensed victualler to public houses began in London in 1897, with a partnership between Dick Levy and Henry Franks. They acted on the then unorthodox assumption that there is as much money to be made out of food as out of drink. Levy and Franks leased pubs from brewers and successfully sold mainly inexpensive but tasty meals to lower-class customers. These pubs were supplied by food companies that Levy and Frank operated themselves. They had expanded to thirty such pubs by 1918,[124] and thereby disproved those who said that workers wanted nothing but alcohol. Typically, the higher profit margins on food than on alcohol generated larger aggregate sales. However, such pubs seem to have been an exceptional phenomenon in the period up to and including World War I.

A large survey in the late 1930s in the northern town of Bolton,[125] finds a different situation in northern pubs: 'As for getting meals in pubs, this is almost impossible'. The picture was thus geographically uneven and demand for good pub food was obviously higher in certain areas of London.

Such licensed companies as operated by Frank and Levy during the first decade of the twentieth century expanded rapidly during the inter-war years. Sometimes giant brewers themselves took the initiative, but this occurred mainly in London. Provincial brewers used well-established catering companies. Rising food sales during the inter-war years were reflected in proliferating numbers of catering companies. For example, Whitbread and Co. leased about 8 per cent of its 580 tied houses to catering companies in the mid-1920s, and Watney leased 10 per cent. Licensees became caterers principally to the middle classes, especially in the new suburban super-pubs.[126]

The discussion of the role of food in pubs, and of the extent to which meals were provided, revives again in the 1960s when a stronger change in this direction becomes apparent. Of the 124,358 catering establishments in 1960, public houses comprised 61,553.[127] Where pubs provided their own meals, they were either prepared in advance by the publican's wife or provided frozen by companies and heated up. Moreover, pubs offered a fairly narrow and homogenous range of dishes.[128] 'Pub grub' included pies and pasties, chicken in the basket, bangers and mash, ploughman's lunch, and Sunday roasts. Big outside-catering companies stepped in where most individual licensees were both disinclined and unable to take on the new role of a provider of meals. But there were exceptions to this uniformity of dishes and the standardization of preparation. 'Tenants and owners of free houses often took a different approach. They still had pride in home cooking.'[129] Also, chains of mega pubs, with a strong food offer, had become prominent. Restaurant-oriented pubs, such as Berni Inn, Beefeater, Vintage Inns, Toby, and Chef & Brewer, are singled out.[130]

Between 1977 and 1984, food sales in public houses grew by 375 per cent and went from 12 per cent of all food-catering sales to 22.5 per cent.[131] Dining in pubs had become the second most frequent choice of venue after eating at home.[132] The world of mass catering clearly had engulfed pubs, and this movement, although providing higher consistency in the quality of the food, came at the expense of freshness, originality, and excellence of meals offered. At this time, meals still consisted mainly of pub classics. Some foreign dishes, such as lasagne and chilli con carne, began to appear on menus from the early 1990s; however, French classical techniques were eschewed.

A more far-reaching change towards food-led pubs came only in the 1990s. It engulfed all kinds of pub, and the provision of meals started to become as important as that of beer, or even outweighed the takings from beer. The latter was the case, for example, in the new branded mega pubs. At the close of the 1990s, pubs headed the list of number of meals taken in commercial establishments, not including snacks.[133] This shift occurred in response to the decline of drinking. A market report by the company Key Note, commenting on the late 1990s,[134] estimates that pub food sales, worth about £1.9 billion, then accounted for around 33 per cent of the eating-out market. The shift was also demand-led in that women and couples, who now counted for a large proportion of the customers, expected meals to be served.

The high street branded mega pubs, which gained ground from the late 1980s and expanded in the 1990s, contributed greatly to this increased consumption of food. Names like J.D. Weatherspoon, Pitcher and Piano, All Bar One, and Slug and Lettuce come to mind. Most sell fairly standard fare, such as burgers, pies, hot dogs, and salads, but also trusted favourites like lasagne and chicken tikka. Some, such as J.D. Weatherspoon, offer some healthy options, as well as lots of craft beers. Although the quality of food in these pubs is more reliable, and the food is cheaper than it is in traditional pubs, the individuality of the latter has been swept away by the mega pubs. Eating out became 'horribly unexciting, predictable and ... almost identical',[135] and they are 'slowly but surely constricting British high streets'.[136] Nevertheless, the mega pubs appeal to a large section of the British population. They have been able to claim a substantial share of the overall turnover from food, and their dominance on towns' high streets may explain why gastropubs were rarely able to become established there.

More traditional food-led pubs were found in both urban and rural areas, and rural pubs were more likely to be destination pubs for the meals offered. Pub restaurants became established in what previously had been the saloon bar. The increase in the quality of meals sold was due to the convergence of a number of influences: the much increased competition from the expanding and diversifying restaurant sector; the development of more cosmopolitan tastes among potential customers, as well as their higher aspirations for the quality of ingredients;[137] and last, but not least, the emergence of a new breed of chef, trained in upmarket restaurants and seeking to set up their own business. Pubs, in many quarters, were still regarded as part of the national patrimony, and their expansion into gastronomically more ambitious food enhanced the value of that patrimony. All this provided the foundation for the development of the gastropub that, from modest beginnings in the 1990s, really took off in the 2000s.

What about the drink consumed in pubs during the twentieth century? After World War I, in the absence of widespread protest, the weakness of beer persisted. Although porter was still drunk in the south of England, in the north mild beer was the universal drink.[138] Bottled beer became increasingly popular. The level of consumption of beer and of drunkenness had dropped, partly due to reduced drinking hours. However, there was variation between areas, with industrial towns having higher levels. Beer consumption rose again during World War II, but there was a further fall in the strength of beer.[139] Drinkers are said to have cared primarily about the price of beer and little about the quality.

After World War II, rising general prosperity led to more alcohol being consumed. However, beer began to lose ground to spirits, and wine became the drink of choice when eating out. Beer consumption became much more diversified. In the early post-War period, so-called keg or, more disparagingly, fizzy beer, which had been pasteurized and was brought up from the cellar by gas pressure, was most widely drunk. By 1976, it constituted 40 per cent of all beer sold in pubs. It was easy to handle and transport and therefore popular with breweries and publicans alike, although its taste left much to be desired. Sales of draught beer, in contrast, had greatly dropped, constituting only 14 per cent of sales. Lager, which had made for only 2 per cent of beer sales in 1959, greatly increased in popularity, to constitute 50 per cent of all beer drunk by 1990.[140]

From the 1980s, more affluent and sophisticated customers demanded more superior beer. More expensive imported beers and domestic cask-conditioned beer gained ground. The latter was both stronger and unpasteurized. An upturn in the consumption of 'real ale' started in the late 1980s, and demand has continued to expand until today. It was partly facilitated by the admission of a 'guest beer' for tenants in tied houses by the Beer Orders Act of 1989.

Millns regards its rise to popularity additionally as part of the consumer shift in taste towards 'authentic values'.[141] This shift parallels that in food consumption and indicates a reaction to the growing homogenization of products sold by the big corporations.

This chapter leads to a number of conclusions about eating out in the nineteenth and twentieth centuries. First, the tremendous economic and technological transformations brought about a number of changes, broadly summed up by the homogenization and degradation of food and the diversification of eating-out venues. While taverns and inns were disappearing, the pub retained a strong presence and even began to branch out into the provision of food. But this latter trend was hesitant and uneven, and the pub encountered a lot of competition from new venues. At the same time, during the nineteenth century, class divisions solidified, and the classes experienced the degradation of food to different degrees.

Gastro-nationalism, directed against French cuisine, continued to some extent but became less chauvinist, and the expanded middle classes showed some cosmopolitan tendencies. In the twentieth century, class divisions became comparatively less pronounced, particularly after World War I. With the improvement in income for the lower classes, more people participated in eating out, and new hospitality venues developed. It was only towards the end of the twentieth century that pubs moved more fully towards embracing dining. The quality of food, in general terms, did not improve greatly until the end of the twentieth century. The gradual improvement in pub food in the last few decades has been well summed up by Thornton: 'Pub food has blossomed from the curled-up sandwich of the 1960s, through the Chicken in the Basket of the 1970s and 1980s, to the refined pub restaurant and impressive gastropub of today.'[142] But by then pubs met competition from a host of new eating-out venues, particularly from the turn of the century.

Moreover, English cooking became confronted with other national cuisines—a phenomenon that reached new heights during Britain's pronounced global economic and cultural integration since the 1980s and into the twenty-first century. Diners and chefs with more cosmopolitan tastes began to proliferate more widely and, to some extent, became a cross-class phenomenon.

Endnotes

1. Perkin, H. 1969, *The Origins of Modern English Society*, 3–4. London: Routledge, Kegan Paul.
2. Drummond, J. and Wilbraham, A. 1939, *The Englishman's Food. A history of five centuries of English diet*, 334. London: Jonathan Cape.

3. Paston-Williams, S. 1993, *The Art of Dining. A history of cooking and eating*, 267. London: The National Trust.
4. Perkin, 1969, 22.
5. Drummond and Wilbraham, 1939, 331.
6. Girouard, M, 1984, *Victorian Pubs*, 60. New Haven and London: Yale University Press.
7. Drummond and Wilbraham, 1939, 390.
8. Burnett, J. 1966, *Plenty and Want. A social history of diet in England from 1815 to the present day*, 54. London: Thomas Nelson and Sons.
9. Paston-Williams, 1993, 267.
10. Burnett, 1966, 91.
11. Perkin, 1969, 144; Tombs, R. 2015, *The English and their History*, 481. London: Penguin Books.
12. Perkin, 1969, 92.
13. Tombs, 2015, 481.
14. Burnett, 1966, 167.
15. Burnett, 1966, 51, 53, 167.
16. Mennell, S. 1985, *All Manners of Food. Eating and taste in England and France from the Middle Ages to the present*, 135. Oxford: Basil Blackwell.
17. Otter, C. 2015, 'Industrializing diet, industrializing ourselves: technology, food and the body, since 1750', C. Helstosky ed., *The Routledge History of Food*, 220–48. London, New York: Routledge.
18. Drummond and Wilbraham, 1939, 340.
19. Hayward, A. 1899, *The Art of Dining*, 152. London: John Murray.
20. Drummond and Wilbraham, 1939, 363; Burnett, 1966, 72, 209.
21. Shore, E. 2007, 'Dining out; the development of the restaurant', P. Freedman ed., *Food. The history of taste*, 301–31. London: Thames and Hudson.
22. Newman, G. 1987, *The Rise of English Nationalism. A cultural history 1740–1830*, 149. London: Weidenfeld and Nicholson.
23. Acton, E. 2011, *The Elegant Economist*. London: Penguin Books. Contains extracts from Acton's *Modern Cookery for Private Families*, first published in 1845.
24. Spencer, C. 2002, *British Food. An extraordinary thousand years of history*, 281. London: Grub Street.
25. Shore, 2007, 313.
26. Mennell, 1985, 76.
27. Perkin, 1969, 142.
28. Burnett, 1966, 57.
29. Burnett, 1966, 170ff.
30. Burnett, 1966, 57.
31. Rogers, B. 2003, *Beef and Liberty*, 172. London: Chatto & Windus.
32. Spencer, 2002, 281.
33. Cited by Richardson, S. and Eberlein, H.D. 1925, *The English Inn, Past and Present*, 43. London: Batsford.
34. Acton, 2011, 1.
35. Burnett, 1966, 189.

36. Rogers, 2003, 167.
37. Tombs, 2015, 411.
38. Burnett, 1966.
39. Rogers, 2003, 170.
40. Rogers, 2003, 183.
41. Shore, 2007, 321–2.
42. Whiting, S. 1853, *Memoirs of a Stomach, Written by Himself, that all who Eat may Read*, 98. London: W.E. Painter.
43. Cited by Clair, C. 1964, *Kitchen and Table*, 238. London, New York, Toronto: Abelard-Schuman.
44. Mennell, 1985, 79.
45. Perkin, 1969, 418.
46. Burnett, 1966, 71.
47. Rylance, R. 1815, *Places of Alimentary Resort*. London; Hayward 1899 [but first written in 1835 and 1836]; Newnham-Davis, N. 1899, *Dinners and Diners*. London: Grant Richards.
48. Ing Freeman, J. ed. 2012, *The Epicure's Almanack. Eating and drinking in Regency London*, xi. London: The British Library. First published by Ralph Rylance under the title *Places of Alimentary Resort* in 1815.
49. Ing Freeman, 2012, 4, 6, 11, 13.
50. Harrison, B. 1973, 'Pubs', H.J. Dyos and M. Wolff eds, *The Victorian City. Volume I*, 176. London and New York: Routledge.
51. Ing Freeman, 2012, 43, in her introduction to the *Almanack*.
52. Ing Freeman, 2012, 43.
53. Ing Freeman, 2012, 45.
54. Ing Freeman, 2012, 30–1.
55. Ing Freeman, 2012, 113.
56. Ing Freeman, 2012, 48.
57. Burnett, J. 2004, *England Eats Out. A social history of England from 1830 to the present*, 87. Harlow: Longman.
58. Burnett, 2004, 87.
59. Ing Freeman, 2012, 213.
60. Clair, 1964, 149.
61. Ing Freeman, 2012, 216.
62. Burnett, 2004, 102.
63. Ing Freeman, 2012, 200.
64. Shore, 2007, 321–2.
65. Spencer, 2002, 289.
66. Walker, T. 1928, *The Art of Dining*, 7. London: The Cayme Press.
67. Walker, 1928, 33.
68. Walker, 1928, 50.
69. Ing Freeman, 2012, 32.
70. Ing Freeman, 2012, 230, 265.
71. Ing Freeman, 2012, 169.
72. Ing Freeman, 2012, 147.

73. Ing Freeman, 2012, 109.
74. Ing Freeman, 2012, 132.
75. Ing Freeman, 2012, 49.
76. Burnett, 2004, 89.
77. Cited by Clair, 1964, 150–1.
78. Burnett, 1966, 69–70.
79. Burnett, 2004, 103ff.
80. Burnett, 2004, 103, 110.
81. Clark, P. 1983, *The English Alehouse. A social history 1200–1830*, 313. London and New York: Longman.
82. Clark, 1983, 120–1.
83. Burnett, 2004, 103–25.
84. Spencer, 2002, 298.
85. Jennings, P. 2011, *The Local. A history of the English pub*, 130. Keele: Keele University Press.
86. Girouard, 1984, 11.
87. Burnett, 1966, 147.
88. Ing Freeman, 2012, 190.
89. Girouard, 1984, 206.
90. Girouard, 1984, 200.
91. Wilson, R.G. 1998, 'The changing taste for beer in Victorian Britain', R.G. Wilson and T.R. Gourvish eds, *The Dynamics of the International Brewing Industry since 1800*, 95. London: Routledge.
92. Burnett, 1966, 12, table 4.
93. Burnett, 1966, 58; Paston-Williams, 1993, 286.
94. Drummond and Wilbraham, 1939, 343.
95. Spencer, E. 1897, *Cakes and Ale*, 207. London: Grant Richards.
96. Burnett, 1966, 178, 180.
97. Burnett, 1966, 178.
98. Tombs, 2015, 627.
99. Burnett, 1966, 214–15.
100. Burnett, 1966, 236.
101. Burnett, 1966, 255.
102. Burnett, 1966, 233.
103. Burnett, 1966, 235.
104. Burnett,1966, 268, 269.
105. Burnett, 1966, 270ff.
106. Burnett, 1966, 277, 278.
107. Burke, T. 1947 [1930], *The English Inn*. London: Herbert Jenkins Ltd.
108. Burke, 1947 [1930], 160.
109. Burke, 1947 [1930], 172–4.
110. Batchelor, D. 1963, *The English Inn*, 27–30. London: B.T. Batsford.
111. Fothergill, J. 1931, *An Innkeeper's Diary*, 170. London: Chatto & Windus.
112. Fothergill, 1931, 186.
113. Fothergill, 1931, 170.

114. Fothergill, 1931.
115. Fothergill, 1931, 134.
116. Fothergill, 1931, 154.
117. Selley, E. 1927, *The English Public House As It Is*, 31. London: Longmans, Green and Co. Ltd.
118. Selley, 1927, 69–74.
119. Gutzke, D.W. 2004, *Pubs and Progressives. Reinventing the public house in England 1896–1960*, 226. DeKalb, Illinois: Northern Illinois University Press.
120. Selley, 1927, 32.
121. Selley, 1927, 34.
122. Gutzke, 2004, 227.
123. Gutzke, 2004, 142.
124. Gutzke, 2004, 142, 143.
125. Mass Observation, 1987 [1943], *The Pub and the People. A Worktown study by Mass Observation*, 209. London: Cresset Library.
126. Gutzke, 2004, 143.
127. Burnett, 1966, 278.
128. Nixon, J. 1983, *The Public House*, 12. Hove: Wayland Publishers.
129. Nixon, 1983, 12.
130. Jennings, 2011, 219; Thornton, T. 2014, *Brewers, Brands and the Pubs in their Hands*, 64. Kibworth Beauchamps: Matador.
131. Jennings, 2011, 219.
132. Nixon, 1983, 12.
133. Jennings, 2011, 218–19.
134. Barker, L. ed. 2001, *Public Houses. Market report plus*, 7. London: Key Note.
135. Thornton, 2014, 77.
136. *The Observer Magazine*, 06.08.2017: 22.
137. Key Note, 2003, *Public Houses. Market report*, 9. London: Key Note.
138. Haydon, P. 2001, *Beer and Britannia*, 269. Stroud: Sutton Publishing.
139. Haydon, 2001, 282–3.
140. Haydon, 2001, 288, 289.
141. Millns, T. 1998, 'The British brewing industry, 1945–95', R.G. Wilson and T.R. Gourvish eds, *The Dynamics of the International Brewing Industry since 1800*, 155. London: Routledge.
142. Thornton, 2014, 229.

Part II
The Rise of the Gastropub

5

Publicans Between the State and the Brewers: A Subordinate Relationship

Chapters 1 and 2 have focused mainly on the relationships between publicans and their customers in past centuries. As small entrepreneurs, publicans' business success was also crucially shaped by the way the state regulated and taxed their pubs, as well as by the terms on which they became connected to their suppliers of alcohol, the giant brewers.

State Regulation of Pubs

Throughout most of the period covered in this book, establishments that sell alcohol consumed on the premises have had regulation of their trade imposed on them. Regulation and control have weighed much more heavily on pubs than on the other two types of hostelries and, given their chief customer base, on the working class. Pub regulation is therefore not unreasonably regarded as an instrument to control the working class.[1] Another state instrument to influence pubs is taxation. Regulation has an exceedingly complex history, with much variation through the four centuries. For the earlier centuries, only some of the most significant Acts and their effects will be covered. The bulk of the chapter deals with more recent regulation and taxation of pubs that have continued to shape their economic fortunes at the present time and form the background to the rise of gastropubs in the twenty-first century.

Regulation from the Seventeenth to the Nineteenth Century

From 1660 onwards, regulation imposed by the central state has been executed by justices of the peace/magistrates at the county level and has been complemented by legal control through the courts and, in later times, the police. Brewster Sessions issued or withdrew licences annually, and the middling sorts or so called 'chief citizens' and church ministers brought continual pressures on magistrates at parish level to repress alehouses they regarded as causing disorders,[2] though not always with great success.[3] A licence usually was tied to the restriction of the opening hours and to a proscription of certain activities within pubs, such as gaming, handling stolen goods, tippling, and meeting with prostitutes. Licensing was never a merely technical administrative measure. As Clark points out, from the seventeenth century onwards 'official intervention and supervision played an influential role in deciding the numbers, location, organisation and activities of alehouses and public houses'.[4]

The chief motivation for government intervention was to influence publicans in such a way as to reduce both drunk and disorderly and alleged subversive behaviour of drinkers. Concern about this behaviour came from organizations that viewed the alehouse as a competitor—particular religious organizations—or as subversive to the established order and politicians' reputation. This latter concern was expressed mainly by the 'better sorts' and by politicians and their mouthpieces in the press. Alehouse drinking was additionally seen as causing poverty and as increasing the expense on poor relief.[5] Another motive for state intervention, particularly from the eighteenth century onwards, was the preservation of the sobriety and health of industrial workers, as well as of soldiers. In the nineteenth century, some elements in the Temperance Movement had perhaps altruistic motivations also, being mindful of the socially harmful impact of alcohol consumption on the drinkers and their families,[6] though fear of disorder was never far away. At the current time, the adverse effect of excessive alcohol consumption on health is the main preoccupation.

A big milestone in the history of regulation came in the 1820s and the early 1830s. In 1828, the Licensing Act was passed. This Act consolidated existing licensing law and remained the basis of the licensing system until 1910.[7] The Act enabled justices to refuse new licences and withdraw existing ones, furnishing them with an efficient instrument to reduce unruly houses. This set aside almost 300 years of legislative history,[8] during which justices' power had been less intrusive. This measure was very effective in reducing drunkenness and it enhanced the respectability of the working class. As the Act made publicans responsible for drinkers' good conduct and asked for accountability, it imposed conditions that only the owners of the larger and better-managed pubs could fulfil out of their own means. It thereby drove many publicans into the arms of the brewers, creating 'tied houses'.[9]

The Beer House Act 1830 liberalized the sale of beer in an effort to counteract the much-bemoaned spread of gin consumption. This Act took a step backwards and allowed almost anyone to sell beer, provided they obtained an excise permit, but not a licence. This led to a rush of setting up new beer houses, usually much more poorly endowed than the public houses. The latter continued to require a full licence to sell wine and spirits, as well as beer. Additionally, the duty on beer was repealed. As the Reverend Thomas Page put it: 'If Satan himself had had a seat in the counsels of the nation, the Beer Act was the very kind of measure which the great enemy of mankind would have suggested.'[10] The politicians behind the Act, however, justified it by claiming that it would benefit the working classes. However, an 1869 Act bowed to widespread pressure and introduced the licensing requirement also for beer houses. Beer houses subsequently declined rapidly.[11] The more regulated public house had not been irreparably damaged by the competition from the beer house. By 1870, people talked again about the 'golden age' of the public house.

In the late nineteenth century, the more relaxed attitude by the authorities towards public houses evaporated again. A new regime of strict regulation of the public house was a response to campaigns by a combination of social, political, and religious forces. A series of measures to curb public drinking and suppress political radicalism was enacted, and licences were selectively withdrawn.[12] The Sunday Closing Bills of 1883, pushed through by the Temperance Movement, were the first of many to restrict Sunday drinking hours.[13]

Regulation in the Twentieth and Twenty-First Centuries

Another important spurt in regulation occurred during World War I, in order to keep fighting men sober. A Central Control Board, created in 1917, was given powers in designated areas vital to the war effort to place restrictions of all kinds.[14] This time it included a substantial cut in opening hours, as well as a weakening of the alcohol content of beer. The price of beer also soared. Most of these restrictions were retained even after the War; Jennings concludes: 'All these changes appreciably altered the world of the pub and helped to change its character for much of the rest of the century.'[15]

After World War I, in the 1920s and 1930s, it was unanimously observed that alcohol consumption and drunkenness had significantly declined,[16] and hence no drastic new regulation was contemplated. Despite some increase in drinking during World War II, the longer-term trend proved to be downwards.[17] At the same time, the brewing industry had faced relentless contraction.[18]

At the end of the twentieth century, when pubs and drunkenness were no longer regarded as a danger to social order, the licensing system became liberalized once more as part of the general trend towards market liberalization. In 2001, this new government stance towards pubs also became reflected in the transfer of the responsibility for licensing from the Home Office to the Department of Culture, Media and Sport. Two years later, the old licensing system by justices was discontinued and transferred to local authorities. The Licensing Act of 2003, extending opening hours, was heralded as helping both breweries and licensees, as well as customers. However, in permitting longer opening hours, the Act has been connected with new surges in drunkenness and has been indicted for going against all the warnings on the harmful impact of alcohol on health. However, the alliance between the government and the breweries against the working class had come to an end.

Liberalization of the licensing process led to a very considerable increase in licensed premises. A substantial lengthening of opening hours for the first time since World War II benefited particularly the town centre mega pubs. An increase in drunkenness, particularly among young people and now also women, has attracted widespread condemnation. Robert Tombs probably speaks for many when he says, 'town centres across the land were regularly taken over by the shambling hordes of the tipsy'.[19]

Concern about alcohol consumption and binge drinking is now focused mainly on health consequences. The free and unregulated flow of beer and alcohol from pubs and, more so, from supermarkets is raising serious concerns. It has greatly increased the incidence of liver disease and the costs of treatment for the NHS. The half-hearted measures by neoliberal governments to reduce health hazards, relying on voluntary self-responsible industry action, is deemed to have been ineffective, according to a recent study by the Institute of Alcohol Studies.[20] Police powers were increased to cope with the ensuing drunken disorder, and now, as then, no other business is so closely watched by the police authorities as the pub.

Taxation of Pubs

From the very beginning, a second important aspect of government control of pubs was the raising of revenue for the state. The revenue raised in the process of imposing high taxes on alcohol became a very substantial part of government income. The excise machinery was already a well-developed and efficient money-raining machine in the late seventeenth century and has continued to be a favoured state strategy up to the present day. For much of the eighteenth century, excise on drink was a principal pillar of the British treasury[21] and enabled governments to fund the wars both against the French and the Americans during that century. At its highest level, during the wars with France, such tax counted for over half of the state's revenue, and through the succeeding century it came to around a third.[22] With the reduction of drinking from the end of the nineteenth century and the accelerating closure of pubs during the twentieth century, this income has been somewhat reduced. But it remains nevertheless true that tax on drinking, in various forms, furnishes governments with a substantial income that rarely meets with much criticism. By foregrounding the issue of public order or, more lately, consumer health, such imposition of taxes on alcohol can occur with relative impunity.

Even though licensing laws were relaxed at the beginning of the twenty-first century, excise duty remained a very popular government instrument right up to that time. It remained the second highest in Europe. Brewers claim that, between 1979 and 1993, excise duty, together with VAT, increased the price of beer by 59 per cent in real terms.[23] Yet, consumers have not been greatly deterred by this increase in prices.

High and discriminatory taxing of pubs continued into the twenty-first century. Tax on beer has been continually rising since 2008, when the beer tax escalator, positing the automatic rise in the price of beer by 2 per cent above inflation every year, was first introduced by the Labour government.[24] This meant that the cost of an average pint of beer of £3.22 included 54 pence VAT and 55 pence of excise duty, making it the dearest pint in the European Union (EU).[25] This taxation strategy united pubs and breweries in strong opposition. The most disastrous effect of taxing on pubs has been its discriminatory nature, with supermarket sales of alcohol being far less taxed than those in pubs. This has occasioned a serious displacement effect, with people 'tanking up' with cheap supermarket alcohol before visiting pubs at night (for more details on this differential taxing strategy, see section The Pub Sector in the Twenty-First Century). Pubs also pay more VAT than other small and medium-sized enterprises.

Pubs and the Brewing Industry

Historically, the conditions for running a public house and the livelihood of publicans were nearly as strongly influenced by the giant breweries as they were by state regulation and taxation.

From the 1700s onwards, large brewers were a considerable force, although there was much geographical variation. Breweries supplied most of the public houses' beer, and fixed prices among themselves. Brewers were often not only leading figures in local politics[26] but, through powerful lobbying, also became influential in Parliament. Moreover, politicians realized that they had complementary interests. The state used breweries to keep order among ale and beer houses by gradually eliminating the weaker ones and by excluding those of bad repute.[27] Breweries were thus co-opted by the state as guardians of public order.

However, the interests of brewers and the state diverged when it came to the duty charged on beer. The lobbying power of large brewers, for most of the time, prevented these charges from becoming too high. The breweries fared particularly well when the Tories were in Government. The Tories were 'accepted friends of the drink interest', and the Liberals its enemy. The alcohol graph, as well as the pub rebuilding graph, rose and fell with Tories in government.[28] The following ditty by Sir Wilfred Lawson, a Liberal Party politician, cited by Girouard,[29] sums up the results of the 1896 election as follows:

> 'Tis Beer, as is to statesmen known,
> Supports the altar and the Throne,
> T'Was Beer this Parliament returned
> And the great Tory triumph earned.

The powerful position of the brewers versus publicans became further consolidated when independently-owned houses gradually became tied to particular breweries. Samuel Johnson commented in 1781 that ownership of pubs by the larger breweries offered the latter 'the opportunity to grow rich beyond the dreams of avarice'.[30] The 'tied system' was not at first a strategic goal of breweries, but developed as publicans became indebted to brewers. However, it became an ingenious device to further strengthen brewers' monopoly and gain free rein over beer prices. As publicans obtained unfavourable terms from the brewers they were tied to, they tried to even out the situation by increasing the adulteration of their beer.[31]

Writers are not agreed on the timing and scope of the 'tied houses' system, which developed unevenly according to socio-geographical context. According to Brandwood et al.,[32] this movement started in London from the seventeenth century onwards. High prices of land and of leasing, as well as of equipping a pub, first drove London publicans into the brewers' arms. Burnett,[33] in contrast, claims that the practice began in the eighteenth century. It is agreed, however, that, by 1850, the majority of pubs were held in this way,[34] and, over the course of the century, a few major brewers came to dominate the market. Jennings further suggests that the brewing interest was significant only in the major cities.[35] The capital, in particular, provided a large and concentrated market where the brewing industry was in the vanguard of industrialization.

From the 1870s, brewers started to list on the stock market and, with their new-found cash, bought other smaller brewers and acquired many more public houses. Most pubs were now leased by breweries. By 1900, only 4 per cent of publicans brewed themselves, and by 1913, as many as 95 per cent of houses were tied, according to the Brewers' Society.[36] By eliminating many medium-sized companies, breweries had become large powerful companies, spearheading the British movement towards corporatization.

At the beginning of the nineteenth century, brewing was already being carried out along mass production lines in London and a few other urban centres, using the new steam technology.[37] By 1815, the eleven leading London brewers were turning out two million barrels of fairly uniform beer from other than brewery suppliers. Wines, though, still had to be bought through breweries.

However, this legislation did not release many publicans from dependence. Very few of the pubs relinquished were bought by sitting tenants.[48] Instead of being owned by the big brewers, many became owned by big pub companies, or pubcos, as they came to be called. The latter were of two types:

1. Financial services (e.g. Namura) or property development companies that do not involve themselves directly in the pub business. They were said to be 'nothing more than property companies deriving revenue from rent'.[49] In their hands, pubs became financial assets that were bundled into packets, securitized, and traded frequently, leading to a constant churn.[50]

2. Pub companies, whose main business it is to acquire, develop, and manage pubs as a business while remaining free from the control of brewers. Examples of pubcos are Enterprise Inns, Discovery Inns, and, the largest of them, Punch Taverns, which had more than 9,200 pubs in its estate by 2006.[51] Their hard-nosed chief executives were often former brewery managers who took out huge loans to buy large numbers of pubs.[52] Two of the biggest, Punch Taverns and Enterprise Inns, consequently 'are battling to stay on top of huge debt mountains'.[53] The pubcos were remote from their licensees and became 'a target for widespread resentment and disaffection among publicans'.[54] Pub companies are a heterogeneous collection. Some have a common format for all their pubs, others aim at a range of brand identities. Some of them favour managed over tenanted pubs to secure their brand strategy.

This greater diversification of ownership has not greatly improved matters for publicans and their customers. Most pubcos, using their centralized purchasing power, entered agreements with a specific brewer whereby, in exchange for a price rebate, they tied themselves to that brewer. However, price savings are not passed on to customers, and pubcos are said to have made huge profits through the gap between what they pay breweries for bulk purchasing and what they charge licensees of pubs.[55] Like breweries before them, the large pubcos are said to force their tenants to buy beer from them at inflated prices, and many charge rents for premises above market rates.[56] Pubcos were an unwanted by-product of the Beer Orders Act.[57] Verticalization, with all its attendant evils, continued by the back door.

Moreover, many breweries retained a pub estate of tied houses that became only reduced in number. Even after the Beer Orders Act of 1989, introduced to destroy brewers' exaggerated market power by de-verticalization, brewers found ways to maintain high prices and dependency among tenants.[58] Breweries changed tenancy conditions, causing a marked deterioration in relations a year—around one-fifth of national production. Three years later, it was found that they operated a cartel for fixing both the price and the strength of porter. Significantly, only one conviction for adulteration of beer was ever obtained against the great houses.[38] However, outside London, small and medium-sized brewers prevailed during the first half of the nineteenth century, although breweries in towns like Burton, Norwich, and Liverpool were quite large. By 1914, only forty-seven firms accounted for 45 per cent of all beer brewed, with the ten largest producing a quarter of the total.[39]

During Victorian times, brewers' money had important influence on pubs' interiors, which were made splendid—with mirrors, brass fittings, painted glass, and light fittings—to make the pub enticing to drinkers.[40] The architectural splendour of pub buildings was often in stark contrast to the poverty of the drinkers who frequented it. Brewers aroused a lot of hostility, both among publicans and among their customers. They became depicted as ruthless, monopolistic, and profiteering businessmen foisting inferior beer on the public at high prices. Any publicans who protested were in danger of losing their licence.[41]

Despite the fall in the number of pubs and the amount of beer consumed after 1870, the brewers did not lose their dominance.[42] If anything, they became more powerful after the merger mania of the 1950s when the industry became further concentrated. By 1967, according to a Monopolies Commission report on the supply of beer, the then six largest brewers—Bass Charrington, Allied, Whitbread, Watney Mann, Courage, and Scottish and Newcastle—accounted for 70 per cent of all beer production between them and owned over half of the on-licences in Britain.[43] From the 1970s, breweries countered the decline in beer drinking by diversification through conglomerization and international expansion and by further take-over activity. One response to counter these developments was the founding, in 1971, of the Campaign for Real Ale (CAMRA).[44]

It was only in 1989 that the state—in the form of the Conservative Secretary for Industry, Lord Young—at last moved against the brewers' monopoly, embodied in the 'tied houses' system. The report on the brewers, published by the Monopolies and Mergers Commission (MMC), implied 'the domination, manipulation and neglect' of pubs by brewers.[45] This move against the big brewers occurred despite the fact that the brewers had made large donations to Party funds and against the protest of nearly 100 Conservative MPs.[46] The introduction of the Beer Orders Act, following the thorough report by the MMC, compelled breweries that owned more than 2,000 pubs to sell off half of the number exceeding that figure by 1992. About 12,000 pubs were disposed, and the proportion of beer sold to the free trade rose substantially.[47] Tenants of tied houses were additionally allowed to sell a guest beer—a cask-conditioned real ale—and to buy non-alcoholic drinks with tenants, and many long-serving licensees left the trade at that time in protest against higher rents.[59] Many breweries and pubcos no longer seek to replace tenants who come to the end of their contract. The property boom during the first decades of the twenty-first century has made the sites on which pubs stand often more valuable for alternative development than retaining the pub in operation.

Nevertheless, the level of concentration in the brewing industry has fallen, and the industry has become more diverse. Five of the major companies left brewing altogether, turning themselves into pubcos or other highly diversified entertainment conglomerates, and twelve substantial companies closed.[60] Many smaller regional and local brewers now make up the industry, with around twenty-seven family brewers now providing its backbone.[61] This indicates the reduced profitability of brewing and the comparatively high gains connected with pub/real estate ownership, particularly in cities. Examples of big breweries that turned into pubcos are Mitchells and Butlers, Brakspear, and Whitbread.[62] At the current time, the former Big Six brewers have become reduced to the Big Four. Moreover, most of the big brewers are now foreign-owned.[63]

Legislation in 2002, offering tax incentives for breweries making fewer than three million litres of beer per year, has provided the impetus for the founding of micro-breweries, usually brewing craft beer/real ale. This movement towards brewing and drinking local micro beers, also supported by CAMRA, took off very quickly. It appeals to the same customer demand for small local producers using more natural production methods as in the field of gastropub food.

The duty rises on a sliding scale—so that middle-sized companies still pay less than large multinational corporations (MNCs). The number of breweries grew from 140 in 1970 to 1,700 in 2016. The tax break may shave off as much as a fifth of their costs for micro-breweries, giving them a 25–30 per cent price advantage. The 1,300 micro-breweries now found all over Britain are becoming competitors to the old established big brewers.[64]

But neither medium-sized nor micro-breweries are very satisfied with their revenue. Medium-sized breweries claim that 'they are the squeezed middle between multinational drinks companies and state-subsidized microbreweries'.[65] Twickenham Fine Ales—the oldest micro-brewery at twelve years—says many micro-breweries are struggling. Customer loyalty is difficult to gain, with drinkers constantly wanting to try new ales. Pubs support this thirst for novelty by constantly changing their guest beers.

In January 2012, MPs unanimously passed a motion criticizing the government's lack of action on pubcos' treatment of pubs. The pub companies, however, opposed any statutory code of conduct imposed on them.[66] After continuing protest from industry stakeholders, a statutory code of practice was finally published in 2016 for pubcos/breweries with more than 500 pubs in their estate, while a voluntary code was introduced for companies with pub estates below 500. This code renders the continuation of the tie system voluntary for licensees and gives tenants the right to opt for the charge of a 'Market-Rent Only'. The legislation also established an independent pubs adjudicator who would enforce a statutory pubs code for England and Wales. The code has been hailed as a 'New Dawn' for the industry by its trade paper.[67] It is, however, too early to say whether these new codes, together with the abolition, in the 2013 budget, of the 'duty escalator' for beer and the cut in price of a pint by 1 pence, will improve the economic situation of pubs substantially.

With the giant English breweries finally in decline themselves, pub companies have taken their place to exploit publicans tied to them. After being squeezed for centuries between the state and the large breweries, the rapid decline of pubs has finally achieved some reprieve from the state. Whether the state's recent intervention on the side of publicans will curb the power of pubcos and, if so, whether it has come in time to halt pub decline, remains to be seen.

The Pub Sector in the Twenty-First Century

Figures issued by the British Beer and Pub Association (BBPA) for 2014, for a total of 51,900 pubs,[68] detail ownership status of pubs as follows. They attribute ownership of 9,800, or 19 per cent of pubs, to breweries; 17,500, or 34 per cent, to pubcos, and 24,600, or 47 per cent, to independent owners (see Table 5.1).[69] Hence, although independently-owned pubs constitute the single largest group, the proportion of tied pubs (either to a brewery or a pubco) still form the majority. Of the brewery-owned pubs, about half are run by employed managers (rather than by tenants) and of the pubco-owned ones, just over a third are managed. Of the independent owners of the so-called 'free houses', some lease the pub to a tenant, while others are owner managers of pubs. (The BBPA statistics do not make the latter distinction, nor do they single out the community-owned pubs.)

Table 5.1. Pub ownership in 2014

Type of owner	No of pubs	% of pubs
Brewery	9,800	19
Pub company	17,500	34
Independent owner	24,600	47

Source: British Beer and Pub Association 2015, 68.

Although pubs have been closing for many decades, closures have accelerated significantly in the twenty-first century. Since 2000, the total number of pubs has fallen by 15 per cent.[70] A peak closure time was between January and June 2009, when fifty-two pubs ceased trading every week,[71] showing the impact of the recession. Statistics from CAMRA suggest that in 2015, an average of thirty-three pubs per week closed,[72] and in 2016 this rate of attrition continued. There are now about 48,000 pubs in Britain, down from about 70,000 in 1980.[73] Losses have been heaviest in urban areas, particularly in pubs outside city centres, which were traditional drinks-led community locals.[74] It is widely held that purely drinks-led pubs were the most likely to go under and that, except in a few exceptional areas, they are no longer viable today. Moreover, the biggest growth in turnover in 2016 came from an increase in food sales.[75] What this means for pubs' business model will be discussed below.

Despite an accelerating decline of pubs, in socio-economic terms, they still feature prominently in the contemporary economy. In 2016, the value of the total pub market was estimated at £21.55 billion.[76] Pubs still provide a highly significant share of employment—higher than do either restaurants or hotels[77]—and they continue to be embraced by a significant proportion of the population. In 2017, women constituted a slightly lower proportion (49 per cent) than men of pub visitors in general, and their proportion shrank to 45 per cent in premium (the highest priced) pubs.[78]

The ownership of pubs by breweries and, also by pubcos since the 1989 Beer Orders Act, connected with the infamous beer tie and the higher beer prices charged to tenants/lessees, is considered by many industry insiders as one important contributory factor to pubs' endangered economic viability. Brewers' wholesale prices are appreciably higher for tenants than for independents. CAMRA claims that '[tied] licensees pay up to 50 per cent more for beer than a free-of-tie publican'.[79] What is more, these prices have increased significantly in recent years. A 2015 report on this problem by a Parliamentary Committee (Business and Transport Section) states:

> The evidence to the Committee shows that the wholesale prices offered to tied licensees have increased at a much faster rate than the wholesale prices to the free trade or the off-license sector with the result that lessees of tied pubs are at a significant competitive disadvantage.[80]

Additionally, it is suggested that pub companies/breweries charge tied pubs 1.3 per cent more rent than is paid by free-of-tie tenants.[81] The parliamentary report concludes: 'This could be a major factor in the failure rate of tied public houses in recent years'.[82]

The fact that many more tenanted than privately owned pubs prove economically unviable further supports this conclusion. An IPPR survey, published in 2011, found that landlords in 57 per cent of tied, as opposed to 43 per cent of landlords in free houses, said they were struggling financially. There were 46 per cent of tied landlords, as opposed to only 22 per cent of free ones, earning less than £15,000 p.a.[83]

Many of my interviewees confirm this negative view of pubcos and big breweries: pub closures are due to 'the big heavy hand of the pubcos. They basically were property companies and squeezed the margin. The economics of this fell apart with the recession'.[84] 'The tenanted model failed so badly. They only worry about shareholder value and raise the rent when you do well.'[85] An independent Cambridgeshire publican, who had previously run a tied pub for two years, commented scathingly: 'Greene King and Enterprise Inns—I wouldn't touch them. They are greedy.' The Cambridgeshire owner of several gastropubs spontaneously exclaimed: 'I would run a mile from Greene King.' A rural Suffolk pub, tied to Adnams, has to subsidize the price of beer in order to prevail in the competition with local freeholder pubs. Their drink margins are quite a bit lower than their food margins because 'Adnams take 10 per cent of turnover'. A London pub, tied to the pub company Enterprise Inns informs me: 'There is a tie on all our taps, at an inflated price... We bear all the risks.'

However, the 'tied' model and government taxation are by no means the only reason for the decline of pubs. The first and most fundamental reason is that the British, known as heavy drinkers in centuries past, have greatly reduced their *public* intake of alcohol. Figures from the BBPA show the amount of beer we drink per capita is down from 113.9 litres in 1990 to 66.2 litres in 2013.[86] Drink-driving convictions have fallen by 41 per cent in England and Wales since 2000.[87] An Office for National Statistics (ONS) study, spanning ten years, found that, in 2013, one in five adults and 40 per cent of 16–24 year-olds described themselves as teetotal.

This decline in alcohol consumption is attributed to successful campaigns that stigmatize drunk driving and connect heavy drinking with health hazards and an irresponsible use of the NHS. However, the positive response to such campaigns must also reflect the changed composition of society and the rapid expansion of the middle class. Young working-class men, because they are no longer concentrated in the same workplace in large numbers, have stopped drinking in the same pub, and this has undermined the group culture of hard drinking. Additional social reasons for the decline in pub visits include the availability of many other entertainment venues, including home entertainment such as television programmes, video games, and engagement in social media. Most recently, rises in living costs, together with stagnating wages, also have played their part in curtailing spending on non-essentials.[88]

People who still wish to consume a large amount of alcohol can obtain it far more cheaply from supermarkets, due to differential taxing by governments of alcohol consumed in pubs and alcohol from supermarkets drunk at home. In 2016, for the first time since industry records began, more beer was sold by supermarkets and off-licences than by pubs. A comparison with 2000 shows that, then, two-thirds of all beer was consumed in pubs.[89] This development is driven by the big difference in price between the two types of venues, with an average price increase of 38 per cent on the price of lager drunk in pubs between 2005 and 2015.[90] This is yet another example of government favouring big business at the expense of small enterprises like pubs. Many of my publican interviewees comment with bitterness on what they regard as unfair competition from supermarkets that has increased in recent years. 'Supermarkets have completely destroyed the drinking pub.'[91] The smoking ban, introduced in 2007, is said to have acted as an additional accelerator of pubs' decline.

Last, several commentators lay the blame on pubs themselves, suggesting that there are still too many pubs competing with each other. Thus, a market report on the sector suggests that 'there are probably still too many pubs in operation for the market to support'.[92] The parliamentary committee report on pubs and the beer tie agrees: 'There may be up to 6,000 surplus pubs in the UK forming 12% of the market.'[93] But such a claim ignores their uneven closure and their disappearance, particularly, from large swathes of countryside.

Others claim that pubs have only themselves to blame for closure. The *Good Pub Guide*, in 2014, created a furore when, after forecasts of further major closures, they commented that it 'was high time they closed their doors to make way for more energetic and dynamic licensees' and that 'bad pubs at the bottom of the pecking order' are 'happy with indifferent food, drink, service and surroundings'.[94] Several of my interviewees, too, suggest that the landlords of failed pubs have not done enough to make their pubs attractive to potential customers, who now have much raised expectations of what a night out should provide. 'I think they have not kept up with the times, have remained mainly wet-led. You need an attraction to get people out of their own houses where they drink.'[95]

The survivors—of whom my interviewees are prime examples—demonstrate very clearly that, to keep their customers, landlords/ladies often go to great lengths to keep them satisfied. They continually diversify and update their offers and introduce new attractions to customers who can be claimed by many other entertainment venues. They hold quiz or jazz nights, offer facilities to view major sporting events, do occasional gastronomic dinners, run a cookery school, maintain a petanque pitch or organize a communal sing-song at Christmas time. There appears to be a continuous pressure to think up new attractions, on top of good beer and food. It is obviously not easy to make a profit, particularly in a rural pub. A gastropub is not a business that enables its owner/tenant to get rich quickly, but more often is a labour of love. When asked about the profit aimed for, the following response is not untypical: 'It [the profit margin] is terribly tight, there is no room for profiteering. Profit also is very uneven through the seasons. This is a very competitive industry, and there is constant pressure to keep prices down.'[96]

In sum, the 'great pub dying' has many social and economic causes, particularly improvements in leisure time provision and raised legal and social intolerance of drunkenness. Viability is additionally undermined, particularly in London, by private property companies that charge excessive rent for their pubs.

In the 2010s, as a consequence of the much increased incidence of pub closure, a new category of ownership was brought into being, namely the community-owned pubs. This still very modest trend towards community pubs has been facilitated by a new law that allows pubs to be named as assets of community value by the local council if people nominate them as such. It has additionally been aided by the popularization of new ways of financing that raise money from a group of small investors who value the setting up/preservation of a particular local enterprise and do not necessarily expect a large return on their investment.[97] According to CAMRA, in 2014 more than fifty pubs across the UK were being run by their communities.[98]

Such rescue operations are motivated not merely by the wish to preserve a community hub, but also a distinctive building. The pub is viewed as an asset that adds character to a place and stems the steady onward march of homogenization of towns/villages and of people's consumption habits by corporate chains. However, a transfer of pub ownership to a local community and the longer-term success of such a pub is a very complex matter. Hence, the overall number of community-owned pubs has remained small. It has not become a significant device to stem the pub dying.

Endnotes

1. Smith, M.A. 1984, *The Public House. Leisure and control*. Manchester: Centre for Leisure Studies, University of Salford; Nixon, J. 1983, *The Public House*. Hove: Wayland Publishers; Haydon, P. 2001, *Beer and Britannia*. Stroud: Sutton Publishing; Jennings, P. 2011, *The Local. A history of the English pub*. Stroud: The History Press.
2. Wrightson, K. 1982, *English Society, 1580-1680*, 227. London: Hutchinson.
3. Hailwood, M. 2014, *Alehouses and Good Fellowship in Early Modern England*, 78ff on the seventeenth century. Woodbridge: Boydell Press.
4. Clark, P. 1983, *The English Alehouse. A social history 1200–1830*, 340. London and New York: Longman.

5. George, D. 1925, *London Life in the XVIIIth Century*. London: Keegan Paul, Trench, Trubner & Co. and New York: Alfred Knopf; Clark, 1983; Jennings, 2011.
6. Jennings, 2011, 52.
7. Jennings, 2011, 56.
8. Clark, 1983, 333–5.
9. Smith, 1984, 9–10.
10. Cited by Jennings, 2011, 57.
11. Clark, 1983, 338.
12. Clark, 1983, 256–7.
13. King, F.A. 1947, *Beer has a History*, 143. London: Hutchinson's Scientific and Technical Publications.
14. Jennings, 2011, 183, 185.
15. Jennings, 2011, 189.
16. Jennings, 2011, 194.
17. Jennings, 2011, 193.
18. Millns, T. 1998, 'The British brewing industry, 1945–95', R.G. Wilson and T.R. Gourvish eds, *The Dynamics of the International Brewing Industry since 1800*, 142. London: Routledge.
19. Tombs, R. 2015, *The English and their History*, 830. London: Penguin Books.
20. *The Observer*, 08.11.2015: 4.
21. Clark, 1983, 3; Jennings, 2011, 135.
22. Jennings, 2011, 135.
23. Millns, 1998, 155.
24. *Mailonline*, 04.03.2013.
25. *Mailonline*, 04.03.2013.
26. See, for example, Riddington Young, J. 1975, *The Inns and Taverns of Old Norwich*, 7. Norwich: Wensum Books.
27. Clark, 1983, 182; Smith, 1984, 10.
28. Girouard, M. 1984, *Victorian Pubs*, 214. New Haven and London: Yale University Press.
29. Girouard, 1984, 85.
30. Cited by Brandwood, G., Davison, A. and Slaughter, M. 2011, *Licensed to Sell. The history and heritage of the public house*, 20. Swindon: English Heritage.
31. Burnett, J. 1966, *Plenty and Want. A social history of diet in England from 1815 to the present day*, 83. London: Thomas Nelson and Sons.
32. Brandwood et al., 2011, 17.
33. Burnett, 1966, 83.
34. Clark, 1983, 184; Jennings, 2011, 97ff; Brandwood et al., 2011, 17.
35. Jennings, 2011, 97.
36. Jennings, 2011, 100.
37. Burnett, 1966, 103.
38. Burnett, 1966, 83.
39. Burnett, 1966, 83.
40. Girouard, 1984; Jennings, 2011.
41. Jennings, 2011, 101.

42. Jennings, 2011, 202.
43. Millns, 1998, 143.
44. Jennings, 2011, 220.
45. Thornton, T. 2014, *Brewers, Brands and the Pubs in their Hands*, 34. Kibworth Beauchamps: Matador.
46. Crompton, G. 1998, 'Well-intended meddling: the Beer Orders and the British brewing industry', R.G. Wilson and T.R. Gourvish eds, *The Dynamics of the International Brewing Industry since 1800*, 162. London: Routledge.
47. Crompton, 1998, 164.
48. Crompton, 1998, 165.
49. Haydon, 2001, 314.
50. Thornton, 2014, 142.
51. Jennings, 2011, 220.
52. Haydon, 2001, 312.
53. Thornton, 2014, 211.
54. Thornton, 2014, 154.
55. Thornton, 2014, 206.
56. CAMRA, 2015, at http://www.camra.org.uk/home.
57. Thornton, 2014, 50.
58. Crompton, 1998, 164.
59. Crompton, 1998, 162.
60. Crompton, 1998, 164.
61. Thornton, 2014, 221.
62. BBPA (British Beer and Pub Association) 2015, *Statistical Handbook*, 72, at <http://www.beerandpub.com/news/new-bbpa-statistical-handbook-paints-comprehensive-picture-of-the-drinks-sector>.
63. Thornton, 2014, 221.
64. *The Observer Magazine*, 08.11.2015: 52.
65. BBPA, 2015, 72.
66. Helsey, M. and Seeley, A. 2015, *Pub Companies, Pub Tenants and Pub Closures. Background History (up to 2014)*, Standard Note SN6740, 33. London: House of Commons Library, Business and Transport Section.
67. *The Morning Advertiser*, 21.07.2016.
68. A 2017 MCA pub market report puts the number of total outlets lower, at 47,548.
69. BBPA, 2015, 68.
70. BBPA, 2015, 68.
71. Smithers, R. 2014, 'Pubs closing at rate of 31 a week', *The Guardian*, 12.08.2014.
72. *The Guardian*, 31.01.2015.
73. McVeigh, T. 2016, 'Landlords appeal to regulars: carry on drinking'; *The Daily Telegraph*, 31.03.2016: 17.
74. Helsey and Seeley, 2015.
75. *The Morning Advertiser*, 22.06.2016. Abridged version available at https://www.morningadvertiser.co.uk/Article/2016/06/23/MCA-UK-Pub-Market-Report-2016.
76. *The Morning Advertiser*, 22.06.2016.

77. Key Note 2003, *Public Houses. Market report plus*, 28. Hampton: Key Note.
78. MCA 2017, *Pub Market Report, 2017*. Abridged version available at http://www.mca-insight.com/market-intelligence/market-reports/the-uk-pub-market-report-2017/554174.article.
79. Key Note 2013, *Pub Market Report*. Hampton: Key Note.
80. Helsey and Seeley, 2015.
81. Key Note, 2013, 31.
82. Helsey and Seeley, 2015, 6.
83. Helsey and Seeley, 2015, 9.
84. Owner of Essex coastal pub, 2016.
85. Landlord of Suffolk rural pub, 2016.
86. BBPA, 2015, 92.
87. BBPA, 2015, 8.
88. Key Note, 2013, 10.
89. BBPA 2015.
90. BBPA 2015.
91. Owner of Essex rural inn, 2016.
92. Key Note 2013: 28.
93. Helsey and Seeley, 2015, 24.
94. Smithers, 2014, 3.
95. Publican of Cambridgeshire pub, 2016.
96. Cambridgeshire owner of two rural pubs, 2015.
97. Boffey, D. 2015, 'Hands off our Pub! Towns battle developers to keep the local open', *The Observer*, 19.04.2015: 12–13.
98. *Big Hospitality*, 23.04.2014, at http://www.bighospitality.co.uk/Hot-Topics/Pub-Trends.

6

The Gastropub and its Divided Identity: Drink, Food, and Sociality

This chapter analyses the dual organizational identities of gastropubs as both pubs and restaurants and explores the resulting tensions/conflicts, as well as the synergies and opportunities of the dual focus. This entails the consideration of four important aspects of gastropubs. I focus first on how publicans balance the demands of drinkers with those of diners. I then explore how committed they are to satisfy both kinds of demands, as well as considering what strains and tensions are involved in the balancing act. The second aspect is what kind of food gastropubs are offering, in terms of its style and complexity, and the ambiguity surrounding this activity as well. Third, I explore how these two aspects impact on, and shape the sociality developed in, gastropubs. Fourth, and finally, I ask how publicans conceptualize the dual organizational identity for themselves and how they present their organization to potential customers by means of labelling their establishment.

Before this exploration of gastropubs' organizational identity, I place them into the wider context of pubs in the twenty-first century. Chapter 5 showed that, since the Beer Orders Act of 1989, pubs, particularly tied pubs, have been squeezed hard economically, both by the pub companies (pubcos) and by the state. This, together with social reasons and a decline in drinking, has led to a continuous and alarmingly high rate of pub closure, particularly of mainly drinks-led pubs situated in suburban areas and in villages.

Publicans have reacted to the multiple onslaught on their livelihood by diversification of what they offer. After many centuries of concentrating mainly and even solely on alcoholic drink, they have moved to make food a prominent part of their business portfolio. The percentage of food in turnover has increased from 8.8 per cent in 1990 to 30.1 per cent in 2012—an increase of 21 per cent—whereas, for other products, market share has remained fairly stable.[1] The necessity to sell food is emphasized both by the trade press and by all my interviewees. The 2013 market report by Key Note confirms that

The Gastropub and its Divided Identity

'the long-term trend is towards dry-led establishments, that is pubs that derive the majority of their revenue from food sales'.[2] The sentiment expressed by a chef in a rural Essex pub that 'a pub would die if you did not serve food', sums up what nearly every publican in my sample feels. This turn towards meals responds, at the same time, to a significant change in demand; namely, the much increased incidence of eating out, rather than cooking at home, during recent decades. As Paddock et al, have shown,[3] in 2015 eating out has become a regular and normalized social activity, and almost everyone in their large sample was familiar with it. While there are many more restaurants than pubs catering for eating out,[4] pubs have greatly increased their share of this market.

Given the low capabilities of publicans in providing food in the past (as shown in Chapter 4), it is interesting to investigate how various kinds of pubs have handled the transition during this century and what kind of food they are able to provide. There is a very large variety among pubs in the food they offer and in the proportion of turnover it constitutes. The type of food offered ranges from mainly snack food, via bought in frozen meals, to proper meals and elaborate menus. Much food served by pubs, particularly by the large chains, is still not cooked on the premises but comes from a central hub. It is often delivered frozen and only reheated in the pub kitchen and is thus lacking in taste and originality. Such food preparation relies neither on a well-equipped kitchen, nor on the presence of a skilled chef, but simply requires storage and refrigeration facilities. Some of my interviewees talk about this food with horror. Where the quality of food has significantly increased, such as in some of the city centre mega pubs, standardization of meals may detract from their appeal.

My interest in this chapter is solely with that still relatively small, but growing part of the pub sector where meals are freshly cooked on the premises by a professional chef (often with an *haute cuisine* background) from produce comparable in quality to that of a good restaurant and mostly locally sourced. Moreover, the sale of food constitutes a significant proportion of the pub's turnover. For a definition of the illusive concept of quality, I have relied mainly on the Michelin Pub Guide, *Eating Out In Pubs*, as well as judging the quality myself by eating in nearly all the pubs where I have conducted interviews.

Some Features of the Gastropub

What, then, distinguishes the institution of the gastropub (also referred to as pub restaurant) from the conventional restaurant? Such a distinction is not easy to make and in some cases not clear-cut. *First*, and foremost, despite a strong focus on food, publicans reserve a space in proximity to the bar for customers who wish only to drink. *Second*, they offer one or more menus that feature not only sophisticated dishes but also bar meals and/or traditional English food, and all at a high level of quality. *Third*, they preserve a pub atmosphere by keeping some elements of pub décor, such as a prominent bar with several beer pumps, open fires, simple wooden (and often oddly assorted) furniture, flagstone floors, and a garden or terrace, as well as eschewing table cloths. *Fourth*, publicans offer a relaxed and more casual service and implicit code of behaviour. *Fifth*, their prices, relative to those of upmarket restaurants, are competitive, both for food and, more so, for wine, and are pitched at a level that will not deter the main customer base of pubs. All this combined leaves some room for the development of a type of sociality conventionally associated with pubs, and described at length in Chapter 2. Establishments qualify as a gastropub if their landlord/lady adheres to all or most of the above criteria. Drawing on my sample of forty gastropubs, in London and in thirteen different counties, I will examine each of the above aspects in turn. First, however, some general features of my sample.

My data confirm that the gastropub is still a relatively young institution, acquiring critical mass only in the twenty-first century. Table 6.1 shows the year when interviewees had opened their gastropub. Most of the pub restaurants visited are businesses founded since 2000. Only three started up in the 1990s. I was able to interview the landlord whose pub, The Eagle in Clerkenwell, was the first to be called 'gastropub' in 1990. The owner of a rural Rutland gastropub, opened in 1991, says: 'There was nothing in the market like this when we started.'

This recent emergence reflects both the increased expectations towards food among the English and the availability of higher-level chefs to meet, as well as strengthen, these expectations. Such chefs, operating as head chefs, have been trained by the upmarket restaurants that became prominent from the early 1990s onwards and were often rewarded with one or more Michelin stars.[5] Their presence, as both owners and head chefs, is very prominent in my sample of pubs. However, the recruitment of good chefs remains very challenging.

With the exception of London gastropubs, they are mainly among rural or suburban destination pubs, and some of my rural pubs are in very small villages (with only 200–300 inhabitants) and/or in fairly isolated locations.

Table 6.1. Period when licensees started their current business

1990–1999	7
2000–2005	7
2006–2010	13
2011–2015	13
Total	40

The population of these villages is generally affluent, with a higher weight of NRS (National Readers' Survey) grades A and B (professional and managerial strata) than in the British population as a whole.[6] A driver of this development has been a flight by young chefs from the astronomically increased property prices in cities, and particularly in London. Such pubs are usually very handsome and large properties, often centuries-old former inns. Of the pubs visited, eleven date from before the eighteenth century, eight from the eighteenth and nineteenth centuries, and only one was built in the twentieth century, while the remainder could not be dated. Several of them were formerly part of an estate owned by the local gentry/aristocracy, and one is still owned by the local aristocrat. There are also historical connections with monasteries that dominated a village in earlier centuries, and, in London, with a livery company that built the pub in the early nineteenth century and still owns it. Such pubs, in addition to churches, are usually the only local buildings in the neighbourhood that provide a link with Britain's historical past and the forms of ownership characterizing these periods. Thoroughly renovated by their owners, the pubs lend distinction to the area in which they are located.

Relationship Between Drinking at the Bar and Dining

Gastropubs have a dual organizational identity, but, despite regarding both identities as vital, the two identities are ordered and dining tops the hierarchy. Hence, all the pubs I visited give more space to dining than to drinking. Yet, all the publicans, except five, nevertheless preserve a space for guests wishing to drink only. This consideration for 'mere' drinkers is extended even though drinking at the bar constitutes only a small part of their income—between 5 and 20 per cent. A *small* crowd of 'drinkers only' is not necessarily due to an unwelcoming landlord. It is influenced also by the size of the village community. In rural pubs, the ban on 'drink-driving' makes being a local inescapable, and most of the villages in which they are based have a population of only a few hundred people.[7]

Publicans have found various ways to divide the space available to them into open and more secluded spaces. Many publicans do not take reservations for the bar and are instead working on the principle of 'first come, first served'. They do not set up tables for lunch or dinner there, but welcome both drinkers and diners. Some pubs maintain a small reserved area for drinkers near the bar in the middle of the pub. Both strategies favour integration and even aggregation of identities. A degree of compartmentalization is adopted in the next two approaches: a bar area divided from the dining room in a small, separate room, but the circular bar is still shared with the dining room; or a room at a different level, usually on the ground floor, through which dining only customers must cross. Last, unlike restaurants, nearly all pubs (thirty-five in my sample) have a garden and/or terrace which, though weather-dependent, greatly increases the number of covers as well as spaces for drinkers. 'This place lives and dies on sun shine' one publican told me, and 'living' here refers to greatly increased revenue.

Publicans have found different solutions to preserving the two-fold business focus and maintaining a dual organizational identity. Yet, for nearly all of them it has created a business with a 'split personality' that creates more or less psychological discomfort for the landlord/lady. They have to spend a lot of effort to manage the integration of identities. An East End publican, for example, who goes to considerable length to preserve the bar service of this once traditional boozer—long-time local drinkers, for example, pay a lower price for their beer—nevertheless finds it his greatest concern 'to get the customers right...to preserve a balance between the boozers and the dining room'. However, customers who prefer the dining room to the boisterous sociality of the bar—among them City Boys[8] for whom a special list with more expensive wines is kept—must nevertheless cross the fairly narrow bar space. Hence, he and his partner have to try to keep the level of inebriation in bounds and 'are very strict with bad behaviour'. The manager of a Suffolk inn that attracts a much more middle-class clientele nevertheless finds the dual focus of dining pubs a challenge: 'We are both a village pub and a restaurant. It is hard to get the balance right. Villagers may question our prices.' The last quote also indicates that publicans have to consider different external stakeholders—local and further afield destination diners—who hold divergent expectations. A different kind of tension between the demands of the bar and kitchen is experienced by a Worcestershire publican/chef, who realizes that drinkers want the publican behind the bar, but cannot always satisfy their demand because he, as head chef, is needed in the kitchen.

Publicans display varying degrees of willingness and enthusiasm for the preservation of the old pub function, and some no longer care to maintain both identities. Thus, a small number of publicans keep the space for drinkers only grudgingly or not at all, as most of the profit comes from the food side of the business. 'We only take "drinks only" customers during the week, and they can always sit outside.'[9] This pub derived only 5 per cent of its profit from such customers. A pub in Wales, recently bought by a couple with restaurant experience, keeps a space for drinking, but eschews the pub 'spirit': 'I try to avoid the pub feeling.' Some landlords/ladies keep up the semblance of a pub simply because it is expected by the villagers: 'We initially had an area kept just for drinkers, but it did not pay...We would like to use the word "restaurant" more but it would be frowned upon.'[10]

A second and much larger group (thirty-five) of publicans really value the 'bar' function and like and embrace the atmosphere it creates. 'The atmosphere of a pub is important to me'[11] and 'I have worked quite hard at keeping it a pub'[12] are a couple of the remarks made to me. The latter publican reinforces this position when he says that he calls his establishment 'a pub, with a restaurant attached'. 'A gastropub', he adds, 'would be a restaurant, with a bar attached.' Another chef-owner of a rural Suffolk pub tells me that, on buying the pub three months before the interview, they reinstated the bar area. Although the income from it is no more than £100 a day, he finds it to be 'really good for the pub restaurant'. Drinkers often come back for food as well. The landlord of a rural Essex pub 'is passionate to keep the pub' and has gone to some lengths to preserve the ambience of a traditional pub. An Oxfordshire rural pubkeeper answers my question of what distinguishes his establishment from a restaurant with 'the fact that the welcome is the same for drinkers and diners'. A London publican, too, despite maintaining a very upmarket dining room and menu, embraces the pub atmosphere: 'I have worked as a student in pubs and have always been a lover of the English pub...the future is in casual dining, and the pub is the perfect melting pot.'[13] This stance is confirmed by the fact that the pub has become a real hub for local people, hosting all sorts of community clubs and associations.

Some publicans are ambivalent and/or found the dual focus initially difficult to accept. Even when they embrace the dual focus, publicans may find it difficult to manage it on a day-to-day basis. A Cambridgeshire village publican at first was strongly oriented to provide high-end food, and rented the pub because he wished to open a restaurant: 'I am here for the food, rather than the beer.' After eighteen months in the pub, he has nevertheless come around to the recognition that a village pub needs to cater for local demand. He renovated a space by the bar, reserved for drinking customers: 'A village pub should be welcoming.' The manager of another Cambridgeshire pub with a relatively small bar area finds it a real challenge to allocate the space between the two groups of customers during the week, when the dining room is closed: '[It is challenging] accommodating everyone with different expectations, to decide [on use of tables] between diners and drinkers. I don't know when walk-ins will come. It is hard to decide between the two groups of customers, but I like the diversity'. A more extreme case of conversion is represented by 'a Thai restaurant' in a pub'. The ethnically Thai landlady and chef, who are strongly wedded to a Thai identity in terms of food, décor, and even dress for front-of-house staff, nevertheless have come around to the view that the village needs a community centre—'we need to keep it for the local people'—and have made available a space for drinkers. Moreover, they now recognize that what at first appear to be mere drinkers may become diners in time: 'I did not like it [drinking at the bar] at first, but now I think it works well. They come into the bar, and they smell Thai food, and they come back [for dining].' All these publicans indicate that they see some synergy between the two kinds of business.

A Kent publican represents a particularly interesting case of identity ambivalence. On the one side, he sees himself mainly as a restaurateur. He chose the pub—which was awarded a Michelin star—because it is not situated in a village, in order to avoid locals telling him what to do with it, i.e. preventing him from developing his high-end food. His 'drinking at the bar' trade is very small, and he does not 'do' pub staples at all. On the other side, however, he fully embraces the pub ambience, particularly its relaxed and casual nature. Until recently, he has kept the brewery-owned pub, by his own admission, in a somewhat 'grotty' state and has scorned the refinements aimed for by other Michelin-starred places. A lot of ordering occurs by going to the bar. He does not believe in any kind of staff uniform, has his two menus and his wine list chalked up on blackboards only, and maintains two open fires. In sum, there is clearly a pub environment and ambience without, however, any availability of pub food.

Most of the above landlords/ladies run pubs in areas with largely middle-class housing so that the social gulf between drinkers and diners is not very big. More effort to combine the drinking and dining side has to be made by London publicans, where the constituency of patrons is more socially diverse. A particularly sustained effort has been made by the two chefs who run 'the last proper local pub on [London's] Hackney Road'. It was formerly just a local boozer—a pub on an estate built in the Victorian period for the working class by the philanthropist Lady Burdett-Coutts. My interviewee describes the pub as 'a boozer with a high level of noise' where 'old boys who have been drinking here for twenty years still come in every day'. They drink Foster's rather than real ale and may knock back up to ten pints per sitting. They are mainly older males, and their wives may still come to call them home. The traditional pub environment has been faithfully preserved and just improved 'for greater comfort—this is still a pub'. Yet, the relatively confined space of the bar must make it difficult to keep the different social worlds of drinkers and discerning diners from colliding. The food is fairly robust, but it nevertheless must appear as strange to the working-class boozers as their drinking habits do to the middle-class diners. For the two landlords, despite their very real good will vis-à-vis the drinkers, these inherent, though not necessarily open, clashes of taste appear to be of some concern. They are passionately committed to providing a distinctive dining experience and 'are not interested in promoting alcoholism'. There is a hope that the changing demographics of the neighbourhood may gradually 'allow us to change the balance' and thereby lessen the sometimes stark contrasts. However, such long-time mere 'boozers' are now the exception in pubs: 'Locals who prop up the bar and provide entertainment are gone',[14] and the 'boozer and wife-beater is a dying breed'.[15]

To sum up, publicans of gastropubs, in trying to create both a restaurant and preserve the pub function, face the dilemma of balancing revenue against the best use of space for both activities while creating an atmosphere that benefits both drinkers and diners. As I shall explore next, a dilemma presents itself equally strongly in the choice of food offered and the types of menus adopted.

Menus and Food Offered: Ambivalence and/or Uncertainty About Culinary Style

At a time when a plurality of cooking styles and food from different national origins around the globe jostle for the attention of the chef and the diner, described as menu pluralism,[16] it is hard for chefs to develop their own distinctive styles of cuisine. The chefs of gastropubs not only share this problem, but have it magnified by the demand to develop both a sophisticated cuisine that makes the pub a dining destination and a menu that incorporates bar food. The bar food consists mostly of relatively simple, traditional English dishes that are valued by a significant proportion of the customers, such as fish-and-chips, pies, and sandwiches. Pubs are compelled to offer several menus because they 'need to be flexible for different customer groups and occasions'.[17] 'The make-up of the food is very complex—it is a broad spectrum.'[18] 'This is a very big and complex operation.'[19]

Each type of food embodies different culinary styles, and thereby carries the danger that a distinctive culinary identity becomes obscured. The aggregation of organizational identities causes concern and discomfort, particularly as highly-trained chefs, difficult to recruit and to replace, are held to be important internal stakeholders. Publicans have dealt with this dilemma in a variety of ways. The landlady of a Welsh pub, who has recently managed to recruit a talented head chef, regards him as a more important stakeholder than the village customers. The latter, in a recent survey of their views, have asked for more bar food, but the landlady is not disposed to accede to their demand. A Yorkshire chef, in contrast, who came to the pub from a fine-dining restaurant, points out: 'I think you have to adapt to customer needs. I use less expensive ingredients and local produce. We are a business. As I get older, I don't mind so much [doing bar food as well].' A Cambridgeshire landlord who is mainly intent on providing complex dishes, and most enjoys cooking for the gastronomic menu, nevertheless came to recognize that: 'I have to do simple dishes at lunchtime. There is an expectation of pub meals.' Yet another chef, representative of several other chefs, perceives no dilemma at all: 'It is no problem for me [to cook both more complex dishes and traditional pub food].

I can put as much love and attention into fish-and-chips as into *haute cuisine* [dishes].' Thus, aggregation of organizational identities is handled in different ways by internal stakeholders. It is evident that acceptance of dual identities has taken time for some chefs, and a few have opted for the deletion of one culinary identity.

One may argue that these latter publicans no longer run a gastropub, but a restaurant. Yet, most of them still display a great attachment to the 'drinking at the bar' side of the pub and fully recognize its value for the overall ambience of the place. A north London pub with very upmarket food, heavily inspired by French and Italian cuisine even in its bar snacks, nevertheless describes itself on its website as offering 'outstanding food and service while retaining a traditional pub atmosphere' and as 'welcoming diners and drinkers alike'. That this is not mere window-dressing, but reflects the publican's personal values, becomes clear during the interview. 'We wanted the physical environment of the pub... the atmosphere is really unique. It's buzzing, really lively. That's what I am most proud of.'

At each end of the continuum, pubs either offer predominantly sophisticated cuisine or mainly pub classics (Table 6.2). Those that try to satisfy both customer bases—the majority of my respondents—either offer two different menus or divide one menu into different sections. As pub classics tend to be staples and restaurant-type dishes to be more subject to change, the latter may also be offered on a daily changing blackboard list of *Specials*. These Specials, as one respondent puts it, 'are more ambitious', while another describes the blackboard as a means 'to showcase the finest quality food, what the chefs are most proud of. It is the very opposite of the "Offer" menu' (a reasonably-priced set menu available during the week). Several chefs prepare a few 'special meals' during the year where the gastronomic menu, accompanied by matching wines, gives them an occasional chance to display their skill and creativity to a higher degree.

High-level chefs, because they are hard to recruit and retain, are important internal stakeholders and are therefore provided with opportunities to satisfy their professional expectations, as well as being expected to provide traditional pub classics. They have to balance cooking the inventive and/or complex gastronomic food they love to cook with what will sell. Integrating the demands of the different types of food poses varying degrees of discomfort for many of the chefs, as well as for publicans. One respondent, whose head chef

Table 6.2. Proportion of pub classics/bar snacks of all food offered (in %)

None	1–20	21–40	50/50	50+	No answer	Total
4	10	9	9	9	3	40

is Michelin-trained, emphasizes the dilemma this dual focus poses. He points out that preparing traditional English pub food is not satisfying for such an accomplished chef: 'It is a challenge. It is a slow transition. You lose a lot of custom if you change too quickly.' Another publican, who employs both a Michelin-trained chef and a 'highly talented *MasterChef* winner' in the kitchen, also acknowledges the dilemma: 'This is an area of confusion. Are we confused, or the whole sector of the market? It becomes quite difficult to decide where we are.' He further mentions the considerable adjustment this demanded from the chefs: 'The chefs would initially complain about making "fish-and-chips", but they now understand.' This acceptance was eased by the fact that there is some division of labour in this kitchen between those preparing pub classics and those doing more complex dishes. An Oxfordshire publican of a Michelin-starred gastropub (not in my sample) met with the resignation of his talented head chef and four other chefs when, after facing a decline in bookings, he wanted to respond more to customer demand for 'pub grub'.[20] A Suffolk publican with an excellent Michelin-trained chef is very aware what an asset he is to the business: 'Keeping the chef [is the greatest challenge I face]. I am going to make him my partner. I spend time massaging his Ego and give him a lot of autonomy.'

Yet, several chefs have reached a compromise, particularly if they are also the owner/lessee of the pub. The wife of a Suffolk chef tells me: 'G. has trained as an *haute cuisine* chef but he has adapted to local demand. We do different sorts of food—traditional dishes and Specials [on the blackboard] which will be more upmarket.' G. further has had opportunities for cooking more upmarket food in the substantial external catering the pub does (25 per cent of their income) and by putting on periodic gastronomic, wine-matched dinners for a small group of local connoisseurs. This 'allows him to do more creative cooking'.

In yet another group of pubs, the dilemma is partially solved by a spatial division between dining rooms and bar, each served by its own menu. A London pub employing a chef trained by Prue Leith, who is still attached to French regional cuisine, aims to capitalize on his training and experience by turning the pub into a dining destination. But at the same time, the separate menu for the bar area will cater for simpler local demand by offering a number of traditional pub dishes. Or from the chef-patron of a pub with a rating of 7 in the *Good Food Guide*: 'It is my own business. We now look at what people want to eat but appreciate it at a higher level...I don't mind doing the bar food but I do it at a higher level. It has to have the same integrity.' These chefs manage to integrate the demands of a dual organizational identity most of the time.

However, the bulk of meals sold is not of the traditional fairly basic English variety. More sophisticated and more complex dishes may belong to a variety of national styles of cuisine, of which Modern British is one. As culinary styles have symbolic properties that express meaning, namely the identity of the chef and the pub, chefs are concerned to develop a distinctive and clearly recognizable style. Their style is, however, only partly shaped by running a gastropub, but is heavily influenced by their training and past experience. Most of the chefs have a professional background of having trained and/or cooked in upmarket and even Michelin-starred restaurants, as well as having spent a *stage* in France. They have learnt to use French techniques of preparation. 'X got trained classically. He has used the techniques to adjust simpler dishes and giving them that "wow" factor.' A Lake District chef agrees: 'French was a good foundation. You can experiment on this basis. I keep French [culinary principles] in my head.'

Yet, most of the chefs are prepared to keep down the level of complexity and refinement of their dishes in favour of more robust pub-like dishes. Some chefs have adjusted easily, while others have changed over time, taking note of customer demand: 'I like to do French cooking, but I had to change.'

Some chefs manage to integrate the two identities by declaring themselves prepared to apply their skills to basic English bar food, such as fish-and-chips or burgers. Several point out to me that their fish-and-chips are not of the ordinary sort, but use the best and freshest ingredients, as well as sometimes slightly modern twists in their preparation such as making the batter with beer. A Welsh pub serves its burger on toasted focaccia bread, with blue cheese and onion marmalade and sea salt fries, and a Suffolk landlord described his beef burger thus: 'It is an elevated version. 100 per cent good beef, in a light brioche bun.' Another pub staple, steak, may be lifted into the realm of luxury food by serving a Chateau Briand steak with a red wine or a peppercorn sauce. Likewise, sandwiches often are a bit more special, such as smoked salmon and crab with lemon mayonnaise, or roast beef with tomato, watercress, and horseradish mayonnaise. The traditional English apple tart may be slightly jazzed up by being served with a green apple sorbet. One chef speaks for many when he says: 'I apply restaurant preparation for pub dishes.'

Constant innovation and artifice, found among upmarket restaurant chefs, is rarely extolled by gastropub chefs. The publican of The Eagle, the first London gastropub, points out: 'It is "robust" and never "exquisite" food.' The chef of a rural gastropub says: 'We are more substance over style.' An Essex chef tells me: 'There is not so much emphasis on presentation [as in a restaurant], more on flavour and sourcing.' A London pub produces 'unfussy dishes' and opts for 'simple presentation', while a Cambridgeshire chef describes his food as 'hearty and wholesome'. Gastropubs generally aim for greater simplicity, without completely abandoning inventiveness. The greater simplicity of their dishes is not merely to match the robust pub environment. It is additionally dictated by the much greater number of customers they cater for, compared with high-end restaurants. Numbers of covers their pub restaurants can cater for in the bar and the restaurant, as well as the number of weekly meals actually served, are usually significantly higher than in conventional restaurants. The numbers in Tables 6.3 and 6.4, furthermore, exclude the often considerable number of meals served on outside tables during good weather, as well as in private dining rooms. More than 500 weekly covers served is not unusual among the larger pubs restaurants in the right location, i.e. near population centres. Such numbers rule out a highly elaborate style. One pub owner describes his food like this: 'It is not fine dining, it is high-end casual dining.' As Albert Roux once observed, the English pub restaurant will become the equivalent of the French bistro. Or, maybe, the rise of bistronomie in France from around 2005 onwards copies many features of the gastropub, but labouring under lesser identity problems.

Chefs' narratives of culinary identity are often ambiguous. Several are not able to put a label on their cuisine or are vague in their description. When asked to define his culinary style, one chef tells me: 'It is however I feel in the morning. I struggle with labelling. I do not watch what other people do.' A similar response comes from the chef-owner of a Suffolk country pub: 'It is so hard to say [what my culinary style is]. I worked for so many different chefs and have had so many different influences, including Indian ones.'

Quite a few chefs embrace a plurality of culinary styles: 'Modern European, but I do Asian things as well. There are no rules, we are not strict.'[21] A Hertfordshire chef cooks 'English, French and rustic Italian food'. Or, from a chef who had worked in continental Europe: 'The food is traditionally

Table 6.3. Number of covers pubs can cater for

<50	3
50–75	15
76–100	11
>100	11
Total	40

Table 6.4. Weekly number of covers actually served*

<300	5
301–500	9
501–750	5
751–1,000	5
Not asked	16

* I asked about weekly covers only after twenty-four interviews had already been completed.

Table 6.5. Chefs' culinary style

No clear style	Modern British	French and British	Modern European	International/Asian	Total
10	14	6	6	4	40

British rural food. There is a little bit of continental influence but I try to keep the Spanish and Portuguese influence to a minimum.'[22] However, overall, Asian influences are only slight (see Table 6.5). The fact that the majority of chefs—fourteen respondents—claim to practise a Modern British style 'to match', as one landlord states, 'the nature of the pub', will be explored further in Chapter 7 when I examine culinary nationalism.

A somewhat schizophrenic approach to the food served is additionally complicated by the division between the week-day and the Sunday menu. Yet, nearly all chefs (thirty-six out of forty)—whatever their professed style—offer an English 'proper' Sunday lunch, with one or more roasts with trimmings on the Sunday menu. The Sunday lunch time trade constitutes a very significant part of their overall income—it is their 'bread and butter', as one chef explains. Customers expect it, and Sunday roast dinners consistently attract a large number of diners, up to 550 covers in a London gastropub on some Sundays and at least 100 covers in most pubs. A national competition for the Best Sunday Roast Dinner, sponsored by *The Mirror*, has doubtlessly contributed to this popularity. On Sundays, the chef largely has to put his high culinary aspirations on one side or, at most, can display his *haute cuisine* credentials for some of the starters and desserts. A rural Lancashire chef, whose refined food has received a rating of 7 in the *Good Food Guide*, is frank about the adjustment required when cooking large numbers of Sunday traditional lunches: 'I do what people want. I run one type of establishment for four days a week and a different type of establishment on a Sunday.' Again, two different culinary identities have to be integrated in some way—that of a traditional English institution and that of a fine-dining establishment. It is managed by compartmentalization—this time in a temporal sense—or by deletion. Another rural chef, however, who cooks food to an exceptionally high standard (he had been awarded a Michelin star at the time of the interview), is not prepared to make a compromise even on Sundays. Despite the high financial reward of offering traditional Sunday lunch, he does not wish to offer it: 'It is very hard to do a roast around bits of halibut and similar more refined dishes.' Rather than compromising, he prefers to scrape by with a low and uncertain profit.

The continuing importance in British eating-out habits of meat and two vegetables has been noted also by other, earlier studies of eating out, such as those of Warde and Martens[23] and of Beardsworth and Keil.[24] The significance of these choices in symbolic terms will be discussed below. In sum, publicans/chefs are very aware that a section of their customers expect to find both pub classics and/or English dishes on their menus, and most try to accommodate this demand, even though it causes some chefs psychological discomfort.

Chefs realize that some diners are conservative in their eating habits, while others are eager to try new dishes and tastes, and even one and the same person, depending on the circumstances, will embrace traditional dishes at one time and at other times opt for novelty. A significant segment of modern diners is what has been described as omnivore. One way in which chefs can please both themselves and the diners who wish for something more than just plain English food, while not offending the traditionalists, is to restyle something English by adding a few surprising and even innovative foreign elements to the main ingredient, such as a more exotic accompaniment or merely a foreign flavouring. Warde and Martens,[25] too, noted that a prevalent consumer strategy was distinguished by 'the search for small differences which confer a touch of individuality without taking a person too far from the group norm is a most important consumer strategy'.

Gastropubs try and distinguish their cooking and culinary style from restaurants also by practising a pronounced localism in their sourcing, opting for the freshness of the produce and local specificity to distinguish their culinary style. Additionally, interviewees like to see their pubs as embedded in the local community, and to support local farming and business. As many of the pubs in my sample are situated in rural areas, local sourcing comes more easily than in the mostly urban restaurants. The way their localism is linked to signalling the Britishness of their pub will be explored in Chapter 7.

Moreover, in their sourcing practices, chefs of rural pubs use a lot of personal ties to obtain their high-quality and fresh ingredients. Thus, for example, pub customers may also become suppliers and friends, emphasizing the closer and denser networks that still obtain in rural areas. A chef in rural Hertfordshire, for example, tells me that he has used the same local butcher for fifteen years and that he has 'a local guy for game'. The owner of a Cambridgeshire rural pub tells me that 'a local guy brings pigeons he has shot, as well as fish caught in a near-by lake'. Even in urban pubs the bring-and-barter phenomenon is known, with, for example, a huntsman bringing in game in exchange for food and drink in a Bedford pub restaurant.

The most extreme case of local sourcing is found in pubs where food comes from their own farm/garden, where foraging is extensive, and/or where in-house artisan-style production of foods—by baking, preserving, and smoking food stuffs—is prevalent. Thus, a rural Suffolk pub, in the summer, is 75 per cent self-sufficient. The publican not only grows his vegetables, salad leaves, herbs, and fruit, but also raises his own pigs, sheep, goats, ducks, geese, and turkeys on five acres of land adjoining the pub. Any fruit left over is bottled or pickled and turned into sorbets. The legendary *Sportsman*, on the Kent coast, not only forages on the sea shore and in near-by woods, but also engages in substantial in-house production, making its own bread and butter, as well as smoking fish and meat in-house. A number of other pubs also make their own terrines, ice creams, breads, butter, pickles, etc., and may even brew their own beer. The chef proprietor of a north Essex country pub with a garden of one acre declares it a 'vanity project' which does not necessarily pay, but can be a useful marketing tool. A London pub, situated at a very busy road junction, carries this trend of self-provision *ad absurdum*. Its owners grow herbs and salad greens in its very small, and probably thoroughly polluted, roof garden.

To sum up this section, chefs betray a notable degree of uncertainty and/or ambivalence about the food they serve. This is due to two main factors. First, providing simple English bar food and Sunday roasts as well as more complex and original dishes makes it difficult to develop a clearly articulated culinary style. Second, even within their more ambitious cuisine they have problems of culinary identity. Many wish to match the style of their cuisine to the traditional British institution of the pub and thus portray themselves as offering Modern British food (this is further discussed in Chapter 7). They inevitably come up against the fact that British food, for several centuries, has not had a *haute cuisine* character nor an inspiring culinary tradition.

Drinking in Gastropubs

The number of pure drinkers varies between days of the week, being usually the highest on Friday nights. Overall, heavy drinking is rare in gastropubs. People who want to indulge in it either frequent the few remaining boozers or, in the case of young people, visit the city centre mega pubs. Beer is still a mainstay of pubs and is now divided into the traditionally sold keg and bottled beer and the relatively new cask beer. There has occurred a major shift in consumption towards the twice-fermented and non-pasteurized cask ales—the so-called real ales—often from micro-breweries. One publican informs me that the change in demand occurred only about four years ago. Whereas Key Note claim that cask ale now has 52 per cent of the market,[26] the BBPA cite only 8.2 per cent for 2015.[27] The former estimate seems to be more credible than the latter.

Real ale has fermented in the vessel from which it is served, and the carbonation is entirely natural, not forced. Cask beers do not keep well once opened and generally require more attention than keg beers. All the publicans interviewed nevertheless keep one or more real ale, and the busier urban pubs will stock a large number. A London publican, for example, stocks eight draught beers from London craft and micro-breweries. Many vary the cask beers they stock by having a succession of guest beers, as the demand by drinkers for novel real ales seems inexhaustible.[28] The number of cask beers pulled depends on whether pubs are tenants of breweries/pubcos (where only one guest beer is allowed) or free houses, and on the volume of their general trade. For some publicans, the sale of real ales is connected explicitly with the authenticity they also aspire to in their food: 'I won't choose a beer that is not authentic' and 'good beer may become as important as good food', or 'having different cask guest beers is rather like changing the menu for food'. One publican does special events where food is matched to various ales, and another issues a beer list in addition to the wine list.

Serving meals, however, has significantly changed the drinking habits of customers. In all the pubs visited, a large majority of evening diners now drink wine, rather than beer, with their meal. However, many men start the evening with a beer—often at the bar—and then continue with wine, capitalizing on the flexibility of the pub environment.[29] They thereby also bridge the gap between a pub and a restaurant. However, this greater predilection for wine, according to a publican formerly employed in the wine trade, does not go together with a lot of knowledge of wine. This is confirmed by another publican: 'Even the professional classes find wine selection intimidating.'

Wine lists, in most of the establishments interviewed, are simpler than in upmarket restaurants. More importantly, they are very competitively priced, with low-priced (in the tens and twenties of pounds) to medium-priced (up to £35) wines predominating. The most expensive bottle of wine stocked, in most pubs, is below £50, although there are notable exceptions. A small number of landlords, who are particularly interested in wine, keep a few very highly priced bottles, even if they sell them only once or twice per year. Overall, then, the much lower prices for wines than in restaurants of comparable standards makes eating out in a gastropub a more affordable option.

The Nature of Service and the Sociality Encouraged

What sets the gastropub apart from a high-level restaurant is not only the food and drink served. The nature of the service that pubs are able to provide and the encouragement of a specific sociality traditionally associated with pubs are other prominent distinguishing elements. While the service can easily be described, it is less straightforward to ascertain whether the old pub sociality has been preserved, or whether the strong move to dining inhibits it to a significant degree.

The sociality cultivated among drinkers at the bar is now only a minority feature of gastropubs, as the number of diners—particularly in country pubs, but less so in big urban centres—often far outnumbers that of pure drinkers.

The number of 'drinking only' patrons varies considerably, from being very small—fifteen to twenty people (in most of the pubs visited) constituting 'a core local drinking crowd'—to being quite large (in several London locations and at weekends). However, the availability of the 'drinking at the bar' option is taken up also by many diners before they sit down or before they leave. 'There is a good mingling between people [who drink and who eat] —they are mainly from the village.'[30] 'I think the difference [between a restaurant and a pub] is on arrival. In a pub you go to the bar and order a drink and then try and grab a table. There is more freedom and flexibility.'[31] In the original gastropub, The Eagle of Clerkenwell, not only drink but also meals are still ordered at the bar, and this 'facilitates meeting people at the bar'. Even if you do not go to the bar, you can order draft beer and always real ale, thus benefiting from being in a pub restaurant. 'Local beers enhance the evening's experience. It pleases all members of the party—the blokes like the beer and usually have a beer first.' Also, customers cannot be neatly divided into drinkers and diners, but will come for a drink one evening and for a meal another.[32] Thus, an interviewed customer of a village pub in Cambridgeshire visits the pub on a Friday night to drink at the bar with friends, while his visits on a Sunday are devoted to enjoying a meal with his family. The fact that many customers easily integrate different expectations about gastropubs also eases the integration of different organizational identities for publicans.

Last and most important, the bonhomie created by drinking at the bar—in many of my pubs—spills over into the rest of the premises and is embraced by the landlord/lady because it spreads the 'proper' pub atmosphere. Eating in a pub restaurant differs, a Worcestershire publican points out, 'because you get the noise of the bar. It is a lot more relaxed'. Conversely, where old-style boisterous drinking around the bar has survived and diners have to cross the drinking space when arriving and leaving, this can also cause the landlord concern, especially as diners and drinkers may come from very different social groups.

Yet, it cannot be denied that the move to dining, and the 'small group' formation it entails, has undermined the old type of pub sociality to some extent. With its predominantly collective outlook and its broad inclusiveness of anybody who cares to join the drinkers, it is fundamentally different from the private and exclusive party gathering around a dining table. The former, in turn, goes with a more boisterous sociability. Seasoned drinkers who liked the old 'boozer' atmosphere will be deeply disappointed with what gastropubs have made of their old haunts. They would probably agree with the food critic A.A. Gill, who opined that 'food and pubs go together like frogs and lawn-mowers, vampires and tanning salons, mittens and Braille'.[33] Yet, even habitual bar flies prefer a gastropub to losing the pub altogether.[34] It is also worth remembering that alcoholic lubricants of sociability are, in any case, not what they were in the past—the quantity drunk and the level of drunkenness have decreased significantly in comparison with the past—although some of the London gastropubs prove to be an exception to this rule.

Moreover, sociality is not only developed by drinking together, but also by sitting at the same table to eat. The resulting commensality is associated with the development of reciprocal commitment among the diners.[35] 'Sharing food is held to signify "togetherness", an equivalence among a group that defines and reaffirms insiders as socially similar.'[36] In a similar vein, Freud observes: 'To eat and drink with someone was at the same time a symbol and a confirmation of social community and of the assumption of mutual obligations.'[37] One of my publican interviewees also recognizes this: 'The essence of eating out is the social side, it reinforces the bonds of humanity. What makes human beings is sitting around the table and eat together and speak.'[38]

Fischler additionally points to the renewal and strengthening of ties of family and friendship and the way it overcomes individualization, albeit in a less gregarious manner. As Fischler observes: 'Commensal festive occasions periodically bring together families dispersed in the course of life.'[39] They restore loosened links of kinship and bring together households dissolved with the dispersal of generations.[40] While it is widely feared that '"in eating without meals" eating has been de-socialised',[41] Sunday pub lunches with friends or family are important in at least partially re-socializing meals. In this way, the meal retains its symbolic significance.

These insights are confirmed by the empirical results of two large-scale British studies of eating out, conducted by Warde and Martens[42] and by Paddock et al.[43] When they questioned their interviewees on the pleasures of eating out, they consistently found that people valued the conversation around the dining table as much or even more than the food consumed. They confirm that food is tasty only because of the pleasure derived from eating it in good company. Warde and Martens find that 'eating out is more convivial than eating at home' because it provides for a more equal exchange around the table,[44] particularly for women, who gain a better chance to concentrate on communication rather than providing food. They rightly point out that, when looking at eating out, to have shared lively conversation and passed time in congenial company is often neglected.[45] Hence, although commensality constitutes a less gregarious and exuberant type of sociality, it is, at the same time, less superficial and may encourage stronger bonding. Warde and Martens conclude: 'Eating out is a major and expanding conduit for sociable interaction.' The practice of eating out provides a context for sociability and the maintenance of social networks of close relationships.[46]

Importantly, commensality and the atmosphere that surrounds it in pub restaurants differs in many ways from that in conventional restaurants with a similarly high level of cuisine. The casual, relaxed, and impromptu sociality of the bar has coloured also the service and atmosphere of the pub dining room. Customers may sit anywhere in the pub and can choose whether they want to be close to the more animated, loud, and sometimes 'rowdy' bar sociality, or whether they want to sit at a more secluded table where conversation can be conducted relatively undisturbed. They may choose to dine in the restaurant/dining room on certain occasions, such as for a family or a special celebration meal, but opt for a meal in the bar on other occasions.

Owners of gastropubs offer a new kind of service, pairing culinary erudition with an inviting and easy-going manner, and they offer flexibility. Every publican interviewed emphasizes the casual and relaxed atmosphere in the dining room. 'It is more friendly and less formal, more laid back...we have lots of friends here', as compared with the restaurant this Suffolk landlady had worked in before. Or: '[We provide] informality with food of quality and without fuss or high cost. We need this to be local with immediate comfort.' 'The service is more relaxed. To be engaging is more important than perfect service.' '[This pub differs from an upmarket restaurant in that] it is more informal. You can switch from eating to drinking, and you can go to the bar.' 'We offer quality without formality. Customers can use the pub as they choose. It is very flexible.' A Suffolk landlord, whose pub combines a prix-fixe menu of two courses for £15.00 with a collection of original paintings on the walls, well sums up the wide appeal of the gastropub: 'They [the customers] are looking for something more price-friendly and informal, yet we are posh enough for a calendar date.' Additionally, close ties between landlords/ladies and their many repeat customers are still common.

It is widely assumed that social bonds cannot easily develop between diners on separate tables. Publicans, in contrast, are at pains to point out synergy between the bar and the dining functions and to down-play the seemingly different organizational identities attached to each function. A good number of my interviewees identify both casual and arranged meetings between friends in the dining room, as well as the making of new friends across tables. Even a London publican finds 'that everybody knows each other. They have done all their life-cycle events in this pub'. The pub atmosphere and the presence of regulars among diners means that tables are often pushed together to increase sociability.[47] People talk across tables and afterwards go together to the bar.[48] The landlord of a small, rural Berkshire pub restaurant finds that 'people join together as if they were in a bar. The restaurant lends itself to it. It happens quite a bit'. In sum, bar and dining room of gastropubs are inter-related in many ways and thus serve to sustain at least some of the traditional pub sociality.

A greater informality manifests itself additionally in both the service and the décor. Front-of-house staff, with some notable exceptions, are not professionals—most of them are in casual employment and often have received only brief and basic training. One landlord is quite frank about this: 'The service is not as good [as in a conventional upmarket restaurant]. I can't get the staff.' A pub manager endorses the problem around training of front-of-house staff: 'There is so much turnover, when do you train? You have to keep it simple enough so that everyone knows what is going on.' Staff are more casually attired—there is no requirement for a house-style uniform in any of the pubs, but merely a demand for neat black clothing, an apron, and, in a few cases, a pub badge. Several interviewees allow jeans. Practicality and hygiene trump attractive appearance: jewellery and make-up are sometimes forbidden and flat shoes mandated. Customers, likewise, can enjoy a relaxed dress code. A Cambridgeshire publican comments: 'Customers are getting the eating-out experience but don't have to really dress up and be on best behaviour.' Another Cambridgeshire pub owner describes the resulting ambience like this: 'It's that homely, relaxed feeling. You can bring your dog in'.

Front-of-house staff pride themselves on their friendliness and approachability and on the absence of pomp. Tradition-bound formalities are totally rejected. According to the manager of a rural Suffolk inn: 'We don't use "Sir" or "Madam", and we don't place napkins on laps, and we don't hover around. We interact with customers when necessary.' 'You can have a good meal in a non-stuffy environment', according to a publican in rural Oxfordshire. A Lancashire publican agrees: 'No stupid rules. You shouldn't feel obliged to serving staff in any way.' The more casual nature of the service is also paralleled by the greater flexibility of the menu, which is much less constrained by the rules of fine dining. A Worcestershire publican tells me: 'In a sense, I could put anything on the menu. I do not have the rules you have in Michelin-starred restaurants. They are a lot more constrained.' A Yorkshire landlord agrees: 'We are happy for guests to have just a sandwich and a drink. There is no stipulation whatsoever of what to have.' Or, '[in a pub] you can be more multi-faceted, very adaptable'. A rural Cambridgeshire landlord pinpoints the use of the blackboard as an important means for gaining menu flexibility: 'With blackboard dishes, we can run out, but we must never run out with "a la carte" dishes. The blackboard gives us supreme flexibility, plus informality.'

Wine lists are not intimidating, and there are no sommeliers. Prices of wines are kept low, compared with those of upmarket restaurants. The flexible and casual style extends also to reservation, which, in many pubs, is not necessary. Several publicans tell me that only a very small proportion of diners ring to reserve a table, which, of course, eliminates the possibility of advance planning for the kitchen. The manager of a rural Suffolk inn points out that this informality attracts people and makes them dine more often—it takes a less momentous decision to eat out at the pub than at a restaurant: 'Lots of couples come once a month. They would not do this in a restaurant.' This is endorsed by other publicans: '[The gastropub enables] eating out without making an event of it.' 'You have a wide and easy choice.... You are not expected to consume in a prescribed way.' One London publican claims that lifestyle changes entail a greater flexibility in the use of time and that the pub can satisfy this requirement by offering a wide range of food and drink options, from a cup of coffee to a meal from a gastronomic menu. This emphasis on the more relaxed and casual nature of service and the format of dining again betrays an effort to aggregate identities. An increase in impromptu decisions to eat out is also a prominent result of the large survey of diners undertaken in 2015 by Paddock et al.[49]

Last, the physical environment in pubs, particularly in the bar section, continues to set gastropubs apart from upmarket restaurants. Most landlords have preserved the basic physical elements of pubs: that is, wooden furniture, often assorted rather than matching—what several respondents refer to as 'shabby chic'. In one pub even the dining plates—bought from car boot sales—are assorted and are proudly presented as a 'design feature'. In many pubs there are large wooden settles, flagstone floors, and, particularly, open fires. 'We have two fires—they are an important part of the atmosphere. This gets at the difference with a restaurant again.'[50] Open fires, or at least wood-burning stoves, are found in all but five of the pubs I visited. Additionally, the ubiquitous presence of a garden or terrace also sets the pub apart from the restaurant. It is an environment that encourages family visits, with several pubs even providing a playground.

But this traditionalism goes together with some modern touches, in that pubs are, on the whole, lighter and less cluttered, with an absence, by and large, of Victorian coloured glass and mirrors and polished brass. Colourful cushions are scattered around settles and settees, and shelves of cookery books may be found in quite a few pubs. In a few cases, the pub has been completely renovated, and traditional features, such as assorted wooden chairs and the use of old materials for a remodelled bar, have been combined with very contemporary designs, such as bright turquoise leather banquettes and modern lighting.

Gastropubs are distinguished from traditional boozers in that few keep a television set (though the landlord may bring in a computer for special events) or any gaming machines and juke boxes. Pub games, such as darts or snooker, are also largely absent. Whether these absences are due to lack of space (as some interviewees suggest) or are part of an attempt to lift the social tone of the pub is not clear. Another area where the social tone has been lifted up from what was found in purely drinks-led pubs are in the toilet facilities. A Cambridgeshire publican tells me: 'Loos are a litmus test for a distinction of the dining pub from the wet-led pub. Ours are more like restaurant loos, and ladies' toilets have a higher quality.' My own experience is that this remark may be generalized to all of the gastropubs in my sample.

Dining rooms are often situated in the former saloon or lounge. They usually lack the features of the bar and are kept simpler, more consistent in the furnishing, and more modern. Although tables are usually without cloths, chairs are upholstered. In a few cases, this simplicity goes together with a stunning chandelier and some original paintings. In sum, considering the service and particularly the ambience of the bar area and the dining room, the gulf between the two in sociality, in many of the gastropubs, is not as deep as may be imagined. Landlords, while not denying the differing organizational logics of the bar and the dining room, at the same time are keen to underline both the cognitive and behavioural similarities between them and the resulting synergy. The effort referred to in the last two paragraphs, to both preserve some vital elements of the traditional pub and to obliterate others, is another expression of the divided identity that characterizes the gastropub, but, in some cases, simply introduces modern taste into a largely traditional physical environment.

Publicans' Views on the Term Gastropub

Finally, how do publicans view their establishment, and what do their views reveal about organizational and personal identities? Few publicans are fond of the term 'gastropub' and reject it for a variety of reasons. As one London publican says: 'We are definitely a gastropub, but we do not use the term.'

A Rutland publican tells me: 'We are pigeon-holed as a gastropub, but I hate the word—we are more unique.' The landlord of an upmarket, rural Essex pub pleads:

> I can't stand the term gastropub—it suggests indigestion. We are stuck between a restaurant and a pub. I wish the industry would come up with a new, better term. We are a gastropub, but I wish we could be something else.

Why, then, has the term gastropub, coined in the early 1990s, largely fallen out of favour? The landlord of a rural Suffolk pub believes that the big chains have appropriated the label and that it has become too ambiguous to use. A London publican agrees: 'The gastropub has become a victim of its own success. They [pub chains and supermarkets] redefined what you could do. It [the label] became too common.' This view is quite widely shared by other publicans. It constitutes an effort to achieve an organizational identity which distinguishes them from potential competitors in the market and permits them to assert their superiority, particularly to pub chains. Table 6.6 shows the labels publicans favour.

Table 6.6. Labels adopted by publicans*

Gastropub	10
Pub	7
Pub with/and restaurant	4
Pub restaurant	6
Pub that serves food	1
Pub and dining room	2
Pub and kitchen	1
Food-led pub	2
Dining pub	2
Restaurant	4
Restaurant in/with pub	3
Restropub	1
Inn (offering food)	3
Undecided	1
Total	47

*Several interviewees offered more than one label.

The notion of the gastropub and the dual identity it entails is not just difficult for the publican, but also for some customers. An astute London publican, whose pub offers upmarket food, observes: 'If someone comes in for a pint, it is confusing. They then work out what kind of place this is and what kind of people we are. They then look at the menu. I can pretty much tell.'

The term 'gastropub' attracts only ten votes. Four call themselves restaurants, and seven simply call themselves a 'pub'. A number of other composite labels are adopted, with fourteen giving priority to the 'pub' function and five placing greater emphasis on the 'restaurant' function. Three pubs with rooms choose to call themselves 'inn'.

In sum, the dual focus of the pub offering both drink and food, both traditional fare and more refined contemporary cuisine, both communal and secluded sociality, becomes reflected also in the difficulty to label the resulting establishment. There is still a search for a name that distinguishes the pub restaurant not only from a conventional restaurant, but, equally strongly, from lower-level pub chains. Chefs regard themselves as being authentic in their sourcing practices and even as creative in their cooking, and thus distinguish themselves from the standardized and homogenized pubs catering for the masses. Talking about a divided identity encompasses many of the ambiguities around the hospitality of gastropubs.

To conclude, drinking at the bar, although greatly reduced in scale, continues to be a feature of all but five pubs in my sample. Publicans, above all, continue the facility because the lively and inclusive sociality of the bar spills over into the dining room in many ways, provided the two are not completely spatially separated. Most licensees have thus aggregated the two divergent organizational identities a gastropub entails and have sought to create synergies between them.

The Gastropub and its Divided Identity

The informality of drinking at or in the bar shapes the atmosphere in the dining room/restaurant. In large pubs, where both drinking and much dining occurs in close proximity in the bar area, an intermingling of both types of patrons is, in any case, common. This flexibility afforded by gastropubs sets them apart from conventional restaurants and is one of their most valued features. The very small number of gastropubs that have found it difficult or undesirable to maintain the dual organizational identity and have chosen to eliminate the 'drinking at the bar' facility have given up a valuable resource. They have turned themselves into restaurants in the shell of a pub.

Where landlords additionally offer a menu or part of a menu of traditional pub staples, the pub atmosphere is further enhanced. But this can no longer be taken for granted, with fourteen out of my forty interviewees offering no or very few (up to 20 per cent) pub classics on a daily basis. However, the traditional English Sunday lunch is cooked in all but four places, and fish-and-chips remain on almost all menus. Meals served in the dining room on week-days and Saturdays, in contrast, are no longer traditional, and chefs adhere to a large number of different styles. They are, in the main, European influenced, with only Asian touches here and there. Even the cooking presented as Modern British has little in common with the traditional pub classics offered and often has a more or less overt French influence. However, in most of the pubs these meals are less complex and more robust than in upmarket restaurants, and patrons can choose between pub classics and more elevated culinary styles.

Does publicans' stance on food therefore undermine the institution of the pub? Food in England has greatly diversified in the last twenty odd years and tastes have become more sophisticated and more open to food from other traditions. It is therefore to be expected that this has affected the cuisine of gastropubs as well. It should not be considered a development undermining the traditional pub. Only when food offered becomes too refined, complex, and expensive and deters the less well-off from visiting this type of pub, is one crucial aspect of pub sociality undermined—its inclusiveness. While this seems to have occurred in a very small number of the pubs I visited, it is not the typical outcome.

It is very evident from my interviews that the diversity and range of expectations facing landlords/ladies of gastropubs puts considerable demands on them. They sometimes cause strain and psychological discomfort and often uncertainties about the style of both food and drink and of sociality to be cultivated. They have to work hard to create and maintain synergy between often divergent identities and their behavioural consequences, and try to accommodate the wishes of different groups of stakeholders. However, the dual identity also entails opportunities that the majority of publicans in the sample value. Such opportunities relate particularly to pub sociality and the chance to preserve a more communal, relaxed, and flexible style of relations both between service staff and customers and between different groups of customers. This is valued by publicans both for its own sake and for the enhanced business opportunities it affords in terms of attracting a greater variety of customers to visit their pub.

However, despite the similarity between the pubs in my sample in having a dual organizational identity, managerial responses to the challenges this poses have been quite diverse. In terms of the four-fold classification scheme of Pratt and Foreman,[51] presented in Appendix IV, all four response modes—deletion, compartmentalization, integration, and aggregation—were identified in publicans' handling of the issues that arise from a dual organizational identity. 'Deleting' the pub function is relatively rare, while aggregation of the two functions, and of the values associated with each, is adopted most frequently. The mode chosen seems to depend on personal history and prior status in the hospitality sector and pub spatial lay-out, as well as on personal values crystallized around the institution of the pub. All these taken together influence constant efforts to *create* synergy between the two identities. To achieve synergy is a difficult undertaking. It requires that publicans integrate the organizational logics and behavioural consequences following from different identities. Here, they have to contend with the fact that the expectations of internal and external stakeholders—higher-level chefs and different groups of customers—are sometimes at variance. Hence, this chapter posits the notion of a divided organizational identity for most pubs, despite much success on the part of landlords/ladies in aggregating the two identities. The institution of the gastropub, now in its twenty-fifth odd year of existence, has not yet developed a settled identity.

The organizational identity of gastropubs analysed in this chapter is created mainly by the publican. As gastropubs are very small business organizations, personal and organizational identity overlap in large measure. The next chapter focuses on how the publican perceives the social identity—in terms of class, gender, and national identification—of customers, and how this, in turns, shapes the organizational identity of his pub.

Endnotes

1. Key Note, 2013, *Public Houses. A Market Report*, 16. Hampton: Key Note.
2. Key Note, 2013, 1.
3. Paddock, J., Warde, A. and Whillans, J. 2017, 'The changing meaning of eating out in three English cities 1995–2015', *Appetite*, 119, 12.
4. Naylor, T. 2016, 'Brioche bun has chefs on the run', *Restaurant*, April, 13.

5. Lane, C. 2014, *The Cultivation of Taste. Chefs and the organization of fine dining*. Oxford: Oxford University Press.
6. For an outline of the NRS, please see Appendix II.
7. Interview notes, 2015–16.
8. The term refers to finance professionals working in the City of London.
9. Rural Hertfordshire pub, 2015.
10. Cambridgeshire village publican, 2016.
11. Owner of a large inn in Cambridgeshire, 2016.
12. Worcestershire pub owner, 2015.
13. London, Maida Vale publican, 2015.
14. Owner of a rural Cambridgeshire pub, 2015.
15. Proprietor of a rural Essex pub, 2016.
16. Fischler, C. 1988, 'Food, self and identity', *Social Science Information* 27: 275–92.
17. Cambridgeshire pub, 2016.
18. Cambridgeshire pub.
19. London pub.
20. *Restaurant*, June 2010, 53.
21. Licensee of Cambridgeshire village pub.
22. Rural Essex pub, 2016.
23. Warde, A. and Martens, L. 2000, *Eating Out. Social differentiation, consumption and pleasure*. Cambridge: Cambridge University Press.
24. Beardsworth, A. and Keil, T. 1997, *Sociology on the Menu. An invitation to the study of food and society*. London: Routledge.
25. Warde and Martens, 2000, 159.
26. Key Note, 2013, 9.
27. British Beer and Pub Association (BBPA) 2015, *BBPA Statistical*. London: Brewing Publications Ltd.
28. *Financial Times*, 28.12.2016: 2.
29. Interview notes, 2015–16.
30. Pub in large Cambridgeshire village, 2015.
31. Essex rural pub.
32. Interview notes, 2015–16.
33. Gill, A.A. 2007, *Table Talk*, 35. London: Weidenfeld & Nicolson.
34. Interviews of members of a 'community pub' project, 2016.
35. Fischler, C. 2011, 'Commensality, society and culture', *Social Sciences Information* 50, 3–4: 528–48.
36. Mennell, S., Murcot, A.T. and van Otterloo, A.H. 1992, *The Sociology of Food. Eating, diet, and culture*, 115. London: Sage Publications.
37. Sigmund Freud, 1918: 174, cited by Kerner, S., Chou, C. and M. Warmind eds, 2015, *Commensality. From everyday food to feast*. London: Bloomsbury.
38. Landlord of a rural Essex pub, 2016.
39. Fischler, 2011, 533.
40. Fischler, 2011, 533.
41. Mintz, S. 1985, *Sweetness and Power. The place of sugar in modern history*. New York: Viking.

42. Warde and Martens, 2000.
43. Paddock et al. 2017, 7.
44. Warde and Martens, 2000.
45. Warde and Martens, 2000, 164.
46. Warde and Martens, 2000, 227; Paddock et al., 2017, 7.
47. Worcestershire rural pub, 2016.
48. Yorkshire rural pub, 2016.
49. Paddock et al., 2017, 2.
50. Rural Essex pub, 2016.
51. Pratt, M.G. and Foreman, P.O. 2000, 'Classifying managerial responses to multiple organizational identities', *Academy of Management Review*, 25, 1: 18–42.

7

Social and National Identity: A Focus on Class, Gender, and Nation

Chapters in Part I have pointed out that, notwithstanding a degree of social mixing, the pub, at the bottom of the hierarchy of hospitality establishments, has been a venue predominantly frequented by members of the working classes, whereas taverns and inns attracted the middling and higher ranks in greater numbers. Gender segregation, in both pubs and taverns, was, if anything, more pronounced than that based on class. A third social dimension, the identification of a certain food with national belonging, was a prominent theme in Chapters 3 and 4, where I focused on the perennial contest between French and English cuisine.

In the twenty-first century, the gastropub, offering both good food and drink and a relatively genteel environment, came to distinguish itself as being at the top end of a social spectrum of pubs. In its focus on high-quality food and on a range of good ales and wines, as well as on the predominance of seated rather than standing customers, it came to develop a greater resemblance to the taverns and inns of previous centuries, than to the typical pub. This chapter explores how these various features of the gastropub influence from which social constituencies its patrons are drawn. It is thus assumed that taste in food and the accompanying sociality is still strongly shaped by one's belonging to one or more collectivities.[1]

It will investigate to what degree, if any, the gastropub still has its social base in the working class and to what extent it continues to foster mixing between the social classes. In addition to social mixing between classes, this chapter also examines whether gender segregation has diminished and, if so, to what extent differences in drinking habits between men and women and attendant forms of sociality have disappeared. The last section of this chapter looks at the extent to which food still expresses national identity. This focus on pubs' customers will be preceded by an examination of the social profile of publicans, which, in turn, affects the hospitality cultivated and the organizational identity achieved, as well as the social make-up of customers.

The Licensees of Gastropubs

The gastropubs in my sample are far more often free houses (thirty-one of forty) than tied properties (nine). Of the free houses, nineteen are owned by their licensee and twelve have independent owners and thus are leased by the publican—a phenomenon particularly common in London, with its astronomical property prices. The breakdown of my sample by type of ownership is shown in Table 7.1.

This ownership pattern departs significantly from that of pubs in general where the majority of pubs (53 per cent) is still tied to either a brewery (19 per cent) or a pub company (34 per cent) and thus lacks independence in buying beers.[2] It indicates that publicans freed from brewery/pubco control wish to cultivate an upmarket and individual organizational identity to distinguish themselves, particularly, from the more standardized pubs that are part of chains, as well as from tenanted pubs that are unable to develop distinction in the area of beers stocked.

Several of the owners of free houses had previously been tied to a brewery or a pub company, but, resenting the tie, had bought themselves out: 'We had leased another pub from Greene King before this, but we needed a pub with the potential to do something better, without the tie to a brewery. The way forward was to get a freehold.'[3] 'We bought it [the pub] from Punch Taverns. We had it a couple of years as tenants and then bought it dearly as we had revived the business by then.'[4]

Licensees are predominantly men (thirty). However, quite a few of the independent pubs are owned by couples where the man is the licensee and chef, and the woman acts as front-of-house or landlady. Some of the former inns (eleven) have a small number of hotel rooms, although only four of the eleven call themselves 'inn'. Having accommodation gives owners greater financial security and also boosts the number of diners.

The pubs are run by two distinctive kinds of individuals or couples. The first and smaller group of the forty publicans in my sample (seventeen) consists of middle class, former professional employees, disappointed with their professional activity. They mostly, but not invariably, employ a professional chef. The professions they have given up are mainly business-related ones, such as

Table 7.1. Types of ownership

Free houses	31
of which, owner-managed	19
leased from an independent owner	12
Tied houses	9
of which owned by breweries	4
of which owned by pub companies	5

accounting, marketing, consultancy, and legal and financial services. There is also among my interviewees a sprinkling of former engineers, an interior designer, a theatre director, a history teacher, and even an officer with Sandhurst training. The great majority of these publicans have enjoyed a university education. These kinds of licensees represent a radical departure from historical patterns where pub landlords had merely a basic education and came predominantly from previous lower middle or working class occupations. The licensees of gastropubs are closer in social terms to the owners of taverns and inns of old. They bring new social orientations and cultural values to the business of running a pub, which, in turn, affects the style of hospitality they offer (the organizational identity of the pub) and the patrons they attract. Several of these career changers let it be known that their previous employment was hard to reconcile with their personal values, which, in their view, are better expressed by running a gastropub. Thus, the landlord of a north London pub tells me: 'I never liked banking. It did not fit my politics and values. It was never going to make me happy. I have always liked food and drink, I have liked feeding my friends.' A Yorkshire publican suggests that chefs have come to prefer working in pubs where they can showcase their food in a relaxing environment. Many greatly value the 'association with the communal' that the pub still fosters and the avoidance of exclusivity it affords. A different statement of a value orientation comes from a female Islington publican who cultivates sustainable food and serves only craft beers and organically grown wines: 'I wanted to prove that it [hospitality] could be value-driven.' (She was awarded an MBE in 2009 for Services to the Organic Pub Trade.) The three joint owners of a London pub even aim to stem the number of pubs dying: 'We felt we should do something to address the pub-closing development.' A Kent landlord, too, is mainly value-driven. He does not want to be considered a businessman, but regards his 'creative aspirations as the most important thing'.

This last landlord/chef, however, is a little unusual in that an embrace of a particular style of hospitality, in most cases, goes together with some familiarity with business practices and with knowledge of how to run a pub as a profitable enterprise. However, such a business orientation is mostly tempered by a conception of hospitality where excellence of food and drink takes precedence over purely financial considerations: 'Sufficient profit is sufficient.'[5] For one landlord, the welfare of staff is a particularly strong concern. It causes him to play down a quest for profit when asked about his profit margin: '[It is] less than 10 per cent. If we are fair and pay well, that is sufficient.'

The second group, of twenty-three licensees, contains professional chefs who started their working life in the hospitality industry. Most of them are from working-class backgrounds, and their highest educational qualification usually is their Chef's Certificate; that is, they have either achieved National Vocational Qualifications (NVQs) or a City & Guilds diploma (in the case of the older chefs). These publican-chefs make up for their lower level of education with the possession of a longer and deeper professional experience, and they are often owner-managers. A majority have trained or worked in Britain's best restaurants. This, inevitably, has influenced their culinary style as well as their aspirations for an elevated organizational identity (see Chapter 6 for more details on this). Thus, while not as middle class as many of their customers, their culinary skill and entrepreneurial status has lifted them out of the working class.

They have acquired a pub both for reasons of affordability (as compared with a restaurant space) and/or because of a preference for a pub sociality and for the lifestyle it affords them and their families. Thus, the landlady of a rural Suffolk pub, when asked about the profit rate they aim for, replies: '[The profit margin] is quite low. This is more a lifestyle than making a living... We have much more social life here [than in the high-end restaurant in which they worked before]...lots of friends.' A London publican hints at the same sentiment when he says: 'I look for people I have a lot in common with, to say "hello" and have a drink with.' A Yorkshire publican recently closed a profitable high-end city restaurant to buy his rural pub. He regards it as more compatible with the lifestyle he wants for himself and his young family: 'The costs of running a restaurant are very high. For a young aspiring chef a pub is the better option. You can live above the pub.'

These chef-publicans are not that dissimilar from the career-changing licensees, in that for both groups running a gastropub is more a lifestyle choice that affords intrinsic rewards, rather than constituting a highly profitable business. They differ from publicans more generally, both in previous centuries and at the current time, in that they are formally trained to provide upmarket food. They have overcome the lack of competency common among the run of publicans to provide good-quality and interesting food that goes beyond simple and often pre-prepared bar staples. They have acquired sufficient confidence in their social status to mix also with their middle- and upper-class customers. Social mixing does not merely occur among patrons, but also applies to the interactions of landlord/lady and patrons. A north Essex chef-proprietor who gets quite a few upper middle- and upper-class customers believes that they come because they like the more informal style of the pub, as compared with that of restaurants. Hence, he does not show them deference, but treats them more like friends: 'Everyone comes and intermingles. The whole idea of informality is bred in [in pubs]. They would not dream of doing it [treating the upper-class patron with easy informality] in a restaurant.'

Customers' Social Position

Widespread eating out has been identified as a fairly recent social habit that has become common only in the last two decades of the twentieth century.[6] Sociologists and social historians who have investigated how social class has influenced eating out in restaurants (though not specifically in gastropubs) identify complex motivations.[7] On the one hand, they hold that this is no longer purely a middle-class pastime and that all but the poorest in our society can now enjoy a meal out. Warde and Martens find that only 7 per cent of their sample never ate out.[8] On the other hand, these same authors conclude that eating out is still stratified according to class, and that class distinctions are upheld by pursuing different tastes in the food consumed. Cultural differences in knowledge about food and in taste are now the mechanisms that reaffirm class and status distinctions in subtle ways. But for Warde such class differentiation does not denote affirmation of hierarchy. Instead he identifies a change 'from a system of distinction to one of undistinguished difference'. 'Differences do not inspire emulation or consciousness of inferiority and superiority.'[9] Mennell et al. suggest that 'we have moved from the situation where...we eat food appropriate to status and respectability to a context where...we seek to select that which displays taste, respectability, knowledge and a search for marginal differentiation'.[10] James endorses this position when she suggests that both foreign foods and authentic high-quality British food is still accessed only by the higher classes.[11] Finally, Warde and Martens, coming from a cultural perspective on class,[12] strongly agree: 'Social position and cultural taste most powerfully determine what kind of eating place people go to.' (Their book distinguishes between eating out in pubs and in restaurants, but not between different kinds of pubs.)

My own study of this, drawing on the social categorization of diners by the landlords of gastropubs, shows that, although their customer base is quite diverse, the middle classes far outweigh members of other classes as consumers of the relatively upmarket food served in gastropubs. However, gastropubs are eating out venues that cater for both tastes in simple, but carefully sourced and freshly prepared, food and for more developed tastes in unusual, often foreign, produce and refined dishes. They thus appeal to omnivores;[13] that is, diners who indulge both kinds of tastes either in one meal or on different occasions or at different times of the day of their pub visit (bar food is more likely to be consumed during lunch-time visits). At the same time, they may attract diners from the working classes whose members, however, may choose mainly from the bar menu.

To gauge the class composition of gastropubs' customers, my question to interviewees was deliberately kept general and 'class' was not singled out: 'Is it possible to tell me what social background your customers come from?'

Nevertheless, the majority of respondents gave answers in 'class' terms, referring to both occupational position and, less frequently, to ownership, but rarely to cultural capital—defined by Pierre Bourdieu as education, specialist knowledge, and social poise.[14] References to income also were frequent: '...the food is not cheap here'; 'Predominantly middle class—it is slightly price-led.' Quite a few interviewees initially refer to the great social diversity of their customers as 'all sorts' or 'all walks of life' or 'the ground floor [bar area] is very mixed [socially]. We try to be inclusive', trying to appear egalitarian. However, most amend their answer when I ask about the 'predominant pattern'. 'There is variety, but most are middle class.'[15] Only four of the forty interviewees stick to their label 'very diverse' or 'a complete mixture' as the only categorization. One example is a landlady in rural Suffolk: 'Diners are very varied in terms of social background, they may have lots of money or come from council houses.'

Respondents use the categories of upper or higher, upper middle, middle, and working class, as well as of 'business people' and 'farming people'. Less frequently, they refer to the NRS (National Readership Survey) social grades A, B, and C (upper middle, middle, and lower middle class) widely used for marketing. The NRS classification schemes are close to the occupationally-based National Statistics Socio-Economic Classification (NS-SEC), adapted from the Nuffield class scheme developed in the 1970s (for details of both schemes, see Appendix II). Respondents depart from both schemes in that they additionally refer to wealth and property owned (including cars) and employ a category of 'upper' or 'higher' class. For example: 'In the evenings, the social background is higher middle class. You can tell from cars—we get Range Rovers, Porsches, etc.'[16] They also refer to the character of housing in the pub's vicinity. Only one respondent refers to customers' attire, 'customers come in both working clothes and well-dressed',[17] and a second description refers to people 'with good upbringing', coming close to Bourdieu's concept of cultural capital[18] (knowledge and social skills acquired in a class-related process of education). There are very few references to differences in taste and/or cultural capital. However, one Suffolk landlord responds in terms close to Bourdieu's (1984) distinction between 'the taste of luxury' and 'the taste of necessity'. He distinguishes between the NRS grades A and B, on the one side, and the C1s, on the other, implying that the latter do not really appreciate fine food and privilege quantity over quality: 'The Cs complain that...our portions are small,...the As think they are "huge".'

By far the predominant label given by my interviewees to their customers is 'middle class'. They either refer to 'class' explicitly, or they mention middle-class occupations, such as 'professionals and business people', 'creatives and arty people', academics and managers, artists, architects, photographers, and internet and publishing companies. '[Diners come] from the media, finance and city-based services.'[19] Farming people receive frequent mentions in the rural pubs, and they are usually farm owners: 'There is a large farming community, and we are the social hub of the village shoot',[20] and 'Farmers around here are moneyed and wealthy'.[21] NRS social grades used also usually refer to the upper middle and middle classes: 'We get As and Bs, quite high-class', according to a Suffolk landlord. There are additionally frequent references to 'commuters' and 'well-off retired people' who are most likely to be middle class. The landlord of a Worcestershire pub describes his customers in the following terms: 'They are reasonably affluent. This is a professional commuters' village.' A Suffolk landlord, whose customer base is heavily tilted towards upper middle-class diners, says: '30 per cent of customers are weekenders from London.' The label of 'affluent' and 'wealthy' is also used four times during the interview.

To my surprise, quite a few pubs count upper class people among their customers. When I checked what kind of people they meant, they refer to the local landowner and/or gentry, to titled people, as well as to senior executives from global companies in the vicinity. Thus: 'Predominantly middle class, a reasonable number of upper class, with some Sirs and Ladies.'[22] A north Cambridgeshire publican is proud to count the local lord, 'a baronet and very high-profile landowner and public person' among his customers. The landlord of a south Essex rural pub tells me: 'We get a lot of farming people. Lord X of Y has a big estate—he is a big landowner, and then there is the Lions Hall. There are three big farming families in the area, one of which owns the abattoir. Then there is the owner of the factory making cricket bats, makes half a million [bats] a year. We get every diverse business you can think of.'

'Working class' is not singled out as the only or predominant category of customers by any publican. However, working-class customers are often mentioned as one small constituency among others: 'We get people with middle and upper middle income, as well as a smattering of lower income people.' There is one mention of 'working to middle class' and two mentions of 'a few working class', as well as three references to a working-class occupation, 'butchers in a nearby abattoir', 'plumbers', and 'even poorer people come—builders etc. Pubs have to have soul'.[23] Indeed, London pubs are more likely to attract 'working people' as their exterior does not readily identify them as a gastropub, while gastropubs in villages rarely have this anonymity. References to 'people in working clothes', as well as to people living in social housing (north London pub) or in council houses (Suffolk rural pub) also indicate 'non-middle class': 'This is quite a diverse environment with quite a bit of social housing inserted between the largely posh housing.'[24] When 'the less well-off' are mentioned, it is usually to emphasize that they come less frequently: 'It is affordable for the less well-off for special occasions',[25] or 'families from all social backgrounds come for infrequent "special occasion" meals'.[26] A landlord in rural Yorkshire who gained a Bib Gourmand for his competitively priced set menu receives people with lesser means more frequently: 'It does not cost a lot—the average guy can come in.'

One publican who uses NRS social grades to distinguish between different groups of customers tells me that those from social class C1 (skilled manual workers and lower white-collar workers, or the intermediate class in the NS-SEC classification scheme) form 5–10 per cent of his customers, whereas another publican estimates that 'the upwardly mobile working class come to 10–20 per cent. They now look for good food, without feeling patronized'. The first of these landlords talks about 'upward mobility' of the working class, whose members now regard eating out as an accepted part of their lifestyle: 'We have experienced a monetary enfranchisement of the working class. We have experienced a quasi-Mediterranean movement towards restaurant eating. It is now included in the household budget. It has become a social norm—like owning a car. There is the need [for it] to be accepted to go out [to eat].'[27] In sum, there are many references to members of the upper working class (skilled workers) and lower middle class frequenting gastropubs, but it is also clear that they are a minority among diners and that middle-class diners predominate.

Additionally, incidental allusions are made to the fact that people from the lower social classes (semi-routine and routine occupations) are not among gastropubs' customers, but congregate in another pub in the village more devoted to drinking. 'There is another pub in the village which caters for the traditional pub drinkers. That pub is for volume drinking and slightly more rowdy than our establishment.'[28] In a similar vein, people with low standards of behaviour, a few publicans point out, are not tolerated in their pub: 'I won't have yobbos [in the bar]. I run a clean and tidy ship.'[29] 'The other pub [in the village] sells very cheap, Witherspoon-type food, there is no cross-over. The advantage is that undesirables go there.'[30] Hence, customers do not come 'from all walks of life', but references are mainly to the respectable working and lower middle/intermediate classes while people from semi-routine and routine occupations (category D in the NRS social grades) are not included. While Wouters connects a code of manners to exclude people lower down the social ladder with earlier centuries,[31] 'the rude' are excluded even from famously informal gastropubs today. The latter are a group who, in the literature about the working classes, have been seen to be particularly badly affected by pub closures in their neighbourhood. In interviews in working-class areas conducted by Beider, the author finds that the loss of pubs as places of community interaction is frequently mentioned with nostalgia and profound regret.[32]

Social mixing between classes also occurs in an upward direction, particularly in rural pubs. There, the mainly middle-class customers have the opportunity to meet the local lord, the big land owner, or the owner of a world-class local business. The rules of social politeness, demanding a suspension of any emphasis on status distinctions, were first mentioned by historians to characterize interaction between the rural gentry and the new urban cultural notables in the eighteenth-century tavern. These rules still seem to apply today and not only in villages. The landlord of a London pub tells me: 'Customers are absolutely mixed. We get a local talking to maybe a Hollywood star. We get some very high-profile people here.'

Even when customers from different social backgrounds visit the pub at the same time, they do not necessarily mix. The landlord of a south Essex pub, with both a public school and an abattoir in the vicinity, tells me:

> We sometimes get groups of public school boys from nearby Felstead. They may sit at a table next to one of farmers' sons and farm workers or butchers from the slaughter house. [However], they stand [at the bar] in their own groups.

Such self-chosen social segregation also works in other ways. At lunch in a north London pub, I observed a man in working clothes and with massive tattoos on his bare legs come to the bar for a beer. He took his beer outside and consumed it on a bench on the pavement.

However, the above presents a slightly simplified picture in that the class composition of customers varies according to location (more lower-class customers in London than in rural areas), according to time of day (a more mixed clientele is served at lunch time), and in the pub's different rooms. Where the pub maintains a separate dining room, some spatial class segregation takes place. Several publicans point out that working people are more likely to be found in the bar than in the dining room.

I did not gather data on whether the different social groups order different types of food, such as mainly bar staples or mainly the more elaborate cuisine, but some clues about cross-over eating exist. The huge popularity of both Sunday roast dinners (some London pubs sell several hundred of such dinners) and of fish-and-chips (they are found on every menu), combined with the predominantly middle-class background of patrons, indicates that members from all classes must be partial to this traditional English food. Conversely, members of the middle and upper classes, on different occasions or even within one and the same meal, can indulge both their cosmopolitan attitude to food and their desire for localism. The gastropub again provides extreme flexibility.

We do not know whether members of the lower classes have omnivorous tastes and also order the more sophisticated, non-traditional dishes. The fact that the less well-off visit the gastropub mainly for special occasions would suggest that they, too, have developed a taste for the more refined fare the gastropub offers. Yet, as two landlords spontaneously suggest, there remain nevertheless subtle differences in taste between guests from different social backgrounds. While a rural Kent publican tells me that 'upwardly mobile members of the working class' are more likely to complain about some features of the food he serves, a Suffolk publican provides some detail on the substance of such complaints. These point towards differences in taste on the part of members of different classes, showing a stronger preference by the lower classes for the traditional British way of preparing food.

> The Cs complain that:
> - the pork is undercooked... it isn't but we cook it pink at the bone;
> - that the vegetables are undercooked because they are al dente;
> - about our Roquefort mayonnaise... they just want cheddar in their burger.

At the same time, gastropubs offer the opportunity to members of both the middle and lower middle/upper working classes to express distinction from those who consume the standardized mass-produced food served in branded mega pubs and in fast-food restaurants. Hence, there are dispositions lying behind food choices and, at the same time, behind choices of venue and associated sociality. A gastropub is chosen, rather than a restaurant.

To sum up this section, the evidence presented above points to four main facts about the class composition of gastropub customers, based on the author's interpretation of publicans' views. First, the historical pattern of a predominantly working-class pub customer base has been inverted to one where affluent middle-class customers form the majority of patrons. Second, there is frequent reference also to social mixing between the middle and the upper class, particularly in rural pubs. Similar to pubs of the past, the gastropub still enjoys some cross-class appeal. In many of the pubs, a minority of upper working-class/lower middle-class customers also enjoy a good meal. Several publicans suggest that the food they serve, particularly from the lunch set menu, is affordable for people from all social backgrounds. Others, however, point out that the cost of a meal means it is affordable on a regular basis mainly for middle-class customers and that 'the less well-off' come less frequently, mainly to celebrate special occasions. Third, customers from the very bottom of the class hierarchy (routine and semi-routine occupations) are not singled out by any interviewee, and any disruptive elements—whether they are from the lower levels of the working class or from among boisterous London bankers—are not welcome in gastropubs. Last, the presence in the gastropub of people from different social classes does not necessarily point to actual social mixing.

My results thus partially bear out the claim of Warde and Martens, Mennell, and Burnett that people from all social classes can now afford to dine out,[33] as well as their additional point that venues are selected to 'display taste, respectability, knowledge and marginal differentiation'.[34] Another conclusion, however, is that middle-class diners visit gastropubs because this type of pub truly caters for their omnivorous taste, satisfying both their liking of traditional English dishes and their taste for more complex, creative, and usually foreign-inspired food, depending on the occasion and on the time of day or week. The gastropub, in that way, offers exceptional flexibility, catering for different tastes and even allowing diners to mix food from different traditions and styles within one and the same meal, while championing the freshness and quality of ingredients and frequently local provenance.

The Gender Dimension: Is the Pub Still a Bastion of Masculinity?

Chapter 2 showed that, historically, pubs were widely regarded as a male sanctuary, and women were either excluded from them or were marginalized within them. Both spatial and temporal gender segregation was utilized to preserve the pub as 'a bastion of masculinity'. Informal social norms sanctioning this segregation were strong, and women were barely tolerated among drinkers at the bar. Whereas lone male drinkers were usually made welcome, lone women drinkers suffered stigmatization. Where women were tolerated, there existed differences in the use of pubs between men and women, expressed in divergent drinking habits. While the norms and sanctions of a gender ideology were often actively inculcated, they were also often absorbed by women themselves and were not necessarily recognized as exclusionary.

In addition to ideological barriers to social mixing between the sexes in pubs, there were also material ones. The often sordid appearance of the bar and especially of the toilet facilities, together with the widespread incidence of drunkenness and the consequent absence of any 'social politeness', were enough to repel many women and to curtail the frequency of their pub visits. Men's topics of conversation and indulgence in superficial intimacy proved no attraction either. Although the more genteel pub lounges created in later centuries and aimed particularly at female drinkers reduced women's exposure to these negative features of pubs, this came at the price of gender segregation between bar and lounge.

The following pages will examine whether the marginalization of women has endured in gastropubs and, where it has stopped, on what terms women's greater inclusion in pub sociality has occurred. I study to what extent and how women's greater labour force participation and spending power at the present time, together with a move towards closer conjugal relations and joint participation in leisure activities outside the home, have conquered this former bastion of male separatism and domination as portrayed in the historical analysis. I will highlight not only the changing attitudes of men and women to gender divisions, but also emphasize how material changes in pubs and in the way gastropubs are run have transformed the gender balance and made women feel more welcome in this type of pub.

The rise of gastropubs, together with new attitudes to gender relations that have become less tolerant of the exclusion of one sex by the other, has brought about an astonishing transformation in the gender composition of pub customers and, in the process, of the pub itself. 'The wife-beating boozer is a dying breed. Females now are more independent and assertive.'[35] Female customers are no longer excluded. 'Women are comfortable to come on their own—they told me so. Now they are totally integrated, if in a mixed group', the landlady of a Cambridgeshire pub believes. Other interviewees spontaneously acknowledge that gender relations have changed and that women have even become a mainstay of gastropubs, particularly in the dining room. Landlords/ladies positively encourage the custom of women by cultivating a female-friendly ambience. Such a welcoming environment may include: flowers on the table; inviting toilet facilities; the availability of attractive non-alcoholic drinks, as well as a wide choice of wines by the glass; and a menu that offers some less filling and more diet-friendly dishes.

'We deliberately make the place female-friendly.'[36]

'I received good advice from Jeremy Corbin [his former employer]. He said: "Make sure you look after the ladies in a gastropub. Once you have got a lady who is in for lunch on her own, you have cracked it." I did not understand it at first, but now I know that he meant you have created the right ambience—it is comfortable also for women.'[37]

'The ladies feel comfortable here. We have flowers on the tables and nice hand lotion in the loos. Staff, too, are very welcoming towards women.'[38]

Many women now command a good income of their own and are no longer dependent on a man to finance their pub visits. Women form the largest section of dining customers, and they have more time to come for week-day lunches—often a lean time for pubs. '10–15 years ago they [women] would spend less than men, but now they spend as much. There has occurred a freeing up of their attitudes, particularly among younger women. They now are often more successful in their career than men.'[39] As such, women contribute vitally to the viability of the gastropub, and publicans take active measures to create an ambience that attracts female customers. They are additionally made very welcome because they act as a civilizing influence. Publicans who aim to run a pub with an inviting ambience see the presence of female customers as a vital component of such a civilized hospitality. Women are also viewed by some publicans as more appreciative of the food gastropubs provide: 'If you have six lads at the bar shouting, why have some expensive venison. The women love the food.'[40] Furthermore, the decline in drunkenness, together with the upgrading of the material environment, has made gastropubs attractive to both women and families.

However, even the gastropub is not used by men and women in the same way, and some of the patterns of spatial and temporal segregation still remind the researcher of their historical antecedents. When we distinguish between the two main activities in gastropubs—drinking and eating—or between the bar and the dining room, subtle gender divisions are still revealed.

Drinking at the bar is still mainly a male predilection, with men constituting between 70 to 90 per cent of drinkers in the majority of places in my study. Drinking at the bar mainly reinforces solidarity between men: 'It is very rare to see a woman at the bar' and 'Women hardly ever sit at the bar, but take a table', according to two Cambridgeshire publicans, and 'men are 80% [of drinkers at the bar], with token females at week-ends'. Although there may occur little active exclusion of women from drinking at the bar, the norm that women, on their own, do not drink at the bar, is still widely internalized: 'We don't get lone women come in for a drink.'[41] Two publicans tell me that any female drinkers at the bar usually come in groups: 'If they [women] come, they come in a big group.'[42] Women obviously need moral support to enter this still predominantly masculine sphere. In one London gastropub, they do not drink at the bar but in the conservatory, thereby replicating the old segregation between bar and lounge. However, in a minority of pubs—around a quarter of my sample—women now form half of all drinkers at the bar. These are mainly London pubs. Thus, a London publican comments: 'Women may now come alone. This has changed dramatically. Customers now are very diverse—also gay couples. This diversity reflects the local environment.'

Drinking habits among the sexes differ. In the past, drinking a large number of pints without ill effect was often seen as a sign of masculinity.[43] This view is no longer prevalent, but 'drinking pints at the bar' continues to be a prominent choice among men, but not among the majority of women. 'Men will have a beer as soon as they come in, before they do anything. It is a tradition.'[44] For men, a visit to the pub must still include a pint at the bar, even if this is subsequently followed by wine with the meal. According to the manager of a Cumbrian gastropub, '95 per cent of guys have beer at some point of the evening'. Women order either less alcoholic or more 'genteel' drinks. According to a Cambridgeshire landlady, 'they are more likely to drink cocktails and mocktails and wine and spirits', and '[d]uring the meal, 95% of customers drink wine, but before the meal men will usually have a pint and women will have a G&T or a sparkling wine'.[45]

Although drunkenness has been drastically reduced in most pubs in my sample, men still take more alcoholic drink than women. Women are more likely to consume soft drinks or coffee. Men still feel more entitled to alcoholic drink, with wives and partners often taking on the drive home: 'Women are more inclined to drink wine or soft drinks. They are the drivers home.'[46] 'Women drink more wine and more white wine. Quite often the wife will be the driver.'[47] 'Very few women drink beer. They drink either wine or soft drinks—they are often the drivers,'[48] '[M]en order more beer, whereas women may have things like Elderflower Pressé.'[49]

But even in this area, patterns are seen to be changing, and a small number of interviewees see no marked differences in the drinking habits of men and women. Thus, an Essex publican detects change: 'Yes, they [drinking habits] differ. But women are changing a little bit—they are drinking more cider and beer although the latter are still a minority.' If cocktails are a prominent offering, women will be less restrained in their drinking of alcohol: 'We are not the archetype of a boozer, we sell a lot of cocktails.'[50] Also, women now may come to drink on their own, though not at peak drinking times: 'Ladies come on their own... In the afternoon ladies come in for a glass of wine.'[51] A Suffolk publican even suggests that, if they come on their own, women are likely to drink more.

Additionally, pub-going patterns differ between men and women. Similar to the pattern described for the 1920s by Selley,[52] men visit the pub more frequently and are more likely to come on a week day, as well as at the weekend. However, in contrast to the pattern in the 1920s, most men now do not come every day of the week, but mainly on Friday nights to unwind at the end of the working week, or for a few days during the week. Women, in contrast, are more likely to come on either Saturday evening or at Sunday lunch time. Thus, one informant, talking about their village pub that closed, tells me that '[r]eal regulars were all men', and another customer says: 'On Fridays, which is the main drinking night—to relax after a week's work—men dominate at about 75%. On Sundays, when family lunches are prominent, men and women are present in equal numbers.' A Lancashire publican confirms this: 'Men come more frequently. The husband comes four times [a week], whereas the wife comes once.'

The picture fundamentally differs when we turn to dining (or lunching) in gastropubs. Dining, in addition to uniting families and couples, attracts groups of female friends. A large number of publicans mention that 'women only' groups are frequent among diners, particularly at lunch times and during the week. An Essex publican comments: 'It has been a big transformation [of the pub].' A Kent landlord agrees: 'Yes, a lot of women come, this is a real change, it accelerated in the last 10 years. Women dining with friends may be a major part of customers.' The importance of women's custom to the viability of the gastropub is pointed out by an Essex publican: 'During the week, the majority of the tables are taken by women only, whereas at the weekend it is more mixed.' An Essex landlady confirms this: 'Women only come more often than couples or men during the week.' In several pubs women even maintain a regular luncheon club: 'We have a monthly dining club of ladies.'[53] 'We also have two "ladies only" luncheon clubs that meet once a fortnight.'[54] 'Every third Thursday is Ladies' Lunch.'[55]

For women, gastropubs or pub restaurants are thus friendly places where they feel safe and have opportunities to meet their friends. Several publicans hint that the sociality developed in 'women only' dining groups differs from that cultivated by men at the bar. Whereas drinking at the bar reinforces solidarity between men but real intimacy does not develop,[56] dining is more likely to attract groups of female friends who 'come as much for the chat as for the food'.[57] A Suffolk publican confirms that 'women ... stay longer and chat'. 'Women are now very frequent diners. They spend less and sit longer. But they talk and spread their good experience.'[58] The facts that the conversation between friends is as important as the food they eat and that social interaction is usually prolonged indicates that pub meetings for women serve to kindle and reinforce intimacy of a less superficial type than that cultivated by men at the bar. A Worcestershire publican recognizes this: 'It is about more than just the food. They [women] chat and stay late.' The importance of eating out together for female friendship is confirmed also by the more quantitative work of sociologists.[59]

To sum up, differing gender identities continue to shape the use of gastropubs. Women are frequent and welcome guests in gastropubs, and this type of pub attracts, rather than repels, women. Moreover, as avid diners, women have become an important support to the maintenance of gastropubs' income, and they have affected the adoption of a welcoming ambience. A meal in a gastropub, often at lunch time, is seen to facilitate bonding among female friends. Publicans recognize them as an important customer group who need to be attracted by creating an environment appealing to women. Moreover, it is an environment where the rougher element among male drinkers are screened out or carefully kept in check. Women lend support to publicans' desire to civilize the pub. Publicans thus see female customers as an essential component of the organizational identity they seek to foster, as well as a mainstay of their financial viability during week days. Women's use of gastropubs, however, differs from that of men in several crucial ways. They drink less and partake of less beer at the bar, visit the pub less frequently, and are more prominent among diners than among drinkers. Hence, overall, women now are very welcome and make use of the pub with great confidence. Yet, a certain degree of spatial and temporal gender segregation—some of it reminiscent of earlier centuries—persists also in the twenty-first century. It is probably less the result of coercion and more due to the absorption of deep-seated gender norms by both sexes that inform habitual behaviour.

Segregation of certain social groups is not just a matter of gender, but also of age. Nearly all the pubs distinguish between customer groups by age, with few of them hosting young people under twenty-five years of age, unless they are part of a family group dining together. The only exceptions are some London gastropubs where 'older gentlemen who nurse a pint may be found next to some young trendies'. It is difficult to determine whether this age segregation is the result of young peoples' choice, or whether their absence is due to an insufficient welcome. Both factors may be at work simultaneously. An Essex publican attributes their absence to inclination: 'The young go clubbing.' However, a Yorkshire landlord tells me: 'Obviously, we don't attract the young—we discourage them.' A Cambridgeshire publican also singles out 'a young element in the village who are too rough', and several others attribute the lack of rowdiness in their pub restaurant to the absence of the very young; that is, below twenty-five years of age. An Essex landlord, when asked about the incidence of drunkenness, confirms: 'We don't get the young crowd, customers just get merry.' This attitude to young people appears outdated when we consider that, statistically, drinking alcohol is now significantly less common among younger than older people.

Food and National Belonging

The theme of culinary nationalism was very prominent when I reviewed attitudes to food and practices of eating out in the seventeenth and eighteenth centuries. Food consumption was particularly designed to signal English patriotism in opposition to the popularity of French cuisine, particularly among the upper middle and the upper classes. At the current time, in contrast, most people would consign a culinary nationalism and its attendant hostility to French cuisine to past centuries and instead underline our cosmopolitan and often eclectic food habits.

People reject the idea of an English nationalism because they are thinking of political nationalism, rather than a merely cultural one, encompassing the practices and beliefs of every-day life. Not surprisingly, it is a French sociologist, Claude Fischler,[60] who has focused on a culinary identity and the behaviours motivated by it as part of a national cultural identity. He studies the way incorporation of food may become an important marker of both inclusion in a nation and opposition to another nation whose cuisine is viewed as a threat to national culinary identity. Fischler concludes: 'The very absorption of a given food is seen as incorporating the eater into a culinary system and into the group which practises it.'[61] An alternative term is gastro-nationalism,[62] that also connects food consumption with the demarcation and sustenance of the power of national tradition and attachment.

Yet, many people would object to the notion that, particularly in the face of globalization, the British people display a culinary nationalism of any kind. I contend that food nationalism cannot be denied that easily and will explore how such a culinary nationalism is expressed. I will investigate whether the gastropub contributes to keeping such nationalism alive, or whether, in its cultivation of upmarket dining and often foreign culinary styles, it further marginalizes the so-called Modern British style of cuisine. If elements of a British culinary style can be identified, what do they consist of? These questions do not have straightforward answers, given the dual organizational identity of the gastropub, including a divided culinary focus that encompasses both traditional British food and more cosmopolitan styles of cooking. This task is further complicated by the fact that the British have a curiously broad culinary identity.[63] It is no longer exhausted by roast meat with gravy and two vegetables, plus a fish 'n' chips supper for week days, but has absorbed a multitude of foreign influences. This causes some commentators, including some chefs, to typify British cuisine by its very openness to foreign influences,[64] but this, in my view, only serves to further 'muddy the water'. Such a view is more about typifying an attitude towards British food that tacitly excepts its culinary poverty than about trying to refine a definition of British cooking. Nevertheless, such an analysis must take into account that foreign influences on cuisine are now no longer connected with any one foreign nation, as was the case with the undisputed hegemony of French cuisine in previous centuries, but with the homogenizing influences of globalization.

The culinary identity of gastropub chefs is defined mainly by reference to their more refined cuisine, rather than their bar food, although the skills and habits embodied in the former also spill over into their provision of pub classics and of the traditional 'roast dinner' Sunday lunches they commonly offer. The training of most of these chefs in fine-dining restaurants means that they have been taught the fundamental techniques of French cuisine and in some cases also of Italian and Spanish and, much less commonly, of Indian and Thai cuisine. The French training and early experience still informs their mode of selection and preparation of produce. Chefs realize that their predominantly middle-class customers, particularly the professional classes, now are partial to a more cosmopolitan style of cooking. At the same time, however, they are conscious of the fact that they work in a pub, a traditional British institution, and that their adopted culinary style may introduce an incompatible element. They therefore strive to offer a cuisine that may be seen to fulfil the requirements of being British; that is, to consciously adopt a British culinary nationalism, even if this is often of a fairly shallow kind.

One way for chefs to reduce the cognitive dissonance is to avoid the high complexity and refinement of upmarket restaurants and instead keep the food 'robust' and avoid the taint of 'exquisite'. This effort is visible in most, though not all, of the pubs I visited. Another, fairly common strategy to meet patrons' expectations of finding some British elements on pubs' menus is to label their food as 'Modern British', regardless of the manner of preparation they employ and often of the actual dishes served. Fourteen of the chefs interviewed, the largest single group, choose this response, 'to match the food', as one landlord states, 'to the nature of the pub'. At the same time, many of them realize the incongruity of their response and diffidently point to the pretence of Britishness usually entailed by this label. 'Modern British covers a plethora of different sins.' 'It's one of these terms. No one can pin it down.' Another publican tells me: 'It's Modern British. I am not quite sure what it means. We use local ingredients, combined with ingredients from around the world.' These chefs regard themselves as simply conforming to a convention in the British hospitality industry. The chefs claiming a Modern British style thus express a banal nationalism,[65] i.e. the every-day representations of the nation which build a shared sense of national belonging among British people. At the same time, they try to legitimate their Modern British culinary style. This cannot be done by referring simply to a *traditional* British cuisine. The latter became discredited in the twentieth century, with even former editors of the *Good Food Guide* having condemned it as 'execrable' or 'non-existent'.[66] Instead, the descriptor Modern British has been uniformly adopted to indicate that British food has made great strides in recent decades.

Several of the above chefs add, though, that they still use French techniques. Overall, 'Modern British' retains a significant French component. If one counts in the three restaurants naming 'British and French', as well as a high proportion of those adopting the label 'European', the French influence on the cuisine of gastropubs remains pronounced. Thus, the London publican, cited above as being unsure of what the label 'Modern British' signifies, confides: '... we try to avoid the term "French". It is not a good selling point.' In other words, the identity of the cuisine is somewhat ambiguous, and the adoption of a label is a matter of which interpretation appeals to the views of diners frequenting gastropubs. Historically, a 'love–hate' relationship to French cuisine has frequently prevailed.[67] Even though one cannot now detect any hate, there still is some ambivalence about adopting a French style, which is often embraced surreptitiously. Chefs no longer disparage French cuisine by using the stereotypes applied to it in earlier centuries, e.g. '*soupe maigre*', but instead utilize new ones. These refer to the use of heavy sauces that disguise the real taste of meat or fish and, more generally, of using too much cream and butter. Such stereotypes conveniently overlook the occurrence of '*nouvelle cuisine*' and its strong, though rarely acknowledged, influence on contemporary *haute cuisine*. There are, however, two chefs in my sample who proudly cook exclusively in the French tradition, featuring all the French favourites and peppering their menus with dishes named in French.

When one of these chefs featured an English pudding one day, it became listed as 'Crumble du Jour'. It is significant that both of these chefs have a slightly problematic relationship with the village in which they are located and instead rely on 'destination' diners.

A number of chefs feel themselves on firmer ground by justifying the label 'Modern British' by reference to their strategy of sourcing produce predominantly locally. If the produce is British, they believe, then this lends an aura of Britishness to the dishes prepared, regardless of the techniques of preparation and even of the history of the dish itself being foreign. One London chef, whose website proclaims a 'Classic British' style, responds like this during the interview: 'I kind of struggle with the term. I use great British ingredients and a lot of farm produce.' Another chef agrees: 'Our cooking is Modern British for the guides—95 per cent of the products are British—but the technique used is French.' Local sourcing from, usually, small producers is, indeed, widely pursued, and this strategy gives some support to their adoption of a British aura. It distinguishes gastropubs effectively from their lower cousins, the ordinary pubs, as well as from the more threatening big branded pubs. As an Essex landlord suggests: '... local sourcing is a critical part of the process. It distinguishes us most critically from chain restaurants.' However, it remains debatable whether such local sourcing is a sufficient element of the culinary process to justify the label 'Modern British'.

Both freshness of ingredients and their high quality, as well as the made-to-order nature of dishes, are emphasized again and again. A Suffolk publican tells me: 'We achieve 70 per cent of local sourcing—within 15 miles. It is a delight. We are lucky in Suffolk.' Or from a Cambridgeshire publican: 'We don't do exotics, everything is grown here.' Even London pub restaurants are sourcing from small producers and procuring meat from selected farms: 'We use small suppliers and are constantly on the phone to them. It is all about contact. They want their ingredients respected.' 'We have a relation with a butcher—fabulous—who butchers the whole animal for us, and we build a special menu around it.' Local sourcing, as often as possible, is thus not a mere marketing technique. Gastropubs, mainly situated in the countryside, are well placed for local sourcing; that is, to buy from near-by farms or small holders, particularly in their acquisition of meats, vegetables, and, in season, of game.

A conscious attempt to be as locally oriented in their sourcing as possible, to preserve authenticity, is thus exceedingly common among my interviewees. Authenticity claims linking food to place rest on the assumption that geographic conditions contribute to foods' inherent characteristics and qualities.[68] Claims for authenticity in the food served are made by several interviewees, some of whom, moreover, mention authenticity also in relation to beer. An artisan revival is identified also in relation to English cheeses.

A London publican speaks of: '[A] cottage industry that is taking back craft and is less mass-produced. Production has to be more transparent as people ask where the meat or fish comes from.'

A third and last way of justifying the label 'Modern British' is to refer to Britain's long-standing proclivity of openness to foreign influences and to its liberal embrace of foreign produce and of elements of other cuisines. A tacit reference to Britain's glorious past as an empire never comes amiss. 'It is global cuisine, a fusion of a myriad of influences from all over the globe, from curry to pizza.' One chef, whose menu has many international references, claims that 'the embrace of many international influences is British'. This chef thus borrows a definition of Modern British first promoted by the *Good Food Guide* in the 1990s,[69] and perpetuated in the 2000s by a prominent food writer.[70] However, it is significant that this embrace of foreign influences is usually carefully controlled to exclude too many Asian elements. These are generally admitted only as small accents or, more rarely, are totally excluded. This is probably a reaction to the large presence in the British hospitality industry of Chinese and Indian restaurants and their association with a down-market image. It thus constitutes a strategy of maintaining distinction. This embrace of many culinary cultures interestingly coincides with a persistence to designate one particular cuisine as 'foreign', namely French cuisine.

A more convincing practice of matching the nature of the food sold to the institution of the British pub exists where publicans offer 'bar food' or 'traditional pub classics'. 'Pub classics are good sellers', one landlord suggests. Serving them still occurs in the majority of the pubs visited, but in fourteen pubs this constitutes only a small proportion of food sold, and, in two pubs, no English bar food is available. Bar food ranges from sandwiches and Ploughman's Lunch to simple British every-day dishes, such as cottage pie and sausages and mash. Among traditional dishes on bar menus, first place is taken by 'fish 'n' chips', which is found on almost every pub's menu, even when pubs do not have a separate menu of pub classics. Another traditional pub dish is the meat pie, seen by several publicans as a crucial part of signalling their identity as a pub restaurant: 'Our pie is a signifier of what we want to be.'[71] These are hot pies made on the premises, with usually high-quality meat fillings.

Conversely, in some pubs, bar menus now feature dishes which were once regarded as foreign exotics but have come to be accepted as almost indigenous dishes, such as lasagne, chilli con carne, and chicken curry. Terms like 'antipasti' or 'tapas', too, seem to have entered the English menu language. Thus, even menus of bar classics, in some gastropubs, display a degree of cultural hybridity. However, this is by no means a central feature of these menus. There is thus a certain degree of menu pluralism, but rarely a global mishmash, as far as the menu for bar classics is concerned.

Culinary nationalism is perhaps most pronounced on Sunday lunch menus, where it is expressed by featuring traditional roast meats with roast potatoes, two vegetables, gravy, and a pungent condiment. An ode to the English roast expressing national pride—not so different from outpourings on its magnificence in earlier centuries—is delivered in the amusing, slightly tongue-in-cheek book of Nigel Slater:

> Nothing quite prepares you for the sheer majesty of the English roast. The melting tender meat, the crisp-edged fat, the deep savour of the gravy, and indeed the host of extras that keep the meat company on the plate... A pool of creamed horseradish root, a dab of Norwich's finest yellow stuff, and enough gravy to float a boat. A dog's dinner? Well, yes, but a glorious dinner too, one that allows the nation to think, for one delicious moment, that we have food that is a match for anyone's.[72]

Of the forty publicans interviewed, all but four do Sunday lunch, and of these only a very small proportion do not offer beef. Such a traditional lunch is still widely expected by patrons and constitutes an important contribution to publicans' income. According to a Suffolk publican: 'We always have beef—it is a non-starter not to have it.' 'Beef is most in demand by a factor of two', suggests one landlord, who offers four roasts on a Sunday. He adds that having beef, always eaten with horseradish and Yorkshire pudding, 'is still connected with being English', and a Cambridgeshire landlord shares this view: 'English people still want their beef on Sunday, with all the trimmings.' The landlady of an Essex coastal pub restaurant agrees: 'There is always roast beef [on the Sunday menu]. It is still considered a traditional lunch—the customers expect to see it [on the menu].' Like Fischler,[73] these publicans realize that 'food not only nourishes but also signifies'. Beef, as the above demonstrates, retains its symbolic connection with national identity—not in a demonstrative way, but as part of long-established custom and habit. Such customary practice, and its supporting beliefs, is built up over many generations and derives its legitimacy from its long-established status. Eating a traditional English Sunday lunch, and particularly one containing roast beef, 'has a taken-for-granted nature for those socialized into their acceptance [of eating habits]'.[74] However, it is thereby no less indicative of a national cultural identity. Those, like Rogers,[75] who have announced the demise of this long-established connection, have thus judged superficially.

The fact that roast beef is still the most popular roast chosen shows a remarkable historical continuity over many centuries in associating beef with Englishness. Beef-eating is no longer connected with a 'fiery' nationalism as it was in the seventeenth and eighteenth centuries, when it was often associated with valour in battle; however, it is still linked with pride in English produce and, to some degree, also with an assertion of masculinity. A London publican observes: 'Yes, [on Sundays, we serve] two roasts, always beef—very popular. It is predominantly men who eat it and older people.'

My finding of the enduring popularity of beef replicates that of Warde and Martens,[76] from a larger survey of dining-out habits at the end of the 1990s—beef was the most popular roast eaten by far. De Soucey, to indicate the force of tradition and identification of a food with nation,[77] quotes one of her French respondents as saying: '[W]e have no Christmas without foie gras.' In a similar vein, many of my respondents might well say that 'there is no Sunday without a traditional roast'.

Gastropubs have also revived some old English desserts like lemon or elderflower posset. Bread-and-butter pudding, fruit crumbles, Eton mess, spotted dick, and sticky toffee pudding, too, have re-gained popularity. Such puddings would only more rarely figure on the menus of upmarket restaurants. How one such English pudding, the trifle (which first appeared as a recipe in Hannah Glasse's 1751 cook book), has gone from initial magnificence to degradation in the twentieth century to be redeemed by top chefs in the twenty-first century is instructively detailed by Nigel Slater's witty account.[78]

However, according to one publican, there are now limits to traditionalism: '[F]ew people have the whole traditional menu—soup, roast beef, and apple crumble.' Another publican, too, emphasizes that people 'want to balance tradition and novelty'. Moreover, a meal of roast beef, as I found one Sunday lunch in a South Wales gastropub, may come with a red wine sauce, potatoes roasted in duck fat, and vegetables cooked *al dente*, providing only faint reminders of a traditional roast lunch. Also, fish has been edging up in the popularity scale, diminishing the attraction of the Sunday roast, as has the growing demand for vegetarian dishes. The expectations of customers, the external stakeholders, thus have evolved and are no longer fully compatible with the food once exclusively served by pubs. Hence, Sunday lunch menus are not confined to traditional English dishes, but also cater for customers with more cosmopolitan tastes.

Publicans realize that traditional Sunday lunches are still expected by a section of their customers. At the same time, they know that the majority of their customers—particularly the middle-class professionals—are no longer simply traditionalists, rooted in geographical identity. Many of them have achieved 'portable' identities,[79] and have developed matching cosmopolitan tastes in food, or are omnivores who mix traditional British food with more elaborate or refined dishes. Alternatively, they may embrace the authenticity of fresh, locally produced food, or they may simply select the French, Spanish, or Italian dishes found on most menus.

Overall, gastropubs play a significant role in fostering and securing our attachment to British national dishes, but this is not easily accomplished. It is often more true in the labels given to the food, than in the actual execution of a dish. Nevertheless, publicans make an effort to retain an aura of Britishness around some of the fare they serve, and there exist nowadays few other upmarket hospitality venues that serve traditional British dishes, as well as the Sunday roast lunch. It would not be too far-fetched to claim that most gastropubs make a significant contribution to the preservation of traditional English fare. Moreover, they do it at a high level of quality and thus contribute strongly to the improvement of not only pub fare, but to gastronomy all round and to the raising of our gastronomic reputation abroad.

This chapter has explored how customers' social identity becomes expressed and reinforced by gastropubs' food, drink, and sociality. Publicans try hard to tailor their pub's organizational identity to what they think patrons want, even if, as in the case of a Modern British style of cooking, the labels do not fully correspond with what is actually offered. Nevertheless, the considerable choice in the food these pubs serve enables them to offer and thereby preserve more British traditional dishes—bar staples—than most restaurants.

In conclusion, this chapter has investigated how the food served by gastropubs relates to chefs' and patrons' social identity—class, gender, and national identity—as well as the reciprocal relation between personal identity and organizational identity. Although publicans'/chefs' culinary identity, as the result of training and previous restaurant experience, may sometimes be hard to reconcile with that of diners, most of them try hard to take customers' wishes into account. After all, they are running a business, rather than satisfying their ego. In comparison with the social identity of pubs' patrons in previous centuries—studied in earlier chapters—there have occurred significant changes, mirroring the social transformations experienced after World War II and, particularly, in the twenty-first century. Gastropubs attract more middle class and more female customers, with gender discrimination greatly reduced, though not eliminated. Unlike taverns, they cater for more omnivorous diners who, although still expressing national identification in some of their food choices, also adhere to cosmopolitan choices according to time of day or social occasion, or happily mix the two even in one and the same meal.

Endnotes

1. Warde, A. 1997, *Consumption, Food and Taste*, 17. London: Sage Publications.
2. British Beer and Pub Association (BBPA), 2015, *BPA Statistical*. London: Brewing Publications Ltd.
3. Rural Essex publican, 2016.

4. Rural Cambridgeshire publican, 2016.
5. London publican, 2015.
6. Warde, A. and Martens, L. 2000, *Eating Out. Social differentiation, consumption and pleasure*, 69. Cambridge: Cambridge University Press.
7. Warde and Martens, 2000; Mennell, S. 1985, *All Manners of Food. Eating and taste in England and France from the Middle Ages to the present*. Oxford: Blackwell; Burnett, J. 1969, *Plenty and Want. A social history of diet in England from 1815 to the present day*. London: Thomas Nelson and Sons.
8. Warde and Martens, 2000, 71.
9. Warde, 1997, 190.
10. Mennell, S., Murcott, A. and van Otterloo, A. 1992, *The Sociology of Food. Eating, diet and culture*, 4. London: Sage Publications.
11. James, A. 1997, 'How British is British food?', P. Kaplan ed., *Food, Health and Identity*, 81. London: Routledge.
12. Warde and Martens, 2000, 90.
13. For more information on cultural omnivores and omnivorousness, see Peterson, R. and Kern, R. 1996, 'Changing high-brow taste: from snob to omnivore', *American Sociological Review*, 61: 900–7; and Silva, E.B., Warde, A., Gayo-Cal, M. and Wright, D. 2009, *Culture, Class, Distinction*. London: Routledge.
14. Bourdieu, P. 1984, *Distinction. The social judgement of taste*. London: Routledge.
15. Cambridgeshire pub, 2015.
16. Essex rural pub, 2016.
17. Lake District pub in a wooded walking area.
18. Bourdieu, 1984, refers to upbringing as a vital way to pass on to offspring social poise and confidence and therefore class-bound social advantages.
19. East London publican, 2016.
20. Yorkshire publican, 2016.
21. West Suffolk rural publican, 2016.
22. Cambridgeshire rural publican, 2015.
23. North London publican, 2015.
24. North London publican, 2015.
25. Cambridgeshire publican, 2015.
26. Rural Oxfordshire publican, 2016.
27. Suffolk rural publican, 2016.
28. Rural Cambridgeshire publican, 2015.
29. Berkshire pub restaurant, 2016.
30. Rural Worcestershire pub, 2016.
31. Wouters, C. 2007, *Informalization, Manners and Emotions since 1890*, 12. London: Sage Publications.
32. Beider, H. 2015, *White Working-Class Voices. Multiculturalism, community-building and change*, 122–3, 137–9. Bristol: Policy Press.
33. Warde and Martens, 2000; Mennell, 1985; Burnett, 1969.
34. Mennell et al., 1992, 4.
35. Cambridgeshire publican, 2016.
36. Cambridgeshire publican, 2016.

37. London publican, 2015.
38. Essex publican, 2015.
39. Kent publican, 2016.
40. London publican, 2015.
41. Suffolk publican, 2016.
42. Cambridgeshire publican, 2016.
43. Williams, Z. 2017, 'The last of the big boozers', *Guardian 2*, 23.02.2017.
44. Kent publican, 2016.
45. Oxfordshire publican, 2015.
46. Worcestershire publican, 2016.
47. Yorkshire publican, 2016.
48. South Wales landlady, 2016.
49. West Midlands publican, 2016.
50. London publican, 2016.
51. London publican, 2015.
52. Selley, E. 1927, *The English Public House As It Is*. London: Longmans, Green and Co. Ltd.
53. Cambridgeshire pub, 2016.
54. Landlady of Essex coastal pub, 2015.
55. Landlady of pub in South Wales, 2016.
56. Fox, K. 2004, *Watching the English*. London: Hodder and Stoughton.
57. Worcestershire publican, 2016.
58. West Midlands rural pub, 2016.
59. Paddock, J., Warde, A. and Whillans, J. 2017, 'The changing meaning of eating out in three English cities 1995–2015', *Appetite*, 119: 7.
60. Fischler, C. 1988, 'Food, self and identity', *Social Science Information*, 27, 2: 275–92.
61. Fischler, 1988, 280.
62. de Soucey, M. 2010, 'Gastronationalism: food traditions and authenticity politics in the European Union', *American Journal of Sociology*, 75, 3: 432–55.
63. Slater, N. 2007, *Eating for England. The delights and eccentricities of the British at table*, xviii. London: Fourth Estate.
64. Slater, 2007, xviii.
65. Billig, M. 1995, *Banal Nationalism*. London: Sage Publications.
66. Warde, A. 2009, 'Imagining British cuisine: representations of culinary identity in the *Good Food Guide*', *Culture, Food and Society*, 12, 2: 157.
67. Rogers, B. 2003, *Beef and Liberty*. London: Chatto & Windus.
68. Bell, D. and Valentine, G. 1997, *We Are Where We Eat*. London: Routledge.
69. Warde, 2009.
70. Slater, 2007, xviii; Billig, 1995.
71. Rural Cambridgeshire publican.
72. Slater, 2007, 135–6.
73. Fischler, 1988, 276.
74. Beardsworth, A. and Keil, T. 1997, *Sociology on the Menu. An invitation to the study of food and society*, 67. London: Routledge.
75. Rogers, 2003.

76. Warde and Martens, 2000, 137.
77. De Soucey, 2010, 447.
78. Slater, 2007, 162–3.
79. Goodhart, D. 2017, *The Road to Somewhere. The populist revolt and the future of politics*. London: Hirst.

8

The Future of the Pub: Are Gastropubs the Saviour or the Nemesis of the Traditional Pub?

How has the gastropub affected the pub landscape more generally? Has it been the saviour or the nemesis of traditional pubs? Is the gastropub still a centre for local communities? What has been its impact on British attitudes to 'good food'? There is no easy answer to these questions as the gastropub has several different functions, some of which strengthen the place of the pub in British society and some of which may undermine it. The overall impact on the social institution of the pub is therefore difficult to measure. In the simplest numerical terms, the gastropub has saved a significant proportion of pubs from closure and has even brought back to life some already closed. In addition to answering the above questions and by way of conclusion to the book, this chapter also attempts to forge more explicit links between the historical explorations of the three different types of hostelries and the chapters presenting the gastropub in the twenty-first century.

It is clear that wet-led pubs are no longer viable in all but some city centre locations and that a move to the provision of meals has become inevitable (see the discussion of reasons for closure in Chapter 5). Mere boozers would have closed down even without the appearance of the gastropub. The facilitation of dining at often quite a high level of excellence, as found in the gastropub, is still too much a minority phenomenon in the general pub landscape to have exerted a pervasive influence. (The 2016 Michelin guide to *Eating Out in Pubs* had 590 entries in 2016,[1] but there is probably a larger number of pubs than this qualifying for the term.) The necessary culinary and organizational skills needed to run a gastropub are not widely held. This conclusion does not, however, deny the considerable beneficial influence of the gastropub: on the built landscape, the wider pub sector, and the quest for community, as well as on the upgrading of food and drink and on consumers' attitudes to food.

The Gastropub's Impact on the General Pub Landscape

In many villages, the introduction of a gastropub has prevented the total disappearance of pubs from a village's stock of historic buildings and has preserved the often sole community focus, as well as an interesting historic building. Several pub devotees told me that they moved to their present village because it had a pub that could act as a social centre. Additionally, it is believed that knowledgeable foreign tourists value the 'gastropub' experience. A London publican with many foreign tourists among his customers observes: 'If visiting London, you want to visit a gastropub. A lot of people still enjoy a pint.' A Lake District chef is proud of the fact that a Japanese company filmed their pub and that guests come from all over the world. However, gastropubs are mainly a rural phenomenon. The high prices of urban high street property have driven them from most city centres, as has the competition from mega pubs, enjoying the benefits of scale by operating a more efficient and therefore more lucrative chain model.

The Food and Drink Served by Gastropubs

In general terms, food among the pubs interviewed was invariably of a high standard and in some cases outstanding. (There is now a significant number of gastropubs that have been awarded a Michelin star.) Regarding the price of meals, publicans are trying to perform a difficult balancing act between the costly provision of high quality, individually prepared food and keeping their prices below those of upmarket restaurants with a similar offering. Their food is essentially a 'craft' product, competing with a cheaper industrially produced one. This problem is magnified by the fact that pubs in general have lower prices than restaurants and that patrons therefore expect lower prices.[2] They thus have the costs of restaurants but are expected to charge pub prices, creating another area where their dual organizational identity presents publicans with a serious problem. A good number of publicans manage to offer meals at very competitive prices and aim to 'offer value'. A Lake District chef tells me: 'X [the owner] wants to give value. She does not want to go above [a rate of profit of 65 per cent].' One pub has a Michelin Bib Gourmand award, which suggests high quality at an affordable price, and another publican suggests: 'The food should be affordable—good food should be more democratic.' A London pub aims 'to combine skills and ingredients from the best restaurants in town with a truly egalitarian, good value pub'.

For most pubs, however, prices are only slightly below those in upmarket restaurants or are even at the same level. Publicans are determined that they must not compromise quality by reducing their prices too much. The 'superior quality' of their food is an important component of their gastropub identity. Hence, the relatively low-price ceilings of £10 for a starter, £20 for a main course, and £7 for a dessert, said to be part of the definition of a gastropub by the trade magazine *Restaurant*,[3] do not apply to all the pubs I visited. Moreover, the picture regarding pricing cannot be given by quoting simple price ceilings, but is highly differentiated and thus more complex. Many publicans have worked out a compromise in that the more expensive menu of *Specials* is supplemented by a very affordable *Prix Fixe* menu during week-day lunches when two courses may be consumed for between £12.00 and £15.00. Also, the simpler bar staples sell at very competitive prices. Furthermore, the total bill is reduced by the fact that, in the great majority of the forty pubs, the wine list contains predominantly low- and medium-priced wines.

Gastropubs, given their relatively low weight in the whole pub sector, thus exert only a modest positive influence on the dining pub sector as a whole. Their business format of high quality food, using fresh produce and enjoying individual preparation, precludes an increased incidence, as does the shortage of skilled chefs. Nevertheless, they have managed to make some valuable contributions to the eating-out sector. They have not only introduced diversity into the sector. They also stand out as beacons of individuality and excellence in the sea of mass-produced and highly standardized food offered by most of the brewery- and pubco-owned houses and by the high street chains of mega pubs. As pioneers and leaders in the field of high quality pub food, many gastropubs have influenced establishments in their neighbourhood and thereby raised the general quality level of pub food. Thus, a Lake District pub prides itself on influencing many other pubs in the neighbourhood: 'Pubs in the area take a lead from us.' A Kent publican makes the same claim and points to particular newly-opened local pubs copying his format. A highly-rated Lancashire pub chef agrees: 'I had to set the standards where other pubs would be in ten years time. Other pubs would want to copy my business model. It took me four years to get there.' The chef of the only two-star gastropub, Tom Kerridge, has published a well-received cook book, featuring some of the robust cuisine of his gastropub, that has spread good practice in this way.

Gastropubs pose an example, not only in the provision of meals, but also in the beer they stock. Not being tied to a brewery in the large majority of cases, they have been able to introduce diversity also in the beers they stock. Nearly all of them sell several real ales in addition to the more standard keg beers and lagers. Whereas much of the keg beer and lager is now made by corporate and usually foreign-owned breweries, real ale comes from small, local owner-managed breweries. While the few (seven) brewery- or pubco-owned establishments in my sample can only stock one guest beer, they usually rotate between different real ales. Gastropubs thus have a positive impact on the supplier sector for both drink and produce, favouring smaller and independent suppliers. Last, the gastropubs, due to their larger number of covers, longer opening times, and wider cross-class appeal, have permitted a larger cross section of the population to experience 'good food' than traditional top-end restaurants have been able to do.

Pub Sociality and Contribution to Community Life

However, critics will ask, what is the compatibility of a strong catering function with the traditional sociality fostered by pubs. Moreover, does the upmarket nature of the fare still manage to attract the traditional constituency of the pub—the working classes—or has the pub ceased to be inclusive and to integrate patrons from a variety of social backgrounds? The gastropub, like other social institutions, clearly has evolved and adjusted to a changing society. While it fulfils some of its traditional functions less well, it may have developed some new ones, more fitting to the society it now inhabits.

The nature of sociality cultivated in gastropubs has been examined in some detail in Chapter 6. My conclusion was that gastropubs are not merely commercial undertakings, but most of them remain an important social institution, even if their social character has been in some ways curtailed and/or changed. The gastropub is still sought after as a place for informal and spontaneous socializing with friends and neighbours and for bridging the boundary between work and play, between stress and relaxation. The changed class composition of the 'pub crowd' is largely a mirror of the changes in the world of work, and the gastropub is a response to these changes, rather than a cause of the crisis in the pub sector. The nature of work has changed, with hard physical toil being more exceptional now. At the same time, the reduction of factory work, where large groups of mainly men worked in close proximity and where work was close to home, also has dwindled in importance. The all-male drinking pub in a mining community, for example, found in the 1950s by Dennis et al.[4] (see Chapter 1), disappeared with the demise of the British mining industry. Hence, where once the work collective also formed the nucleus of the leisure collective, this is now fairly rarely the case.

As a consequence, pub visiting, particularly by manual workers, has become less frequent, and the amount drunk has significantly decreased. The resulting sociality has become less boisterous and has consequently permitted a change in clientele, with women having become an important customer base and, for day-time dining, also whole families. The gastropub less frequently attracts a community of drinkers based on a work group, with some exceptions in London where work now is mainly white-collar and frequently of the professional type. As certain areas of London often attract related businesses, it becomes attractive for people who work there to meet formally and informally to exchange information. Thus, the landlord of The Eagle in London's Clerkenwell tells me that he has 'not so much a living community, more a working community—the pub is the social hub for this community', which consists largely of professional employees. City-based employees, too, tend to frequent pubs near their place of work in the east of London. Even in the countryside, an Essex pub, situated near a slaughterhouse, is the drinking and meeting place of its workers. A number of publicans also emphasize that their house provides opportunities for independent and small-scale business owners—a large and growing occupational group in current society—to meet and exchange experiences.

Hence, despite a decline of drinking by groups of manual workers from nearby enterprises, the striving for community is not dead. My questions to interviewees about whether they still see themselves as a centre of the local community and whether they offer any facilities for community activities yielded some surprising answers. *First*, community activities centre not only on village pubs, but also on urban ones. Even Londoners are 'not bowling alone',[5] and community life seems to be thriving. If anything, community activities are more developed in (sub)urban areas, possibly because village halls are not provided there. *Second*, the gastropub has come to offer facilities for a very wide range of community activities. Unsurprisingly, these differ somewhat from those associated with pubs in past centuries. There has occurred a shift from economic and political functions to more social recreational ones, including self-improvement, mirroring our modern leisure society. However, informal meetings by various groups of business men and women still occur. This may reflect the increase of 'small business' activity in the contemporary economy and the often isolated position a self-employed person may find him/herself in. In one rural Essex pub, even a large company located in the neighbourhood holds its staff appraisal meetings in the pub. This occurs not for a lack of company rooms, but because managers appreciate the more relaxed environment offered by the pub. A *third* change is that the clubs are frequented by both men and women and some even by children.

In rural areas, where gastropubs are often the only pub in a large swathe of countryside, they may even serve several villages. Thus, an Oxfordshire licensee, surrounded by villages now without any pub, tells me: 'Most people in the village and in surrounding villages use us as a social centre. We are a big part of the local community.' Another rural publican confirms that bringing the community together is still considered a vital function: 'Absolutely [I see the pub as a social centre for the people of this village]. It should not lose its community identity. I very much believe in it.' An Essex publican is just as keen to serve the local community: 'This is a small village with only 39 inhabitants, and we cater for them. The pub is a meeting place for them.' 'We really try and immerse ourselves in the community. We do fund raising for village concerns.'[6] And elsewhere: 'Chefs are coming to prefer to work in this environment... There is the association with the communal. It is not exclusive.'[7]

The ability of the publican to offer a room for community activities is, of course, limited by the availability of a separate room. In the face of opened up and consolidated bar spaces in many pubs, this is no longer possible in all gastropubs. Nevertheless, a large proportion of publicans offer a room for community activities, either on a regular basis or at certain times of the year, and one publican even makes available his dining room for meetings on the pub's official closing day. Thus, London publicans host, among others, 'a book club and the local choir meeting regularly'; 'workshops run by a group making a terrarium and also a local preservation group, run by creatives'; 'a Mums and Babies Yoga group, a monkey music room for kids, a drama group, and PTA meetings for both local schools'; 'a medical self-help group, and CAMRA meetings'; and 'regular weekly coffee mornings for the over 50s, organised by the local Age Concern'. Another London publican, who hosts a lot of leisure-time groups—'U3A, Friends of the Earth, a chess club, the local theatre club, and a cook book club'—emphasizes that the room is available for free to gain good will. A suburban Bedford pub makes available its Garden Room to 'the Rotary club once a week, and to a walking club once a month' as well as hosting 'a ladies networking group and a mixed networking group'. The publican explains that 'these are people who have their own business and do cross-selling or are just getting their name out there'.

The community meetings hosted in rural areas involve more farmers' groups, as well as meetings of the parish council and of the Women's Institute, but also include all kinds of sports and book clubs. They additionally host 'an investment club, [meetings of] a board of trustees of a local establishment, and a rescue team'; '... and the cardiology unit from Blackburn hospital. We try to be all things to all people', a Lancashire publican explains. A pub in rural Rutland not only caters for the local community by hosting the gardening club, the village committee, the cricket club, and a small-business meeting for people 'who come and chew the fat', they also do a Christmas and a harvest dinner for villagers. Additionally, the publican manages to involve his staff with the population of the small village in a joint cricket team. Hence, the local gastropub is not merely a place to eat, but it additionally integrates individuals into the local community in a way not too dissimilar from past centuries. The gastropub, in many areas, definitely remains a social hub of the local community. Apart from being a social centre, in rural areas it is also a focal point that gives the village an identity, much like a local church.

The importance publicans bestow on the pub as a centre for the local community is also confirmed by the pub regulars I interviewed in two villages. In an Essex village the pub had recently closed and a community action group had tried to get it re-opened, whereas in the other, a Cambridgeshire village, a group of activists had managed to rescue their pub from closure through community action. One activist resident of the Cambridgeshire village tells me: 'The single most important reason why I moved here [is the presence of this pub]. It is a social centre, and I like the facilities it offers. We go there to unwind before we go back home.' The residents of the Essex village expressed similar feelings about their pub: 'The pub is the heart of the community. It is a place to meet other villagers, relax, have a meal. I could go at any time and meet someone, which is nice. Lots of clubs meet there as well.' Another pub regular who moved to the village because it had a pub says: 'The pub was a meeting place, and in a village of this size, it is the only place... it is much more warm and friendly than our village hall. The pub is everybody's front room.' A third resident is sad that 'the village has lost an extremely important asset. I am thinking of moving'.

However, this rosy picture is not found everywhere. Anecdotal information suggests that, in some villages, inhabitants feel that the arrival of a gastropub has robbed them of a community centre and that the food and drink sold does not satisfy everyone's demands. A small number of publicans indicate that their own objectives are not always congruent with the wishes of many villagers. The latter desire either a greater emphasis on the bar or the provision of more traditional bar food, rather than upmarket gastronomic fare. Hence, the relationship between the publican and the village community can be fraught, with resentment felt on both sides. Villagers still think in terms of 'their pub' and do not concede that a small village can no longer guarantee the financial viability of a pub, even when the latter offers food. Many pubs in such small villages are forced to turn themselves into a dining 'destination' for a wider socio-geographical constituency. This means the adoption of an attractive gastronomic menu over and above the pub staples many still retain or, in a few cases, replacing them. It may also signal to members of the lower socio-economic classes that their local pub does not cater for their needs. Many licensees of gastropubs thus are perennially pulled in incompatible directions and find it difficult to develop a settled organizational identity.

Influence on British Attitudes to Good Food

Another major issue is how the gastropub has affected the attitudes of British people towards food, and, related to this, how it has impacted on the hospitality industry as a whole, particularly on its 'eating out' dimension? Has it played a role in raising peoples' expectations towards food? Is the old pessimistic assessment of British diners' attitude, that, when eating out, their main concern is to save time and money,[8] still valid in the twenty-first century?

Or have British palates become more sophisticated and diners more demanding? Do dining customers, who often no longer have the time and/or the inclination to cook at home, nevertheless possess a greater knowledge about good food, seek out innovative dishes, and have a more developed ability to appreciate inventive food? These are, of course, big complex questions to which only tentative answers are possible.

Chefs of gastropubs, despite holding a variety of opinions about their dining customers' knowledge, expectations, and tastes, mainly believe that patrons' sophistication has grown and that they appreciate the food gastropubs provide. 'It [the rise of the gastropub] has to do with the increasing demand for good-quality, reasonably priced food. The English are more sophisticated than they were, they are increasingly familiar with a variety of cuisines.'[9] 'There is a much increased public awareness about good quality food.'[10] A London publican agrees with an increase in knowledge, but is unusual in noting also customers' increasingly adventurous home cooking: 'We get very knowledgeable customers here. They have travelled a lot and know about food. You can't fob them off. Food knowledge has improved so much. They do adventurous food at home.' This pub is situated in an affluent North London location and counts mainly 'arty' professionals among its customers, which may explain the more cosmopolitan tastes and the 'adventurous cooking at home'. A greater demand for local provenance of produce—which gastropubs consciously cater for—is also singled out: 'People come because of the rise in food quality in the last decade and a greater interest in the food's provenance.'

An Oxfordshire publican/chef additionally points to the improved 'supply side' factors: 'The quality of chefs in pubs has risen'—a fact my research fully confirms. The facts that the quality of food eaten commercially has improved enormously and that customers now have higher expectations are shared by several other interviewees. A Suffolk publican sees the 'foodie revolution' as due to both the 'London' factor and the middle-class customer base of his gastropub: 'If you live in a county in commuting distance from London, the level of understanding of food is high and especially if the county is predominantly middle class. Fine food is still the preserve of the middle class.' He may be right about the 'class' influence, but my identification of excellent gastropubs also in the counties of the Midlands and the north of England would suggest that, despite London's undoubted influence, a confinement of good pub food to the south east is no longer warranted.

A Bedford publican attributes the popularity of gastropubs not merely to the food they sell: 'This is the age of people who can't cook and don't know how to cook, but like to go out to explore new foods.' Three landlords from rural Essex and Hertfordshire also mention the decline of home cooking:

'People are going out more, they are getting more lazy.' 'Minimal cookers come—husband and wife after work. It is a convenience during the week.' 'Can't cook tea tonight, let's just nip to the pub after work.' The informality of the gastropub means that this can be a 'spur of the moment' decision as they usually do not need to book. Such an increase in impromptu meals taken, to save the effort of cooking at home, is also a prominent finding from a large survey of diners undertaken in 2015 by Paddock et al.[11]

In sum, these publicans single out increased knowledge about food, a greater adventurousness in ordering dishes, as well as raised expectations about food quality and increased interest in the provenance of the food consumed. The very existence of gastropubs, with their generally quite original gastronomic menus (as opposed to bar menus), bears out that there is considerable demand for such food. The evidence about cooking such food at home is divided, and may reflect the different customer social bases of pubs.

But such a largely positive evaluation about customers' knowledge and expectations from the majority of interviewees is not uniformly held. One publican offers a more pessimistic evaluation:

> There is an aspiration to holding on to high standards, but customers make this very difficult. I don't believe there has occurred a 'Food Revolution' in Britain. The market for high-end food is tiny. Customers make large demands, but have no tolerance for waiting for products started from scratch, rather than being pre-prepared. Our tastes are becoming increasingly Americanized, we are becoming lazy. We employ Slovakians as Kitchen Porters. They are much more enquiring about food [than the English].

One of his Essex colleagues identifies another limitation in customers' attitudes to his food—a lack of appreciation of inventiveness in the food served: 'Standards and quality are higher, but people are still shy of innovative food. Most people, at most, dip only a little toe into novel food. There has to be an element of familiarity.'

While no other interviewees endorse these more negative evaluations of customer attitudes towards gastropubs' more complex and creative food, such pessimistic views about British attitudes to good food are more often expressed by food critics, journalists, and industry bodies, even if often obliquely. One such evaluation is made by Tony Naylor, a journalist at the hospitality journal *Restaurant*,[12] who is very familiar with both high-end restaurants and gastropubs. He, too, emphasizes the recent increase in the Americanization of our food scene, pointing to the undoubtedly real proliferation of eateries specializing in the so-called Luxury Burger. Naylor believes that, after some notable improvements in the first decade of this century, the gains in our food culture are being lost again. His incisive analysis of recent changes and their reasons merit a lengthy quotation from his article:

> Where is the venue serving rigorous... food predicated on the intelligence of its chef and quality of raw ingredients, or, in other words 'serious food'.
>
> In the UK in general, the last decade has seen a fundamental shift in Britain's idea of what constitutes good food. The local and seasonal, worthy and cerebral foodie aesthetic that was dominant prior to 2008 is now in generational retreat. Its adherents increasingly look like a harried religious cult.[13]

Naylor is undoubtedly right about a bigger turn towards convenience food in recent years, with the number of outlets for take-away food substantially increased since 2014, particularly in poorer urban areas of the north west, but also in some southern areas.[14] Industry reports also confirm that consumers rate 'value for money' as one of the most important factors influencing their decision to eat in a pub.[15]

Among the several reasons for the deterioration in the quality of food since 2008, Naylor cites the following: the pressures on lowering prices; an acute shortage of skilled chefs, which means that, by necessity, openings have to revolve around a few easily replicated menu items, such as the now ubiquitous mac 'n' cheese; the prioritization of interior design, attitude, and an exuberant media voice over what is on the plate; as well as the declining financial feasibility of talented chefs' building up a momentum over time.[16]

Naylor's observations ring very true applied to many upmarket restaurants, but I contend that gastropubs are not guilty of the 'gastronomic crimes' he singles out. Although many of them serve a burger, or an equivalent, they also continue to produce 'serious food', painstakingly sourced and prepared from scratch. They do not prioritize design over food, nor presentation over taste. There is no race to the bottom among the upmarket gastropubs I visited; gastropubs are still making a strong contribution to lifting the general image of the British eating-out scene in their championing of freshness and quality of produce, as well as in their upholding of the quality of the finished product. They are additionally asserting individuality in a sea of standardization. Despite their relatively low weight in the pub sector as a whole, gastropubs serve as beacons in the industry, and, given their large customer base in terms of covers served (as compared with upmarket restaurants), their influence on British attitudes to food and on the eating-out scene should not be underestimated. However, it should not be forgotten that they influence predominantly members of the middle and upper middle classes and that consumption of take-away food and a consequent increase in obesity is growing among lower-income groups.[17] British food culture is in no way homogenous, but strongly stratified. However, in rural gastropubs, members of the skilled working and lower middle classes are now gaining a modest presence, and in many London gastropubs cross-class pub visiting is experienced. In sum, the evidence about the degree of appreciation of good and inventive food by the British is mixed, and this research is unable to settle the question of relative progress or deterioration in customers' attitudes to food.

Apart from the superior quality of food served in gastropubs, the latter also make a valuable contribution to preserving a British food tradition, even if the 'Modern British' label is often contrived or is followed only selectively. Gastropubs' most obvious contributions towards keeping a British tradition alive, while simultaneously lifting dishes' quality and therefore reputation, lies in the provision of bar classics and of Sunday lunch, featuring the traditional roast with trimmings. They are additionally keeping up tradition in the area of desserts.

But even in their gastronomically more ambitious cuisine, several of the chefs make an important contribution towards preserving and developing English dishes. A close analysis of pubs' menus of *Specials*[18] shows that the main component of a 'mains' dish—the meat, fowl, or fish—reminds the diner of the simple and fairly plain traditional English cooking. However, the preparation is now more carefully judged and the flavour therefore better preserved. Subsequently, the meat, fowl, or fish are then often lifted into a realm approximating 'haute cuisine' by an imaginative pairing with other ingredients that are neither traditional, nor necessarily British. Chefs may choose a pairing with another (set of) ingredient(s) not usually combined. Thus, a Yorkshire pub combines a mains of 'Yorkshire Wolds Duck with Greengage Plum, Parsnip and Honey', and a Cambridgeshire pub serves a 'Braised Pig Cheek & Belly Faggot with Mouli, Carrot, Udon Noodles, Coriander and Miso Broth'. Alternatively, the main ingredient is complemented and enhanced by the pairing with a more unusual vegetable or sauce, which are often from another culinary tradition. Thus, the 'Roast English Venison' of a London pub is served with 'Salsify and Pistachio Crumbs', and the traditional and humble 'Cottage Pie' in a Cumbrian pub contains oxtail and venison and comes trickled with a 'Red Berry & Portwine Jus'. A Suffolk pub pairs its 'Slow Roasted Shoulder of Lamb' with a 'Jerusalem Artichoke and Potato Dauphinoise', while a 'Tomato and Mushroom Sauce' has ousted the usual British mint sauce. Alternatively, the very English 'Swaledale Lamb Rump' of a Hertfordshire pub surprises by coming with an accompaniment of 'Merguez & Moroccan Chick Pea Stew'. Thus, while the rules concerning the mode of preparation of the main ingredients (such as either grilling, roasting, or frying—and rarely braising—a piece of meat, fowl, or fish) and the flavour principles are preserved, the rules of combining ingredients have been imaginatively changed. While this sometimes leads to eclecticism, it does nevertheless preserve an element of Britishness.

A third and more rarely found way to preserve the British character of a dish is to de- and re-construct a traditional English dish in an imaginative and sometimes witty manner that nevertheless pays homage to a British food tradition. Thus, a starter and a dessert eaten in a Lancashire pub impressed with its imaginative pairings, and its extremely tasty de-and re-construction. The starter featured 'Black Pudding with Crispy Hen's Egg, Bacon Dashi and Piccalilli Puree', while the dessert of a 'Doughnut Ring filled with Apple Puree' astonished by the extreme lightness of the pastry and the subtle but sharply contrasting flavouring of the apple puree. It looked just like a traditional British doughnut, but tasted like an *haute cuisine* delicacy.

Generally, a British tradition is more frequently preserved in the desserts section of the menu, than in the sections for starters and mains. This reflects the fact that, historically, British cooking has had a strong emphasis on desserts, as well as having managed to retain an exceptionally large variety. Thus, tarts, pies, and crumbles proliferate, and possets and syllabubs appear frequently. Yet, even these traditional sweets have often found new partners on the plate to counterbalance their sweetness or stodginess. So, the 'Treacle Tart' of a North London pub comes accompanied by a 'Yoghurt Sorbet & Pedro Ximinez Caramel'; the 'Lemon Meringue Pie' of a Rutland pub is given a taste contrast in the form of a 'Raspberry Sorbet'; and the 'English Strawberries' of a London pub come paired with 'Lemon Verbena Curd, Strawberry Jam & Sorbet'.

I have shown that both in its food and drink, as well as in the sociality and community spirit fostered, the gastropub has made many positive contributions. Whether, in the future, the gastropub becomes the saviour or destroyer of the institution of the traditional pub depends on whether publicans continue their efforts to balance their liking for sophisticated food with preserving the traditional pub function and atmosphere in the face of considerable financial pressure to utilize space for dining. The character of the pub will inevitably change over time, adapting to the evolving society and its members' needs and expectations. Rather than preserving pubs as museum pieces, they have to be allowed to evolve with the time, as they have done over past centuries. If we are to have pubs selling as much food as drink, we should welcome those providing meals at a high level of excellence.

This chapter has shown gastropubs to have a distinctive organizational identity, but alas a still ambiguous or unsettled one. They have incorporated elements from both restaurants and more traditional pubs. However, in their organizational identity, they have moved away from both these types of hostelry. In terms of food, drink, and service, they are far more flexible than restaurants, as well as cultivating a more distinctive ambience and a livelier sociability. In the provision of food and drink, they offer a wider spectrum than the traditional pubs, described in earlier chapters, and they maintain higher quality standards than mere food-led pubs.

In sum, my analysis of today's gastropubs judges them to make largely a very positive contribution to the hospitality industry and particularly to its 'dining' dimension. Due to their still low numerical weight, gastropubs cannot decisively halt the decline of the pub in general, but the gastropub does not act as its nemesis.

From Taverns to Gastropubs?

How far and in what ways does the gastropub reflect and perpetuate the English historical traditions that characterized taverns, inns, and public houses in earlier centuries? What elements of their physical appearance, selection of food and drink, and of the sociality cultivated have been carried forward into the twenty-first century?

The most obvious continuity lies in the pub buildings and some of their interior appearance, such as plenty of beams, flagstone floors, and large open fire places. Many of today's gastropubs have their origin in either a seventeenth to nineteenth century public house (rarely in a modest ale house) and, very often, an historic inn. One London publican tells me that his gastropub with rooms 'is not that dissimilar to a coaching inn—it is a modern take on the coaching inn'. Eleven pubs are in buildings that were formerly inns, and four publicans prefer the label 'inn' to that of 'pub'. When we look at the food and drink being offered, the combination of a substantial meal with the drinking of wine reminds one of the tavern. While some of the English dishes being served may well have been offered to tavern customers in earlier centuries, most of the more upmarket cuisine today bears little resemblance to food served in taverns and inns in previous centuries. Particularly striking is the improvement in the quality and diversity of pub food, compared with earlier centuries. This, according to a large-scale consumer survey, applies to food-led pubs in general,[19] and the influence of gastropubs among them can only have served to heighten this perception. Drinking a draught beer at the bar, in contrast, carries forward some of the traditions of the public houses of earlier centuries, although the changes in the accompanying sociality probably are more striking than the continuities.

While today's gastropub, due to the much reduced incidence of drunkenness, cultivates an incomparably more decorous conviviality, some crucial elements of tavern and public house sociality have been carried forward into the twenty-first century: the relaxed and relatively inclusive hospitality and the extremely informal and flexible nature of consumption of food and drink today have strong echoes of tavern sociality. Due to increasing institutional differentiation, starting already in the eighteenth century, pubs in general, including gastropubs, have, for some time, ceased to be the location where occupational, employment, and political matters are transacted. Hence, today's gastropubs fulfil far fewer social, economic, and hardly any political functions. However, they still serve as informal meeting places for friends and acquaintances, as well as offering room for all sorts of communal meetings and clubs. The fulfilment of social functions predominates, although some pubs still serve as meeting places for people with similar economic interests and are able to facilitate occupational networking. Such networking now no longer solely benefits men, but also women, with the gender diversification of the customer base. In sum, gastropubs, despite their emphasis on more complex food, still retain the ability to be a focus for community life, in both rural and in urban areas.

Gastropubs, like taverns, mainly attract middle- and upper middle-class customers, which shows a marked discontinuity with the traditional customer base of pubs. The change in the class composition of the gastropub's customer base is one of the most striking historical discontinuities, as compared with pubs in previous centuries. In parallel with these changes in the class background of customers, a significant proportion of publicans now come from middle-class professions, and their background exerts a subtle influence on sociality. Most of the chefs of gastropubs are professionals, just as the chefs of many taverns were in the past. However, just as in the past, social politeness, which frowns upon a condescending stance towards members of lower classes,[20] commands that every comer receives a welcome from both the publican and his/her middle-class customers. Whether, in practice, this welcome is always extended is a matter which cannot be settled by this research.

The biggest social change from tavern to gastropub, however, is the greatly reduced gender discrimination and the active welcome and strong presence of women and families, particularly in the dining room, but still less so at the bar. However, copious alcohol consumption, although now much less common, still remains a male privilege or, depending on one's view, vice. Then, as now, drinking beers at the bar expresses masculinity. Female drunkenness among the young still is more frowned upon than that of men.

When we move from class and gender identity to national identification through attendance of taverns and gastropubs, the picture becomes exceedingly complex. 'Fiery nationalism', current in the seventeenth and, more so, in the eighteenth century, is now no longer expressed by the consumption of national foods and drink. This is, on the one side, a consequence of the cessation of enmities with our French neighbours and, on the other, is connected with the fact that a British food tradition has become heavily diluted by a globalization of cuisine. Although, as I have shown, international (mainly French) influences on the fare of taverns and inns were already present in the seventeenth century, such an influence greatly intensified from the early 1960s onwards. It occurred, first, with the arrival of Indian and Chinese immigrants, and became ever more pervasive and diverse (in terms of the number of different national culinary influences) in recent decades. However, despite such a globalization of the eating-out scene, a more banal nationalism,[21] i.e. the everyday representations of the nation which build a shared sense of national belonging among humans, may still be discerned today. It is expressed by many publicans trying to present their food as 'Modern British' and by customers who seek out and appreciate traditional English dishes, whether as bar staples or at Sunday lunches. Such a cleaving towards traditional English food sustains food-led pubs in general and compels gastropubs, in particular, to cater for this demand by offering traditional pub classics in addition to their more ambitious and often foreign-influenced gastronomic fare.

Looked at in historical terms, the evolution of the gastropub in response to economic and social changes in the wider society means that, despite many similarities, particularly with taverns and inns, the contrasts are equally striking. The most valuable historical continuity is the provision of a very informal and flexible sociality, widely viewed as a very British peculiarity. Gastropubs, just as hostelries in the past, can still provide a community focus. This kind of sociality is combined with the provision of food and drink at a high level of excellence, in a distinctive and well-loved environment that links today's customers with patrons in previous centuries.

Endnotes

1. Michelin, 2016, *Eating Out in Pubs in 2016*. Watford, Herts: Michelin; Michelin, 2014, *The Good Pub Guide 2014*. London: Ebury Press.
2. *The Morning Advertiser*, 2016, 'Pub market report: optimism for on-trade growth' (abridged version). Available at: https://www.morningadvertiser.co.uk/Article/2016/06/23/MCA-UK-Pub-Market-Report-2016.
3. *Restaurant*, July 2011: 49.
4. Dennis, N., Henriques, F. and Slaughter, C. 1956, *Coal is our Life*. London: Eyre and Spottiswoode.
5. Putnam, D. 2000, *Bowling Alone. The collapse and revival of American community*. New York: Simon and Schuster.
6. Publican of Essex rural pub.
7. Publican of Yorkshire rural pub.
8. Mennell, S. 1985, *All Manners of Food. Eating and taste in England and France from the Middle Ages to the present*, 83. Oxford: Blackwell.
9. Landlady of Essex coastal pub.
10. Cambridgeshire publican/chef.
11. Paddock, J., Warde, A. and Whillans, J. 2017, 'The changing meaning of eating out in three English cities 1995–2015', *Appetite*, 119, 6.
12. Naylor, T. 2016, 'Brioche bun has chefs on the run', *Restaurant*, April: 13.
13. Naylor, 2016, 13.

14. Cambridge University Centre for Diet and Activity, cited by *The Guardian*, 25.07.2017: 1, 13.
15. *The Morning Advertiser*, 2016.
16. Naylor, 2016, 13.
17. Cambridge University Centre for Diet and Activity in *The Guardian*, 2017: 1, 13.
18. Menus collected from pubs, 2015–16 and analysed by author.
19. *The Morning Advertiser*, 2016.
20. Wouters, C. 2007, *Informalization, Manners and Emotions since 1890*, 132ff. London: Sage Publications.
21. Billig, M. 1995, *Banal Nationalism*. London: Sage Publications.

APPENDIX I
The Concept of Class in Historical Analysis

Class, particularly the notion of a 'middle class', it is argued by a large number of historians, had no salience in the seventeenth and much of the eighteenth century. Because conflict of interests in the context of industrial production had not yet materialized, collective social identities had not yet formed and social divisions were not sharply defined in political terms. Political expressions of class and the consistent deployment of categories of class for political purposes, according to Wahrman,[1] are not found until after 1832. Society was widely viewed in terms of a pyramid, with fine hierarchical gradations of wealth and status at the top of the hierarchy.[2] No sharp vertical distinctions existed, and deference to those at the top of the social hierarchy—the aristocracy and gentry—was pronounced. Consequently, social groupings and their divisions from others in the hierarchy, it is suggested, were only vaguely defined. Hence, instead of social class, social historians talk in terms of social ranks, orders, degrees, and sorts and refer to those in the middle of the hierarchy as the 'middling sort', rather than the 'middle class'. An excellent overview of social categories applied in the various historical periods and the reasoning behind their adoption is provided by Asa Briggs.[3]

Yet, the inequality between those at the top and the bottom of the social pyramid is said to have been much more pronounced in these earlier centuries than it currently is. Nevertheless, many commentators believe that social groups were not yet conscious of any common interest, defined in opposition to another in the hierarchy. Instead, it was held 'that every man had his place within an order' and that there existed a 'bond of attachment' and a 'network of social obligations' between groupings.[4] Such attachment was associated both with duty and with dependence and subordination.[5]

However, this is not the only perception of social divisions held by historians, and dichotomous conceptions of the aristocracy and the masses also are prevalent.[6] Differences in the possession of wealth and status were publicly acknowledged, and a number of analysts have portrayed these social divisions in pyramidical form, even attaching numerical values to each social group delineated. The analyses of Gregory King and Joseph Massie of the eighteenth century, referring to occupation, both show a tri-partite division based on income and status,[7] where a 'middling class' is inserted between the aristocracy and gentry and the much more undifferentiated labouring masses.

Appendix I. The Concept of Class in Historical Analysis

Those studying urban development from the middle of the seventeenth to the first decades of the eighteenth century identify a group of people in the middle of the social hierarchy—between the gentry and the dependent poor—referred to as the urban bourgeoisie, that 'were becoming a substantial section in English society'.[8] The urban professions, who between 1680 and 1730 had experienced an expansion of almost 70 per cent, constituted a major part of it. In many towns they began to play an influential role in aspects of intellectual and cultural life,[9] including the organization of various activities in inns and taverns. An additional component of the middling classes were those strata active in the growing sector of business and commerce as new industries—particularly metal working and textiles—began to take off.

The labouring masses are said to have lived largely in poverty,[10] although their condition and likely internal differentiation is more poorly documented. The elite (peers and gentry) in the seventeenth and eighteenth centuries was tiny[11]—the landed gentry and the top merchants accounted for only 3 per cent of the population in the eighteenth century.[12] Nevertheless, their great wealth and conspicuous consumption, together with their strong political presence, made the elite quite visible, both in the towns and in the countryside. The 'middling sorts' are already portrayed as diverse, containing both the emerging professions (often with artistic and literary leanings) as well as merchants, tradesmen, substantial shopkeepers, master manufacturers, and those in the armed services and civil service.[13] These less wealthy lower echelons had a more tenuous hold on the status of 'middle ranks'.[14] Away from the bigger cities, at parish level, a distinction was made between the rate-paying 'chief inhabitants' who, often with deep resentment, saw themselves supporting the mass of poorer inhabitants.[15]

Where a small proportion of these chief inhabitants had sufficient resources, they, too, had begun to cultivate a gentility that endowed them with social, political, and moral authority. However, although this gave them the basis for being a 'middle sort', it is argued that they still lacked a formative group identity.[16]

It was only at the turn of the eighteenth and, more strongly, in the nineteenth century that a significant change in social perceptions and identities began to occur. On one side, rapid industrialization and the attendant urbanization are seen to have evoked common interests, founded on economic position, and viewing these interests in opposition to that of another social grouping, thereby constituting class. This saw the birth of the term 'working class' and of the notion that its members should band together against their employers to improve their conditions. By the 1830s—a time of much economic turmoil and hardship—recognition of these various social divisions and opposed class interests had become highly politicized, first in Chartism—'the greatest class war England had ever seen'[17]—and, second, in the Anti-Corn Law League, articulating the hatred by yeomen farmers of the landed gentry and aristocracy. At the same time, political mobilization during and after the debates around the 1832 Reform Act are credited with giving birth to a middling class.[18] Class antagonism became widely expressed. Different positions were taken on whether the middle classes should politically align themselves with the aristocracy or the working classes.

Appendix I. The Concept of Class in Historical Analysis

It is correct that the term 'class' was not in usage in the earlier period and that perceived divisions could not be expressed in political terms. A picture of social structure where the lower orders accept existing stark differences in income, wealth, and status as God-given, and therefore immutable, was, no doubt, very common in the seventeenth and most of the eighteenth centuries, but it was not accepted by all the social orders.[19] Consciousness and resentment of social divisions existed and was often expressed and acted upon.

More important, it is clear that, when examining empirical evidence about visits to public houses, taverns, and inns, that, even at that time in history, society was already highly diversified by commerce, manufacture, and the professions. Even then, cultural capital, in addition to economic capital, was important in constituting lines of division between social categories. Moreover, members of the various categories were well aware of both differences in economic and cultural capital, particularly in the bigger towns and, above all, in London.

Such divisions were often noted in contemporary writing. One such division was between the artistic and literary strata, plus the new professions, on the one side, and the aristocracy and gentry, on the other. Resentment was directed particularly against the fact that rich endowment with cultural capital by the former could not be properly cultivated without the command of the economic capital of the latter. These members of the middling classes did not show an unquestioning acceptance of the social hierarchy, but instead often expressed fierce resentment of and opposition to the social elite. The literary elite, for instance, held strongly conflicting feelings between having to secure upper class patronage and, at the same time, resenting this economic dependence.[20] There was a conception among many of the middling classes that the aristocracy was 'a decadent, self-absorbed elite'.[21] The sort of values espoused by this section of the middling sort within their own communities, particularly those engaged in commerce and craft enterprises—industry, thrift, self-discipline, credit worthiness, and domesticity—often stood in stark contrast to those of the aristocracy.[22]

Endnotes

1. Wahrman, D. 1995, *Imagining the Middle Class. Political representation of class in Britain, c. 1780–1840*. Cambridge: Cambridge University Press.
2. For example, Clarke, N. 2000, *Dr Johnson's Women*, 73. London/New York: Hambledon.
3. Briggs, A. 1960, 'The language of "class" in early nineteenth century England', A. Briggs and J. Saville eds, *Essays in Labour History*, 43–73. London: Macmillan & Co.
4. Briggs, 1960, 45.
5. Briggs, 1960, 46.
6. Wahrman, 1995.
7. Cited by Hay, D. and Rogers, N. 1997, *Eighteenth Century English Society*, 18. Oxford: Oxford University Press.

Appendix I. The Concept of Class in Historical Analysis

8. Borsay, P. 1989, *The English Urban Renaissance. Culture and society in the provincial town*, 204–5. Oxford: Clarendon Press.
9. Borsay, 1989.
10. Clarke, 2000, 73.
11. Clarke, 2000, 73.
12. Hay and Rogers, 1997, 18.
13. Hay and Rogers, 1997, 30.
14. Borsay, 1989, 208.
15. Hailwood, M. 2014, *Alehouses and Good Fellowship in Early Modern England*. Woodbridge: Boydell Press (on the seventeenth century).
16. French, H.R. 2007, *The Middle Sort of People in Provincial England 1600–1750*, 266–7. Oxford: Oxford University Press.
17. Tombs, R. 2015, *The English and their History*, 442. London: Penguin.
18. Wahrman, 1995.
19. Cannadine, D. 1998, *Class in Britain*. New Haven and London: Yale University Press.
20. Clarke, 2000.
21. Hay and Rogers, 1997, 191.
22. Hay and Rogers, 1997, 31.

APPENDIX II
Class Classification Schemes

1. National Statistics Socio-Economic Classification (NS-SEC) was adapted from the Nuffield class scheme developed in the 1970s and was used in the 2001 census. It groups occupations by employment conditions and relations, rather than by skill. The full version of seventeen categories can be collapsed down to three, namely: 1. higher occupations (collapsed from higher and lower managerial and professional occupations); 2. intermediate occupations (clerical, sales, and service, small employers, and technical and lower supervisory occupations); and 3. lower occupations (semi-routine and routine occupations). This scheme does not include the upper class. (For further details, see https://www.ons.gov.uk/methodology/classificationsandstandards/otherclassifications/thenationalstatisticssocioeconomicclassificationnssecrebasedonsoc-2010.)

2. National Readership Survey (NRS) social grades, based on head of household, also refer to occupation, but ranked by skill. It consists of six grades, often used for marketing and believed to be a good predictor of purchasing power. It is known by several of my interviewees. It does not include the small upper class (2 per cent), nor the self-employed.

Grade	Social class	Chief income earner's occupation	Per cent of population (NRS Jan–Dec 2016)
A	Upper middle class	Higher managerial, administrative and professional	4
B	Middle class	Intermediate managerial, administrative and professional	23
C1	Lower middle class	Supervisory, clerical and junior managerial, administrative and professional	28
C2	Skilled working class	Skilled manual workers	20
D	Working class	Semi- and unskilled manual workers	15
E	Non-working	State pensioners, casual and lowest grade workers, unemployed with state benefits only	10

Source: http://www.nrs.co.uk/nrs-print/lifestyle-and-classification-data/social-grade/.

APPENDIX III

Pubs Interviewed

Name of pub	Name of village or town	Name of county/London borough
Abbot's Elm	Abbot's Ripton	Cambridgeshire
Axe and Compass	Hemingford Abbot's	Cambridgeshire
Bell	Stilton	Cambridgeshire
Black Bull	Balsham	Cambridgeshire
Bull and Last	London	Highgate
Carpenter's Arms	Great Wilbraham	Cambridgeshire
Cock	Hemingford Grey	Cambridgeshire
Compasses	Pattiswick	Essex
Crown	Birchetts Green	Berkshire
Crown	Stoke-by-Nayland	Suffolk
Crown	Snape	Suffolk
Culpeper	London	Spitalfields
Dawney Arms	Newton-on-Ouse	Yorkshire
Drapers Arms	London	Islington
Drunken Duck	Barngate	Cumbria
Duke of Cambridge	London	Islington
Dunsforth	Dunsforth	Yorkshire
Eagle	London	Clerkenwell
Fox and Hounds	Hounsdon	Hertfordshire
Freemasons	Wiswell	Lancashire
Green Man	Easton	Essex
Hole-in-the-Wall	Little Wilbraham	Cambridgeshire
Malt Shovel	Barston	West Midlands
Marksman	London	Hackney
Mistley Thorn	Mistley	Essex
Mole	Toot Balden	Oxon
New Inn	Beetley	Norfolk
Nut Tree Inn	Murcott	Oxon
Olive Branch	Clipsham	Rutland
Park	Bedford	Bedfordshire
Pheasant	Gestingthorpe	Essex
Queens Head	Troutbeck	Cumbria
Raglan Arms	Llandenny	Wales
Sportsman	Seasalter	Kent
Square and Compass	Fuller Street	Essex
Trusscott Arms	London	Maida Vale
Unruly Pig	Bromeswell	Suffolk
Westleton Crown	Westleton	Suffolk
White Hart	Hartlebury	Worcestershire
White Horse	Whepstead	Suffolk
Willow Tree	Bourn	Cambridgeshire

APPENDIX IV
Dual or Divided Organizational Identity

Organizations are deemed to have dual or even multiple organizational identities when different conceptualizations exist regarding what is central, distinctive, and enduring.[1] These multiple identities may all be vital and essential to the organization. They therefore place opposing demands on members in that they entail the enactment of different behaviours. Different organizational forms embody contrasting rationales and principles and result in the creation of hybrid identity organizations.[2] Adoption of more than one identity therefore may be connected with stress and conflict.[3] Yet, multiple identities also endow organizations with greater flexibility in reacting to customer demands, and thus offer opportunities.

To derive potential benefits from dual identities, they have to be carefully managed. In a small organization like a pub, such identity management falls to the publican or licensee, and organizational identity is often seen as an extension of personal identity.[4] However, publicans as organizational leaders are not completely unconstrained in their development of an organizational identity. Identity management involves the consideration of the views of other important stakeholders, both internal and external to the organization. Where the publican is not the chef, he/she has to get the support of his employed head chef. At the same time, the construction of an organizational identity, if the business is to succeed, additionally has to take on board the expectations and wishes of external stakeholders, that is, of various groups of customers/patrons.

Degrees of synergy achieved between multiple identities depends on how passionately identities are held and what degree of legitimacy they enjoy. Publicans must decide on the degree of compatibility between identities[5] and pay regard to the different values embodied in each identity and the different course of action each implies. Publicans may have to invest valuable resources in negotiating with the various stakeholders about potentially conflicting identities so that they become more convergent. Where dual organizational identities are only imperfectly managed, one may talk about divided identities.

Pratt and Foreman have developed a four-fold classification of management responses to multiple organizational identities.[6] They vary according to the degree of *identity plurality* on one axis and the degree of *identity synergy* on another. These four different ways of dealing with multiple identities are termed: compartmentalization (high on plurality and low on synergy); deletion (low on plurality and low on synergy); integration (low on plurality and high on synergy); and aggregation (high on plurality

Appendix IV. Dual or Divided Organizational Identity

and high on synergy). The first response, *compartmentalization*, utilizes segregation where enactment of identities with a presumed low degree of synergy is spatially or temporally segregated. In the second response, *deletion*, compatibility is believed to be so low that one organizational identity is eliminated. *Integration* of multiple identities, the third response, occurs when managers attempt to fuse the two identities. However, this response mainly considers the cognitive element of identities and may ignore their different behavioural correlates. The result may be an organization where integration, at best, results in ambivalent action, and, at worst, faces the re-emergence of conflict down the line. The fourth response, *aggregation*, attempts to retain multiple identities and aggregates them, while trying to forge links between them. Efforts are made to identify relationships between them and to exploit synergies.[7] Such aggregation is easier when a hierarchy of identities is established that orders them according to salience to the organization and thereby sets organizational priorities. On the cost side, aggregating identities requires managerial effort invested in and maintaining relationships between identities. This four-fold classification scheme of managing responses to multiple or merely dual organizational identities is used, particularly explicitly, in chapter 6, to order and interpret the data gained from interviews with publicans of gastropubs—the managers of dual-identity organizations.

Endnotes

1. Albert, S. and Whetten D.A. 1985, 'Organizational identity', *Research in Organizational Behavior*, 7: 263–95; Pratt, M.G. and Foreman, P.O. 2000, 'Classifying managerial responses to multiple organizational identities', *Academy of Management Review*, 25, 1: 18–42.
2. Whetten, D., Foreman, P. and Dyer W.G. 2013, 'Organizational identity and family business', L. Melin, M. Nordqvist and P. Sham eds, *The Sage Handbook of Family Business*, 480–97. London: Sage Publications.
3. Reed, M. 2009, 'Bureaucratic theory', *The Oxford Handbook of Sociology and Organizational Studies*, 578. Oxford: Oxford University Press; Whetten et al, 2009, 480.
4. Whetten et al, 2009, 482, on family businesses.
5. Pratt and Foreman, 2000, 25.
6. Pratt and Foreman, 2000, 26ff.
7. Pratt and Foreman, 2000, 32.

Index

accommodation
  alehouses 27
  gastropubs 170
  inns 4, 5, 20, 112
Acton, Elizabeth 101, 118nn23, 34
Addison, Joseph 24, 83
Adnams 136
adulteration
  beer and ale 92, 130, 131
  food 73, 86, 100, 105, 111
  wine 109
age of patrons
  gastropubs 184, 199
  public houses 50
aggregation (organizational identity) 217–18
  gastropubs 166
Albermarle, Lord 83
Albert, S. 9, 14nn28–30, 218n1
Albion, Aldersgate Street, London 54, 88
alcohol-free drinks 180–2
ale
  17th century 81
  18th century 92
  19th century 108
  see also real ale
alehouse keepers 38
alehouses
  class 46–7
  eating out 80–1
  historical development 19, 27–32
  as historical forebear of gastropubs 207
  identity and functions 4
  patrons 46–7
  sociality 60, 64
  state regulation of 126
  see also public houses
All Bar One 31, 115
Allied 131
Americanization of tastes 203
Andrews, C.B. 34n33
Andrews, F. 97nn126–7
Anti-Corn Law League 212
architecture 1
  brewers' influence 131

inns 4, 20, 23
taverns 24, 25
Ashforth, B.E. 14nn24–6
Athenaeum gentlemen's club 105
Atherton, Jason 5

Bacchus 27
Bamford, Samuel 43
bar
  gastropubs 143–9, 157–8, 160, 164–5, 181, 207–8
  gender of drinkers 55, 181
  public houses 28, 55, 62
bar food see pub classics
Barker, L. 121n134
bar maids 52
Barron, Monsieur 106
Barrymore, Earl of 45
Bass Charrington 131
Batchelor, D. 14n4, 19, 33nn4–5, 9, 34n34, 111, 120n110
Bayley, P. 61, 70nn161, 166, 179
Beardsworth, A. 11, 15n36, 154, 167n24, 193n74
Bechhofer, F. 11, 15n38
Bedford, Duke of 83
beef
  17th century 75, 79, 80, 93
  18th century 82, 84, 85, 87, 88, 93
  19th century 101–2, 104
  20th century 110
  gastropubs 189–90
  national identity 74, 93, 189–90
Beefeater 115
beer
  17th century 81
  18th century 92
  19th century 108
  20th century 116
  alehouses 27
  bottled 116, 156
  CAMRA 2
  cask 116, 156–7
  consumption 136, 137

Index

beer (*cont.*)
  craft 133
  draught 116, 156, 158
  gastropubs 156–7, 158, 181–2, 197, 207
  and gender 55, 59, 181, 182
  guest 116, 131, 133, 157, 197
  keg 116, 156, 197
  prices 116, 127, 129–30, 131, 135, 137
  public houses 29, 31–2
  taxation 127, 129–30, 134
  tied houses 170
  World War I 127
  see also breweries
Beer Act (1830) 27
Beer House Act (1830) 92, 126–7
beer houses 126–7
Beer Orders Act (1989) 31, 63, 116, 131, 132, 135, 142
Beeton, Mrs 101, 102
Beider, H. 176, 192n32
Belben, Mike 2–3, 14n7
Bell, D. 193n68
Bell, The, Aston Clinton, Warwickshire 111
Bell, The, King Street, Westminster 78
Beresford, J. 47, 67n66, 96nn91–5, 97, 97n124
Berner's Tavern 5
Berni Inn 115
Berriedale-Johnson, M. 94nn22, 29–30, 95n40
Berry, G. 34n49, 66n9, 76, 95nn31, 42–3
Best Sunday Roast Dinner competition 154
Bickham, T. 94nn4–5, 97n139
Big Hospitality 141n98
Billig, M. 193nn65, 70, 210n21
Blumenthal, Heston 111
Boffey, D. 141n97
Borsay, P. 33nn13, 16, 23–4, 37–8, 41, 42, 65n1, 66nn6, 31, 34, 67nn37, 39, 41–2, 48, 214nn8–9, 14
Boswell, James 25, 35nn57, 66, 54, 69n116
bottled beer 116, 156
Bourdieu, Pierre 174, 192nn14, 18
Bowle, J. 95n44
Bradley, H. 15nn34–5
Brakspear 133
Brambleton Hall 85
Brandwood, G. 33nn19, 23, 34n46, 35n78, 130, 139nn30, 32, 34
brandy 92
Brewer, J. 34nn51–4, 35n59, 45, 67nn54–5, 94n9
breweries 39, 129–36, 170
  guest beer 157
  micro-breweries 133, 156
Brewers' Society 130
Brewster Sessions 125
Briggs, Asa 211, 213nn3–5
Briggs, Richard 25

British Beer and Pub Association (BBPA) 134, 136, 140nn62, 65, 69–70, 141nn86–7, 89–90, 156, 167n27, 191n2
Brown's 77
Brunet's Hotel and Tavern, Duke Street 105
Bull Inn, London 80
Burdett-Coutts, Lady 148
Burke, Edmund 24
Burke, T. 4, 14n14, 19, 33nn3, 8, 14, 26–7, 35nn55, 69, 71, 45, 46, 66n27, 67nn43, 52, 56, 58, 78, 94n24, 95n48, 97n109, 111, 120nn107–9
Burnett, J. 35nn72–3, 101–2, 104, 106, 107, 118nn8, 10, 14–15, 20, 28–30, 35, 119nn38, 46, 57–8, 62, 120nn76, 78–80, 83, 87, 92–3, 96–7, 99–106, 121n127, 130, 139nn31, 33, 37–9, 178, 192nn7, 33
Byng, John (later Lord Torrington) 21, 34n32, 47, 90

cafés 41, 107
  see also coffee houses
Cambridge University Centre for Diet and Activity 210nn14, 17
Cameron, David 1
Campaign for Real Ale (CAMRA) 2, 31–2, 140n56
  community-owned pubs 138
  founding 131
  micro-breweries 133
  pub closures 135
  tied licensees 135
Campbell, R. 96n84
Campion, Charles 3
Cannadine, D. 214n19
Carter, Elizabeth 3
cask beer 116, 156–7
Castle Tavern, Paternoster Row 45
Catherine of Braganza 76
Central Control Board 113, 127
Chaloner, W.H. 34nn36–7, 35n56, 69n114
Charles II, King 74, 80
Chartism 51, 212
Chartres, J. 20, 21, 33nn5, 11, 15, 17, 20, 25, 34nn31, 39, 65nn1–2
Chatelaine's 76
Cheddar Cheese, London 26
Chef & Brewer 115
chefs
  culinary identity 149–56, 185–7
  gastropubs 143–6, 149–56, 164–6, 171–2
children, in gastropubs 199
Chinese cuisine 110, 188, 208
chop houses 54, 100, 101, 103
cider 31, 92, 182
Cirrus Inns 5

220

Index

City of London Tavern 103
Clair, C. 97n132, 119nn43, 60, 120n77
Clark, A. 45, 55, 57, 67n53, 68n77, 69nn117, 124, 69n144, 150, 154
Clark, P. 14nn13, 15, 27, 33nn7, 14, 34nn45, 52, 35nn76–7, 80, 82–6, 41, 43, 48, 53, 54, 60, 66nn11–14, 27, 30, 67nn45, 60–3, 68nn78–80, 68n108, 113, 70nn156, 158, 95n61, 97nn108, 131, 107, 120nn81–2, 126, 138n4, 139nn8, 11–12, 21, 27, 34
Clarke, N. 68n99, 213n2, 214nn10–11, 20
class
  alehouse patrons 46–7
  classification schemes 215
  eating out 73, 74–5
    17th century 75–81, 93
    18th century 82–3, 85–8, 91, 92, 93
    19th century 98–103, 106–8, 117
    20th century 98, 109–10, 114, 120
    gastropubs 145, 146, 148, 158, 169, 172–9
  gastropub licensees 170–2
  gastropub patrons 145–6, 148, 158, 169, 172–9, 198, 201–2, 204, 208
  and gender 51–9
  in historical analysis 211–14
  industrialization 48, 98–9, 212
  innkeepers 37–8, 40, 112
  inn patrons 43–4
  methodological approach 8, 9–10
  publicans 38–40
  public house patrons 28, 30, 42, 46–51, 136, 208
  sociality of pub and tavern life 60–3, 64–5
  state regulation of public houses 125–8
  tavernkeepers 38, 40
  tavern patrons 23, 26, 42, 44–6, 49, 208
coaching inns 4, 20, 22, 37, 207
cocktails 59, 109, 181, 182
coffee consumption 92
coffee houses
  18th century 92
  19th century 103, 107
  class 45, 47, 48, 49
  gender 54
  historical development 26, 27
  social mixing 42
  see also cafés
coffee public houses 108
Collingwood, Francis 25
community life, and gastropubs 147, 198–201, 208
community-owned public houses 138, 200–1
compartmentalization (organizational identity) 217, 218
  gastropubs 166

Conservative Party 131
  see also Tories
cookery books
  18th century 73
  19th century 101, 102
  Acton's *The Elegant Economist* 101
  Beeton 102
  Briggs' *The English Art of Cookery* 25
  Collingwood and Woollams' *The Universal Cook* 25
  Farley 87–9
  in gastropubs 162
  Glasse 88, 190
  Kerridge 197
  La Chapelle 83
  La Varenne 74
  Mollard's *The Art of Cookery made Easy and Refined* 106
  Slater 189
  Soyer 101, 102
  Ude 101
  Verral's *A Complete System of Cookery* 90–1
cook shops 79, 81, 107
Corn Law (1815) 99
corporatization 130
cosmopolitanism 12, 184
  17th century 77, 93
  18th century 87, 93
  19th century 100–1, 106, 117
  20th century 116, 117
  gastropubs 177, 185, 190, 191
costermongers 91
County Inns 21
Courage 131
Cox, T. 14nn23, 27
Coysh, A.W. 14n4, 33nn7, 12, 26, 34n41
craft beer 133
Crompton, G. 140nn46–8, 58–60
Crown and Anchor Tavern, the Strand 24, 25
culinary identity 11–12, 153–4, 156, 184–91
cultural capital 44, 45, 174, 213
Cypriot restaurants 110

Daily Telegraph, The 14n6
dance halls 50
D'Archenholz, M. 47, 53, 67n65, 69n109, 82, 87, 89, 92, 96n73, 97nn114, 117, 123, 135, 137–8, 140
Davenant, Charles 94n13
Davidoff, L. 52, 68nn100–1, 70n148
Davison, A. 33n19, 139n30
de Beauvilliers, Antoine 26
décor 1
  brewers' influence 131
  gastropubs 144, 148, 160, 162–3, 180, 181, 204, 207
  inns 23, 112

221

Index

décor (*cont.*)
　public houses 28, 30, 54, 113, 131, 179
　taverns 23
Defoe, Daniel 24
d'Eichthal, Gustave 22, 24, 54
Dekker, Thomas 80
deletion (organizational identity) 217, 218
　gastropubs 166
Dennis, N. 36n111, 69nn134–7, 70nn154–5, 165, 175, 198, 209n4
Department of Culture, Media and Sport 127
DeSoucey, M. 12, 14n19, 15n42, 190, 193n62, 194n77
desserts
　17th century 79
　18th century 85, 89
　20th century 110
　gastropubs 190, 205, 206
de St Clouet, Monsieur 90
Dickens, Charles 22, 106
dining rooms 4
Discovery Inns 132
Disraeli, Benjamin 48, 68n73
Dog, The, King Street 78
Dolly's Eating House and Tavern 103
domestic dining
　17th century 75–6, 77
　18th century 84–6, 87–8
　19th century 100
Dover Castle, London 92, 108
draught beer 116, 156, 158
drink-driving 136, 145
Driver, C. 94nn22, 29–30, 95n40
Drummond, J. 85, 86, 94nn3, 13–14, 21, 95nn41, 64, 66–8, 96nn83, 98, 101–2, 104–5, 97n136, 117n2, 118nn5, 7, 18, 20, 120n94
drunkenness and excessive drinking
　17th century 81
　18th century 92
　20th century 116
　21st century 138
　alehouses 27, 29
　gastropubs 146, 148, 159, 180, 181, 184, 208
　and gender 54, 59, 128
　public houses 27, 29, 47–8, 126, 127–8, 138
　sociality of pub and tavern life 60, 63
Dryden, John 24
Dyer, W.G. 15n31, 218n2

Eagle, The, Clerkenwell 2–3, 144, 152, 158, 199
Earle, P. 34nn47–8, 66n8, 81, 87, 94n23, 95nn60, 62–3, 65, 96nn105–6, 97n107
East India Company 73, 88
eating houses 4, 103, 105, 106, 107
eating out 71–4, 98–100
　17th century 73, 75–82
　18th century 82–93
　19th century 102–9
　20th century 109–17
　French influence on gastronomy 100–2
　see also gastropubs
Eating Out In Pubs 8, 143, 195, 209n1
Eberlein, H.D. 34n38, 118n33
Enterprise Inns 5, 132, 136
Equal Pay Act (1970) 53
Evangelical and Non-Conformist Revival 60
Evelyn, John 78
Evening Standard 3
Everitt, A. 21, 33nn19, 24, 26, 34nn30, 40, 37–8, 44, 65n1, 66nn4, 6–7, 67nn49–50
excessive drinking *see* drunkenness and excessive drinking
excise duty *see* taxation
Eyre, David 2–3

families
　gastropubs 159, 162, 181, 182, 184, 199, 208
　public houses 32, 113
Farley, John 24, 69n118, 87–9
Fielding, Henry 83–4
financial services companies 132
Financial Times 167n28
Financial Times Magazine 14n9
Fischler, Claude 11, 12, 15nn41, 43, 159, 167nn16, 35, 39–40, 184, 189, 193nn60–1, 73
fish
　17th century 76, 78
　18th century 85, 86, 89
　19th century 104
　gastropubs 190
Fleece, Covent Garden 53
food taverns 113–14
foraging 155, 156
Foreman, P.O. 15n31, 166, 168n51, 217, 218nn1–2, 5–7
Fothergill, John 22, 23, 34n43, 111–13, 120nn111–13, 121nn114–16
Four Nations Tavern, Soho 106
Fox, A. 93n1, 94nn7, 11
Fox, James 60
Fox, Kate 1, 14n2, 50, 62, 68nn90–1, 70nn171–2, 176–7, 193n56
Francatelli, Charles Elmé 99
France
　bistros/bistronomie 153
　chefs' training 152, 185
　eating out 25–6, 73, 74
　visitors to England 22, 41, 54
　wars with 74, 82, 99, 128
Frank, Henry 114
Frankenberg, R.F. 69n138
free houses 134–6, 157, 170

Index

French, H.R. 42, 67n40, 214n16
French cuisine
  17th century 74, 75–82, 208
  18th century 82–91, 93
  19th century 100–2, 105–6
  20th century 109, 115, 117
  gastropubs 150–2, 165, 185–7, 188, 190
Freud, Sigmund 159, 167n37
friendly societies 61
front-of-house staff *see* service
fruit
  17th century 76, 77–8, 79, 80
  18th century 85, 86, 89
  19th century 104

games, pub 61
gardens, gastropubs 146, 162
Garrick, David 24, 83
gastronationalism 12
gastropubs
  challenges 137–8
  class 145–6, 148, 158, 169, 172–9, 198, 201–2, 204, 208
  community life 198–201, 208
  culinary style 149–56
  drinking in 156–7
  and dining, relationship between 145–9
  features 143–5
  food and drink 196–8
  gender 159, 169, 179–84, 198–9, 208
  historical forebears 4, 5, 26, 145, 207–9
  impact on general pub landscape 196
  influence on British attitudes to good food 201–7
  interviews 7–8, 216
  national identity 169, 184–91, 208, 209
  organizational identity 142–68
  origins 2–3
  ownership types 170
  saviour or nemesis of traditional pubs? 195–210
  service and sociality 144, 157, 160–2, 163, 166
  sociality 144, 157–60, 163–6, 176–8, 183, 191, 198–201, 207–9
  study questions 5–6
  term 2, 3
  publicans' views 163–6
Gayo-Cal, M. 192n13
gender
  17th and 18th centuries 93
  20th century 115
  alehouse keepers/publicans 38, 39
  alehouse patrons 51, 53, 54
  and class 51–9
  drunkenness 54, 59, 128
  gastropub licensees 170
  gastropub patrons 159, 169, 179–84, 198–9, 208
  methodological approach 8, 9, 10–11
  public house patrons 32, 50, 51–60, 113, 179
  sociality of pub and tavern life 62, 63
  social politeness 42, 179
  tavern patrons 51–60
George, D. 66n16, 70n178, 139n5
German cuisine 105
Germany 41
Gill, A.A. 158, 167n33
gin consumption 92, 108, 126
gin palaces 53
gin shops 27, 92
Girouard, M. 28, 35nn87–8, 36nn90, 97, 101, 39, 49, 54, 63, 66nn20–2, 68nn74–5, 81–2, 69nn121–2, 70nn170, 181, 108, 118n6, 120nn86, 89–90, 130, 139nn28–9, 40
Gladstone, William 99, 109
Glasse, Hannah 88, 190
globalization 12, 185, 208–9
Globe Tavern, Fleet Street 25
Golden Hind, Hythe, Hampshire 22
Goldsmith, Oliver 24, 83
Good Food Guide 3, 151, 154, 186, 188
Goodhart, D. 194n79
Good Pub Guide 137
Goody, J. 95n58
Gorham, M. 49, 68n89
government *see* state
Grande Taverne de Londres, La (Paris) 26, 74
Gray, Thomas 91
Great Depression 99
Great Exhibitions 107
great fire of London 73
Greene King 136, 170
Grey, Sheridan 60
Grosley, M. 22, 34n35, 35n65, 84, 86, 87, 96nn88, 103, 97n115, 135
Guardian, The 3, 14n8, 70n183, 140n72
Gubbins, Nathaniel 106
guest beer 116, 131, 133, 157, 197
Gutzke, D.W. 36n101, 67n44, 113, 114, 121nn119, 122–4, 126

Habermas, J. 33n1
Hailwood, M. 35n79, 41, 60, 66n28, 68n93, 70nn159–60, 138n3, 214n15
Hannerz, U. 12, 15n47
Harrison, B. 119n50
Harrison, Tom 36n102
Harvester 31
Harwich Inn 101
haute cuisine
  18th century 83, 91
  gastropubs 143, 150, 151, 154, 156, 186

223

Index

haute cuisine (cont.)
  recent revival 89
Hay, D. 213n7, 214nn12–13, 21–2
Haydon, P. 14n17, 30, 36nn95, 109, 54,
    67n51, 69n115, 70nn152, 157,
    121nn138–40, 138n1, 140nn49, 52
Hayward, Arthur 102, 118n19
Helsey, M. 140nn66, 74, 141nn80, 82–3, 93
Henriques, F. 36n111, 69n134, 209n4
Hewitt, M. 67n71
Hey, V. 36n102, 70nn146, 148, 151, 154–5
Hind's Head, Bray 111
Hindostanee Coffee House, George Street 106
Hogarth, William 83, 84
home cooking 202–3
Home Office 127
Horse-Shoe Tavern 103
hotels 106, 113
houses of call 61

identity
  culinary 11–12, 153–4, 156, 184–91
  social 8–9, 169, 172–9, 191
  see also national identity; organizational identity
improved pubs 29, 108, 113–14
independently-owned pubs (free houses) 134–6, 157, 170
Indian cuisine 106, 110, 185, 188, 208
industrialization 28, 89
  brewing industry 130
  and class 48, 98–9, 212
  food production 12, 93, 100
Ing Freeman, J. 14n16, 34nn40, 45, 50,
    97n133, 119nn48–9, 51–6, 59, 61, 63,
    69–72, 120nn73–5, 88
innkeepers 37–8, 40, 112
inns
  class 43–4
  coaching 4, 20, 22, 37, 207
  eating out 71, 72, 73
    17th century 78, 93
    18th century 86, 89–90, 93
    19th century 100, 101, 103, 106–7
    20th century 110–13
  historical development 19–23, 26, 32
  as historical forebear of gastropubs 145, 207
  identity and functions 4–5
  patrons 43–4
  sociality 20–1, 42
Inns of Court 73
Institute of Alcohol Studies 128
integration (organizational identity) 217, 218
  gastropubs 166
interiors *see* décor
International New York Times 14n5

IPPR 135
Italian cuisine 87, 105, 106, 185, 190

Jacob's Well Tavern 45
James, A. 173, 192n11
James I, King 44
J.D. Weatherspoon 31, 115
Jennings, P. 27, 28, 30, 33n5, 35nn70, 76,
    36nn89, 91, 93–4, 108, 113, 116, 40, 48,
    51, 56, 57, 58, 66nn5, 14–15, 17–18,
    25–6, 67nn47, 49, 67–8, 70, 68nn76,
    93–4, 69nn110–12, 120, 122–3, 125,
    131–3, 140, 142–3, 70nn145, 150, 173,
    120n85, 121nn130–1, 133, 127, 130,
    138n1, 139nn5–7, 10, 14–17, 21, 34–6,
    41, 140nn42, 44–5, 51
Johnson, Samuel 24, 25, 54, 83, 130
Jonson, Ben 24

keg beer 116, 156, 197
Keil, T. 11, 15n36, 154, 167n24, 193n74
Kern, R. 192n13
Kerridge, Tom 3, 197
Key Note 115, 121n137, 141nn77, 79, 81, 88,
    92, 142–3, 156, 166nn1–2, 167n26
King, F.A. 36n98, 96n75, 139n13
King, Gregory 211
King's Head, Norwich 89–90
King's Head Tavern, Newgate Street, London 103
Kuklick, B. 70n164
Kumar, K. 15n37
Kümin, B. 33n2, 52, 68nn92, 102

Labour Party 129
La Chapelle, Vincent 83
lager 116, 137, 197
landlords/ladies 9
  see also alehouse keepers; innkeepers; publicans; tavernkeepers
Lane, C. 14n22, 15n44, 167n5
Langford, P. 41, 67nn35–6
La Varenne, François Pierre 74
Lawson, Sir Wilfred 130
layout
  gastropubs 145–9, 151, 160, 163, 166, 177, 181
  inns 21
  public houses 28, 30, 43, 48, 55, 179
  taverns 23–4, 42, 44
Leigh, Rowley 3
Leith, Prue 151
Levy, Dick 114
Liberal Party 130
licensing 125–8, 129
Licensing Act (1828) 126
Licensing Act (2003) 127–8

Index

Literary Club 24
Literary Magazine 82
Little, Alistair 3
localism 12, 177
local provenance of produce 112, 155–6, 179, 187–8, 202
Lockett's 76, 77
London at Table (Anon) 54
London Tavern 24–5, 54, 87–8, 103
Lygon Arms, Broadway, Cotswolds 22, 111
Lyons, Joe 107, 110
Lyons Corner Houses 107

Macaulay, Lord 43
Mael, F. 14nn24–6
Mailonline 139nn24–5
Malthus, Thomas 48
Martens, L. 1, 14n1, 64, 70n185, 154, 155, 159, 167nn23, 25, 168nn42, 44–6, 173, 178, 190, 192nn6–8, 12, 33, 194n76
Massie, Joseph 211
Mass Observation 29–30, 33n10, 36nn106–7, 39–40, 49, 55, 61, 66n24, 67n59, 68nn84–6, 88, 93, 69nn127–8, 130, 70nn163, 165, 168–9, 121n125
MasterChef 151
MCA 140n68, 141n78
McCrone, D. 11, 15n38
McKendrick, N. 94n9, 95n69
McVeigh, T. 140n73
meat
  17th century 77, 78–80
  18th century 85, 86, 88, 89, 90
  19th century 99, 101–2, 104
  20th century 109, 110
  affordability 73
  English versus French cuisine 75
  gastropubs 187
  see also beef
Mechanics' Institutes 48
Medcalf, S. 35nn60–1, 87, 88, 97nn118–22
mega pubs
  competition with gastropubs 196
  emergence and growth 31
  food 115, 143
  opening hours 128
  patrons 50
  sociality 64
Mégroz, R.L. 90, 97nn129–30
members of Parliament 23, 44, 47, 133
Mennell, Stephen 23, 34n44, 35n62, 64, 70n184, 85, 94n19, 96n99, 100, 102, 118nn16, 26, 119n44, 167n36, 173, 178, 192nn7, 10, 33–4, 209n8
menus
  19th century 103, 105, 106–7
  20th century 109

gastropubs 144, 149–56, 161, 180, 188–90, 203
  Ordinaries 75, 76–7, 86–7, 103, 107, 110, 113
  Prix Fixe 197
  Specials 150, 151, 197, 205–6
  see also pub classics
Merchant's Tavern, Shoreditch 5
methodological approach 7–13
Michelin
  Bib Gourmand 176, 196
  Eating Out in Pubs guide 8, 143, 195, 209n1
  stars 144, 148, 151, 152, 154, 161, 196
  training 151
micro-breweries 133, 156
Mill, James 51
Millns, T. 117, 121n141, 139nn18, 21, 140n43
Mintz, S. 167n41
Mirror, The 154
Misson, Henri 79
Misson, M. 95nn50–2, 54–5, 57
Mitchells and Butlers 133
Modern British cuisine 12, 152, 154, 156, 165, 185–8, 191, 205–6, 209
Mohamet, Deen 106
Mollard, John 106
Mollard's Old Drury Lane Tavern 106
Monopolies and Mergers Commission (MMC) 131
Morin's Hotel 106
Moritz, C.-P. 67n46, 90, 97n125
Morning Advertiser, The 140nn67, 75–6, 209n2, 210nn15, 19
Moryson, Fynes 79
Mr Smith's Eating-House, Mary-le-Bone Lane, London 104
Muralt, B.L. de 84, 87, 96n90, 97nn111, 113
Murcott, A. 34n44, 64, 70n184, 167n36, 192n10
music 61

Namura 132
Napoleon Bonaparte 101
National Health Service (NHS) 128, 136
national identity
  17th century 74, 77, 78, 80, 93
  18th century 74, 82–4, 93
  19th century 98, 100, 102, 106, 117
  20th century 98, 110
  gastropubs 169, 184–91, 208, 209
  methodological approach 8, 9, 11–12
  taverns 208
National Readership Survey (NRS) social grades 174, 175, 176, 215
National Statistics Socio-Economic Classification (NS-SEC) 10, 174, 176, 215
Navigation Act (1651) 81

225

Index

Naylor, Tony 166n4, 203–4, 209nn12–13, 210n16
Neames, Barry 22, 111
Newcastle, Duke of 90
Newman, G. 11, 12, 15nn39, 45, 82–3, 84, 96nn70, 72, 74, 77, 80–1, 86, 89, 97n110, 118n22
Newnham-Davis, N. 26, 35n75, 102, 103, 119n47
Nixon, J. 121nn128–9, 132, 138n1
Nkomo, S.M. 14nn23, 27
non-alcoholic drinks 180–2
nouvelle cuisine 186
Nuffield class scheme 174, 215
Nun's Head Tavern, near Peckham 104

obesity 204
Observer, The 139n20
Observer Magazine, The 36n115, 121n136, 140n64
Office for National Statistics (ONS) 136
off-licences 137
opening hours 126, 127–8
Ordinaries 75, 76–7, 86–7, 103, 107, 110, 113
organizational identity 8, 9, 217–18
  gastropubs 142–68, 170–2, 183, 191
Orwell, George 12, 15n46
Otter, C. 118n17

Paddock, J. 143, 159, 162, 166n3, 168nn43, 46, 49, 193n59, 203, 209n11
Page, Reverend Thomas 127
Pagliano's 105
Paine, Thomas 61
Paris 26, 54
Parliamentary Committee (Business and Transport Section) 135
Parr-Maskell, H. 33n6, 61, 70n162
Paston-Williams, S. 93n2, 94nn4, 10, 12, 28, 96n79, 118nn3, 9, 120n93
patriotism *see* national identity
Pennell, S. 94n7
Pepys, Samuel 46, 53, 68nn106–7, 75–6, 77, 78, 94n25, 95n33
Perkin, H. 68n97, 70n147, 117n1, 118nn4, 11–12, 27, 119n45
Peterson, R. 192n13
Picard, L. 34n29, 66n27, 68n83
pies
  17th century 78, 79
  18th century 89, 90, 91
  gastropubs 188
Pitcher and Piano 31, 115
Pitt, William 60
Place, Francis 49, 68n83
plague 73
playgrounds 162

Plumb, J.H. 94n9
politeness, social 41–2, 50, 177, 179
politicians and political gatherings 20, 44, 47, 61, 125–8
Pontack's 75, 77, 87
Popular Café 107
port 92, 109
porter 92, 108, 116, 131
Pratt, M.G. 166, 168n51, 217, 218nn1, 5–7
prices
  17th century 76
  18th century 87
  19th century 98, 103, 105
  beer 116, 127, 129–30, 131, 135, 137
  gastropubs 144, 146, 157, 160, 161, 174, 176, 178, 196–7
  mega pubs 31, 115
  porter 131
  public houses 29
  taverns 45
  wine 157, 161
Prince of Wales Coffee House and Tavern 105
Prix Fixe menus 197
property development companies 132, 136, 138
prostitution 53, 58, 126
provenance of produce
  gastropubs 155–6, 187–8
  local 112, 155–6, 179, 187–8, 202
  Spreadeagle, Thame 112
pub classics
  20th century 114, 115
  gastropubs 149–52, 155–6, 165, 173, 177, 185, 188, 191, 197, 201, 209
pubcos 132, 133–6, 142, 157, 170
Pub Improvement movement 29, 108, 113–14
publicans 9
  class 38–40
  gastropubs 163–6, 170–2
  organizational identity 217
public houses
  21st century 134–8, 141–2
  brewing industry 129–34
  character 1–2
  class 28, 30, 42, 46–51, 136, 208
  closures 2, 135, 136, 138, 142
  eating out 71, 72
    17th century 81
    18th century 91–2
    19th century 100, 103, 106, 107–8
    20th century 110, 111, 113–17
    21st century 141–2
  economic value 135
  employees 135
  food *see* pub classics
  future 195–210
  and gender 32, 50, 51–60, 113, 179

226

Index

historical development 19, 27–32
as historical forebear of gastropubs 207
identity and functions 4, 5
numbers 28, 29, 30, 135
patrons 46–51, 135
sociality 1, 2, 5, 28, 29–30, 41, 60–5, 207
state regulation of 125–8
taxation 128–9
see also alehouses
Public House Trust 29
pub restaurants *see* gastropubs
pubs *see* public houses
puddings *see* desserts
punch 109
Punch Taverns 5, 32, 132, 170
Putnam, D. 209n5

Ratcliffe, B.M. 34nn36–7, 35n56, 69n114
real ale
 20th century 116–17
 gastropubs 156–7, 158, 197
 guest beers 116, 131, 133, 157, 197
 micro-breweries 133
 public houses 31
Red Lion, London 92, 108
Reed, M. 218n3
Reform Act (1832) 212
Reform Club 101, 102
reformed pubs 29, 113–14
Restaurant 3, 14nn10–11, 167n20, 197, 203, 209n3
restaurants 4
 19th century 105–6, 107
 appearance in France 74
 class 173
 competition with gastropubs 196
 competition with hostelries 100
 historical development 26
Restoration 72, 73
Richardson, S. 34n38, 68nn95–6, 98, 118n33
Richmond, Duke of 83
Riddington Young, J. 34n28, 66n23, 139n26
River Café 3
road houses 110
roast dinner *see* Sunday roast
Robins, Monsieur 76
Robinson, A. 66n19
Rochefoucauld, Francois 86, 92
Rochefoucauld, Georges 20, 87, 90
Rochester, Earl of 80
Rogers, B. 7, 11, 14n20, 15n40, 95nn40, 49, 53, 56, 59, 96nn74, 76, 78, 84–5, 102, 118n31, 119nn36, 39–40, 189, 193nn67, 75
Rogers, N. 213n7, 214nn12–13, 21–2
Roman Catholicism 74
Romford, Count 87

Roux, Alain 91
Roux, Albert 153
Roux, Michel 91
Royal Proclamation against Vice and Immorality (1787) 47
Royal Society 24
Russell, Gordon 22
Rylance, Ralph 4, 92, 102, 103–6, 108, 119nn47–8

Sabloniere 105
Sandwich, Earl of 76
Saulieu 105
Saunders, B. 94n18, 95nn44–5
Scarfe, N. 33nn13, 18, 96nn87, 100, 97nn112, 128, 134
Scottish and Newcastle 131
Seeley, A. 140nn66, 74, 141nn80, 82–3, 93
self-employed people as gastropub patrons 199
Selley, E. 29, 36nn96, 99–101, 104–5, 49, 55, 61, 63, 67n57, 68nn84–5, 93, 69nn126, 129, 70nn151, 165, 167, 180, 182, 113–14, 121nn117–18, 120–1, 182, 193n52
service
 gastropubs 144, 157, 160–2, 163, 166
 inns 21, 22
 taverns 89
sexuality 52, 53, 58
Shelley, H.C. 35nn64, 67, 71, 87, 95nn34–6, 96n106
Shenstone, William 83
Ship Hotel, Greenwich 104
Shore, E. 118nn21, 25, 119nn41, 64
Silva, E.B. 192n13
Simon, André 109
Sims, George 25, 26, 35nn63, 74, 54, 69n119
singing 61
Slater, Nigel 189, 190, 193nn63–4, 70, 72, 194n78
Slaughter, C. 36n111, 69n134, 209n4
Slaughter, M. 33n19, 139n30
Slug and Lettuce 31, 115
small-business owners as gastropub patrons 199
Smith, M.A. 35n69, 68nn76, 79, 138n1, 139nn9, 27
Smithers, R. 140n71, 141n94
smoking ban 137
Smollett, Tobias 63, 83
social identity 8–9, 169, 172–9, 191
sociality 40–51, 64–5
 alehouses 60, 64
 gastropub licensees 172
 gastropub patrons 144, 157–60, 163–6, 176–8, 183, 191, 198–201, 207–9
 inns 20–1, 42
 methodological approach 9

227

Index

sociality (*cont.*)
  public houses 1, 2, 5, 28, 29–30, 41, 60–5, 207
  taverns 23, 24, 25, 41, 42, 60–5, 207
social politeness 41–2, 50, 177, 179
social rank/identity *see* class
soft drinks 180–2
Soldiers' Dependants' Allowance 55
sourcing *see* provenance of produce
Soyer, Alexis 99, 101, 102
Spanish cuisine 185, 190
Specials menus 150, 151, 197, 205–6
Spencer, C. 76, 94nn6, 15, 17, 20, 95nn32, 39, 46, 96nn82, 96, 105, 118nn24, 32, 65, 120n84
Spencer, E. 120n95
Spencer Mott, Edward 106
spirit consumption 116, 181
spirit vaults 53
Sportsman, Seasalter, Kent 156
Spreadeagle, Thame 22, 111–13
Spreadeagle Inn and Tavern, Gracechurch Street, London 103–4
Stacey, M. 68n87
staff *see* service
Stanley, L.T. 34n54, 35n68, 66n23, 78, 95n47
state 142
  and brewers 129
  as protector of the pub 2
  regulation of public houses 125–8
  see also taxation
Steele, Richard 24, 83
street food 107
Struggler Tavern and Chop House 103
Stuarts 74
Sublime Society of Beefsteaks 82
suburbanization 28, 42
Sunday Closing Bills (1883) 127
Sunday drinking hours 127
Sunday Mirror 1, 14n3
Sunday roast
  20th century 110
  gastropubs 154, 156, 165, 177, 185, 189–90, 191, 205, 209
supermarket sales of alcohol 128, 129, 136–7
Swift, Jonathan 24

table d'hote 20
take-away food 204
Tarleton, Richard 75
Tatler, The 83, 96n83
tavernkeepers 38, 40
taverns
  class 23, 26, 42, 44–6, 49, 208
  eating out 71, 72, 73
    17th century 73, 75, 76–7, 78, 93
    18th century 86–9, 91, 93

    19th century 100, 101, 103, 104, 106
    20th century 110
  gender 51–60
  great fire of London 73
  historical development 19, 23–6, 32
  as historical forebear of gastropubs 26, 207, 208
  identity and functions 4–5
  national identity 208
  patrons 44–6
  plague 73
  sociality 23, 24, 25, 41, 42, 60–5, 207
taxation
  beer 127, 129–30, 134
  breweries 133
  public houses 125, 128–9, 136–7
  supermarket sales of alcohol 136–7
  wine 81, 109
tea consumption 92
tea houses 107
teetotallers 136
Telegraph Eating-House 105
Temperance Movement
  altruism 126
  eating out 108, 113
  gender 58
  public houses 29
  sociality of pub life 61, 63
  Sunday Closing Bills (1883) 127
terraces, gastropubs 146, 162
Thai cuisine 185
theoretical perspectives 8–9
Thompson, L.P. 33nn21–2, 34nn28–9, 47, 62, 66n3, 67n69, 70n174
Thornton, T. 32, 36nn114, 116, 56, 69n139, 117, 121nn130, 135, 142, 140nn45, 50, 53–5, 57, 61, 63
tied houses 126, 130–6, 142, 170
Tiptaft, N. 30, 34nn28, 42, 36
Tlusty, B.A. 33n2, 52, 68nn92, 102
Toby 115
toilet facilities 162–3, 179, 180
Tomalin, C. 94nn8, 26
Tombs, Robert 14n21, 24, 35n58, 36n103, 41, 66nn27, 29, 31–3, 67n64, 68nn72, 95, 103–5, 77, 95nn37–8, 96n71, 118nn11, 13, 119n37, 120n98, 128, 139n19, 214n17
Tories 129–30
  eating out 77, 80, 83
  public houses 47
  social mixing 42
  taxation of beer 129–30
  see also Conservative Party
Torrington, Lord (earlier John Byng) 21, 34n32, 47, 90

Index

tourism 1, 196
trade unions 61
Trafalgar Tavern, Greenwich 104
Trocadero 107
Turnpike Act 20
Twickenham Fine Ales 133

Ude, Louis-Eustache 101
urbanization 51, 86, 98, 100, 212
  inns 20
  public houses 28
Urry, J. 12, 15n47

Valentine, G. 193n68
van Otterloo, A.H. 34n44, 64, 70n184, 167n36, 192n10
VAT 129
Veblen, T. 94n27
vegetables
  17th century 71, 76, 77
  18th century 85, 86, 89, 90–1
  19th century 104, 105
  English versus French cuisine 75
  gastropubs 187
vegetarian dishes 190
Verral, William 90–1
Vintage Inns 115

Wahrman, 211, 213nn1, 6, 214n18
waiters and waitresses *see* service
Walker, Thomas 105, 119nn66–8
Walpole, Robert 82, 83
Warde, Alan 1, 10, 14n1, 15n32, 64, 70n185, 154, 155, 159, 167nn23, 25, 168nn42, 44–6, 166n3, 173, 178, 190, 191n1, 192nn6–9, 12–13, 33, 193nn59, 66, 69, 194n76, 209n11
Watney 114
Watney Mann 131
Whetten, D.A. 9, 14nn28–30, 15n31, 218nn1–2, 3–4
Whigs 42, 47, 77, 82–3, 90
Whillans, J. 166n3, 193n59, 209n11

Whitbread and Co. 114, 131, 133
White Hart Inn, Lewes, Sussex 90
White Hart Tavern, Holborn 25
Whitehead, A. 57, 69n141, 70nn149, 153–4
White Lion, Putney 104
White's Club 49
Whiting, S. 102, 119n42
Wilbraham, A. 85, 86, 94nn3, 13–14, 21, 95nn41, 64, 66–8, 96nn83, 98, 101–2, 104–5, 97n136, 117n2, 118n5, 7, 18, 20, 120n94
William III, King 92
Williams, Z. 14n12, 193n43
Willmott, P. 30–1, 36nn111–12
Wilson, B. 36n92, 97n116
Wilson, R.G. 120n91
wine
  17th century 77
  18th century 92
  19th century 108–9
  20th century 113, 116
  food taverns 113
  gastropubs 144, 146, 150–1, 157, 161, 180–2, 197
  prices 157, 161
  taverns 4, 23, 25, 45, 60, 77, 81, 88
  tied houses 132
Wine Act (1688) 81
Withington, P. 94n16
women *see* gender
Woodforde, Reverend James 47, 84–5, 86, 89–90
Woollams, John 25
Working Men's Clubs 28
World War I 29, 52, 55, 109, 113, 127
World War II 30, 46, 50, 56, 109, 116, 127
Wouters, C. 176, 192n31, 210n20
Wright, D. 192n13
Wrightson, K. 27, 35n81, 42, 66n10, 67n38, 138n2

Young, Lord 131
Young, M. 30–1, 36nn111–12